SYSTEM FAILURE provides a go-to resource for those who seek to understand the problem of the school-to-prison pipeline, as well as for those of us who suffered, first-hand, the policies and everyday practices that maintain carceral conditions in our nation's educational settings.
- Stefano Bloch, University of Arizona

Chapters in this timely and powerful collection deepen our understanding of how schooling processes continue to criminalize and render disposable already marginalized young people. Reminding us that good intentions are often deadly, authors explore the harmful consequences of reformist policies that purport to protect, but instead dismally fail youth, communities, and the radical potentialities of public education. A critical tool for educators and policymakers, SYSTEM FAILURE sparks necessary interventions.
- Erica R. Meiners, Author of For the Children: Protecting Innocence in a Carceral State

Burch and colleagues' critical analysis of the school-to-prison pipeline transcends traditional understanding of the roots of the problem in racialized school discipline policies. While previous scholarship has largely documented the extent of the problem, it has failed to examine policies that make legitimate 'deficit thinking' (e.g., youths need fixing) and the hidden curriculum (the tyranny of low expectations). SYSTEM FAILURE is a much-needed examination of the broad nexus between implicit societal policies that disproportionately impact children of color and children with disabilities in schools and juvenile prisons. For those interested in challenging current practice and their destructive effects on children, families, and communities, SYSTEM FAILURE is required reading.
- Peter Leone, Ph.D., Professor Emeritus, College of Education, University of Maryland, College Park

SYSTEM FAILURE

SYSTEM FAILURE provides a framework for understanding the ways in which education policy across organizational settings contributes to the school-to-prison pipeline, as documented in the literature and as observed by authors in empirical studies of justice-involved youth in regular public schools, juvenile court schools, probation settings, and alternative schools. Burch and contributors argue that education policy fails low-income justice-involved youth in three major ways: maintaining silence around issues of structural racism and civil rights, marginalizing youth voice and culture and language, focusing on schools or the criminal justice system, and overlooking intermediate settings including the role of for-profit and not-for-profit education companies. While the problem of the school-to-prison pipeline has been well documented, the book adds critical detail and description of a policy process that tolerates the school-to-prison pipeline and stalls efforts to abolish it.

The book is intended for educators, students, policymakers, and practitioners interested in a comprehensive introduction to the policy issues as well as advocates doing serious work on the issues.

Patricia Burch is Professor of Education at Rossier School of Education, University of Southern California.

Critical Social Thought Series
Series Editor: Michael W. Apple,
University of Wisconsin—Madison

Mapping Corporate Education Reform
Power and Policy Networks in the Neoliberal State
Ed. By Wayne Au and Joseph J. Ferrare

The End of Public Schools
The Corporate Reform Agenda to Privatize Education
David Hursh

The Critical Turn in Education
From Marxist Critique to Poststructuralist Feminism to Critical Theories of Race
Isaac Gottesman

The Struggle for the Soul of Teacher Education
Kenneth M. Zeichner

College Curriculum at the Crossroads
Women of Color Reflect and Resist
Ed. By Kirsten T. Edwards and Maria del Guadalupe Davidson

Educating for Critical Consciousness
Ed. By George Yancy

Hidden Markets 2e
Public Policy and the Push to Privatize Education
Patricia Burch

Digital Disruption in Teaching and Testing
Assessments, Big Data, and the Transformation of Schooling
Ed. By Claire Wyatt-Smith, Bob Lingard, and Elizabeth Heck

SYSTEM FAILURE
Policy and Practice in the School-to-Prison Pipeline
Ed. By Patricia Burch

For more information about this series, please visit: https://www.routledge.com/Critical-Social-Thought/book-series/SE0807

SYSTEM FAILURE

POLICY AND PRACTICE IN THE SCHOOL-TO-PRISON PIPELINE

Edited by Patricia Burch

NEW YORK AND LONDON

Cover image: BrendaLawlor / Getty Images

First published 2022
by Routledge
605 Third Avenue, New York, NY 10158

and by Routledge
4 Park Square, Milton Park, Abingdon, Oxon, OX14 4RN

Routledge is an imprint of the Taylor & Francis Group, an informa business

© 2022 Taylor & Francis

The right of Patricia Burch to be identified as the author of the editorial material, and of the authors for their individual chapters, has been asserted in accordance with sections 77 and 78 of the Copyright, Designs and Patents Act 1988.

All rights reserved. No part of this book may be reprinted or reproduced or utilised in any form or by any electronic, mechanical, or other means, now known or hereafter invented, including photocopying and recording, or in any information storage or retrieval system, without permission in writing from the publishers.

Trademark notice: Product or corporate names may be trademarks or registered trademarks, and are used only for identification and explanation without intent to infringe.

Library of Congress Cataloging-in-Publication Data
Names: Burch, Patricia, editor.
Title: System failure : policy and practice in the school-to-prison
pipeline / edited by Patricia Burch.
Description: New York, NY : Routledge, 2022. | Series: Critical social
thought | Includes bibliographical references and index.
Identifiers: LCCN 2021046348 (print) | LCCN 2021046349 (ebook) | ISBN
9781032200651 (hardback) | ISBN 9780367366179 (paperback) | ISBN
9781003262077 (ebook)
Subjects: LCSH: Youth with social disabilities--Education--United States. |
Juvenile delinquents--Education--United States. | Juvenile
delinquency--United States--Prevention. | School discipline--United
States. | Educational sociology--United States.
Classification: LCC LC4091 .S87 2022 (print) | LCC LC4091 (ebook) | DDC
371.826/940973--dc23/eng/20211022
LC record available at https://lccn.loc.gov/2021046348
LC ebook record available at https://lccn.loc.gov/2021046349

ISBN: 978-1-032-20065-1 (hbk)
ISBN: 978-0-367-36617-9 (pbk)
ISBN: 978-1-003-26207-7 (ebk)

DOI: 10.4324/9781003262077

Typeset in Bembo
by SPi Technologies India Pvt Ltd (Straive)

To Robert: For a million reasons and also
To Otsu, for being Otsu

CONTENTS

List of Contributors   xi
Series Editor Introduction   xiv

1 System Failure: Policy in the School-to-Prison Pipeline   1
  Patricia Burch

2 'Softening' School Resource Officers: The Extension of Police Presence in Schools in an Era of Black Lives Matter, School Shootings, and Rising Inequality   31
  Erica O. Turner and Abigail J. Beneke

3 The Culture of Power Online: Cultural Responsiveness and Relevance in Vendor-Developed Online Courses   54
  Jennifer Darling-Aduana, Kathy Villalón, and Annalee Good

4 Redirecting the Teacher's Gaze: Teacher Education, Youth Surveillance, and the School-to-Prison Pipeline   81
  John Raible and Jason G. Irizarry

5 Understanding the School-to-Prison Pipeline for Black Probation Youth   100
  Bo-Kyung Elizabeth Kim, Jessenia De Leon, Camille R. Quinn, Patricia B. Logan-Greene, and Paula S. Nurius

6 Exploring the Relevance and Use of Funds of Gang Knowledge among System-Impacted Latino Boys and Young Men: The Case of an Urban Continuation School 118
Adrian H. Huerta and Cecilia Rios-Aguilar

7 Rising Up and Breaking Down: Youth Resilience and Institutional Failures in the School-to-Prison Pipeline 141
Keybo Wyze Carillo and Patricia Burch

Index *157*

CONTRIBUTORS

Abigail J. Beneke is a PhD candidate in the Department of Educational Policy Studies at the University of Wisconsin–Madison. Using conceptual tools from the anthropology and sociology of education policy and critical race theories, Beneke's research links educational policymaking to school-level practice to examine: the racial and economic politics of education reform, school discipline and school discipline reform, and the role of schools and communities in challenging or reproducing inequality in public education.

Patricia Burch, PhD, Stanford University, is a professor of Education at the University of Southern California in Los Angeles, California. Burch's research focuses on issues of equity and justice in education policy. Burch's recent publications include *Mixed Methods Research for Policy and Program Evaluation* (SAGE, 2016), *Hidden Markets: The New Education Privatization* 2nd edition (Routledge, 2021), and *Equal Scrutiny: Privatization and Accountability in Digital Education* (Harvard Education Press, 2015). Burch's work has appeared in the *Journal of Policy Analysis and Management*, *Educational Evaluation and Policy Analysis*, *Teachers College Record*, *Educational Researcher*, and other notable journals. Burch regularly collaborates with government agencies and non-governmental organizations on program evaluation and in improving program design and policy effectiveness.

Keybo Wyze Carillo (IG highkeytv_) is an aspiring actor and artist who has performed throughout New York City and Miami and has appeared off Broadway. At the time of writing, he was a consultant doing workshops for court-involved youth for District 79 in New York City and Counseling in Schools.

Jennifer Darling-Aduana is an assistant professor of learning technologies in the Department of Learning Sciences at Georgia State University (GSU). She researches the equity implications of K-12 digital learning.

Annalee Good is an evaluator and researcher at the University of Wisconsin–Madison (UW–Madison) Wisconsin Center for Education Research. Her areas of expertise include K-12 digital learning and culturally responsive evaluation.

Adrian H. Huerta is an assistant professor of education in the Pullias Center for Higher Education located in the Rossier School of Education at the University of Southern California. He uses qualitative methods to study boys and men of color, college access and (in)equity, and gang-associated individuals. His research appears in *Boyhood Studies*, *Education & Urban Society*, *Teachers College Record*, *Urban Education*, *Urban Review*, and other top journals. Huerta earned his PhD in education from UCLA and is a past recipient of the AERA Minority Dissertation Fellowship.

Jason G. Irizarry is the dean of the Neag School at the University of Connecticut, a professor, and a faculty associate in El Instituto: Institute for Latina/o, Caribbean, and Latin American Studies. His research interests include urban teacher recruitment, preparation, and retention with an emphasis on increasing the number of teachers of color, culturally responsive pedagogy, youth participatory action research, and Latina/o students in U.S. schools.

Bo-Kyung Elizabeth Kim, PhD, MSW, is an assistant professor at the University of Southern California Suzanne Dworak-Peck School of Social Work. Her research focuses on informing service systems and evidence-based practice strategies as alternatives to youth incarceration to reduce mental, emotional, and behavioral health inequity experienced primarily by youth of color.

Jessenia De Leon is a PhD student at the University of Southern California Suzanne Dworak-Peck School of Social Work. Her research interests include juvenile justice youth and their well-being. Specifically, she examines organizational culture that serve justice-involved youth to enhance services provided by community-based organizations.

Patricia B. Logan-Greene, PhD, MSSW, is an associate professor at the University at Buffalo School of Social Work. Her research examines a broad range of issues related to violence and victimization, including the lifelong effects of child adversity, legal system responses, gun violence, and prevention.

Paula S. Nurius, PhD, MSW, is a professor and associate dean at the University of Washington. Her major research interests include processes and effects of stress and trauma focusing on vulnerable and socially disadvantaged populations, life course development, and fostering resilience.

Camille R. Quinn, PhD, MSW is an assistant professor at the The Ohio State University (OSU) College of Social Work. Her research investigates mechanisms that underlie individual and structural barriers associated with recidivism and comorbid mental health disparities, guided by race-based, criminological, and social determinants of health theories, to inform and culturally tailor interventions for youth of color.

John Raible is the associate dean for diversity, equity, and inclusion in the College of Education and Human Sciences at the University of Nebraska-Lincoln. His interests include transracial adoption and family diversity, critical multicultural education in social work and teacher education, and decolonizing educational spaces and practices. Raible and Irizarry have co-authored a number of papers on the school-to-prison pipeline and multicultural teacher education.

Cecilia Rios-Aguilar is a professor of education and associate dean of equity, diversity, and inclusion at the University of California, Los Angeles, School of Education and Information Studies. She also serves as a faculty co-director of Policy Analysis for California Education and as a board member of the Spencer Foundation. Her research is multidisciplinary and uses a variety of asset-based conceptual frameworks and statistical approaches to study the educational and occupational trajectories of marginalized students. Currently, Rios-Aguilar is examining how community college students make decisions about majors, jobs, and careers. Rios-Aguilar obtained her PhD in education theory and policy and her MS in educational administration from the University of Rochester.

Erica O. Turner is an associate professor in the Department of Educational Policy Studies at the University of Wisconsin–Madison. She uses socio-cultural policy approaches, critical theories of race, and case study methods to study how diverse groups, in and out of schools, make sense of educational inequity and negotiate education problems and policies in ways that advance or impede equity and justice in schools. Her award-winning book, *Suddenly Diverse: How School Districts Manage Race and Inequality*, was published in 2020 with the University of Chicago Press.

Kathy Villalón is a PhD candidate in the Department of Education Policy Studies at UW–Madison, graduating in Summer 2021. Her research expertise includes Culturally Relevant Pedagogy and youth and parent activism.

SERIES EDITOR INTRODUCTION

SYSTEM FAILURE comes out at exactly the right time. As Patricia Burch and the other authors included here document, the data on the role of schooling in the school-to-prison pipeline and the racializing practices that guide all too much of it paint a truly tragic picture. Our educational system both participates and supports an entire assemblage of institutions that form the "carceral state."

The authors clearly recognize that prisons are often sites of profit. In many states, there is more money spent on prisons than on all of higher education combined. But it is not only the physical site of the prison or the school that needs our attention. There is an entire system of connections and relations that require uncovering (Alexander, 2012). It is exactly here that this book enters in important ways.

SYSTEM FAILURE critically examines many of the institutions that participate in this process, focusing on a much larger range of educational settings than those that are usually considered. In the process it makes a crucial contribution. As Patricia Burch states in her introductory chapter,

> Abolishing the pipeline requires a wider lens on policy…The book expands scrutiny of policies to school boards, to for-profit education vendors, to probation officers, to schools of education, to prison schools. While typically not considered as such, these outside of school policies are CENTRAL LINKS in the very school-to-prison pipeline that needs to be abolished. The failures and structural racism of these settings (racist pedagogy, watered-down learning opportunities, unfair sentencing practices, etc.) work to MAINTAIN the school-to-prison pipeline. These settings need to be scrutinized and reformed (or abolished) as part of any serious effort to abolish the school-to-prison pipeline. They are part of the system that is failing youth.

For those of us who are committed to challenging these realities, the task is twofold. We need to understand the causes and effects of the connections between education and mass incarceration. Critical data, both quantitative and qualitative, are essential here. But data don't speak for themselves. They require a truly honest appraisal of racial capitalism and of the macro- and microstructures, policies, and practices that are now pervasive in schools and communities. This requires asking and answering substantive questions about what these data mean, about how they connect to a society organized around systemic racism. SYSTEM FAILURE is an indispensable resource here.

While all of this is absolutely necessary, we also need to focus on interrupting these structures, policies, and practices. There are examples of how progressive alliances can be built on the ground to work against these structures, policies, and practices. These alliances may start with educational action and then spread out to other institutions and groups in important ways. They both cut across some of our differences and just as importantly extend to issues outside of education.

One question that is significant here is who the actors are who can play crucial roles in these interruptive movements. In answering this question, we need to include youth themselves. Indeed, students are among those who have often been at the center. The movement by students in Baltimore to interrupt the all too visible school-to-prison pipeline there is a significant example in this regard (Apple, 2013). As Umar Farooq notes, student activists within minoritized communities in that city pressed forward with a campaign to block the construction of a youth detention facility. Coalitions against the detention center were formed, including an alliance with community groups and with the Occupy Baltimore movement. The proposed construction site was occupied. And even with dispersals and arrests, "daily civil disobedience and teach-ins persisted." The coalition's persistence paid off. The state budget did not include funding for yet another youth prison (Farooq, 2012, p. 5).

This example does not stand alone. A number of possible actions and actors are pointed to in the chapters that are key elements in *System Failure*. But just as noteworthy is that the authors also make visible the tensions and complex contradictions associated with them. A better understanding of this adds to the value of this book.

These tensions and contradictions push us to remember that creating alternatives is not automatic and success is not guaranteed. Reforms can have hidden and complicated effects (see, e.g., Apple, Gandin, Liu, Meshulam, & Schirmer, 2018). Transformations in policy and practice require long-term dedicated and creative actions, actions that often involve alliances among actors in multiple settings, including youth themselves, in interrupting the structures and everyday realities that create the pipeline (see Baldridge, 2019). And all of this also requires engaging in serous critical analyses of what is actually happening and what is being done now as steps toward powerfully interrupting those structures and everyday realities.

But let us be honest here. This is a time of neoliberal assaults on the public sphere, a time when education and so much else is being commodified and seen as a source of profit (Burch, 2021). We face the growing power of authoritarian populist and racist nativist movements throughout the country. Among the effects of this are such things as the denial of the existence of systematic racism, the often cynical and manipulative attacks on Critical Race Theory and the 1619 project, and legislation in all too many states forbidding the necessary teaching of a truly honest history and analysis of the structures of inequalities and the movements to challenge them in the United States. All of this will make substantive interruptions more difficult to accomplish.

The fact that legislatures in so many states are controlled by politicians who may be less than sympathetic (to put it mildly) to essential transformations points to the serious political as well as educational work that needs to be done to counter elements of the racial state and to honestly confront the multiple causes and effects of the school-to-prison pipeline. Recognizing all of this must not lead to cynicism. Indeed, it should have the opposite effect. The struggle over existing policies and the establishment of critically democratic alternatives is ongoing right now. And this book is part of the ongoing process to act back. Patricia Burch has brought together a group of committed authors who assist us in generating both a better understanding of what reality is like and in confronting some of the most critical areas of policy and practice that are currently the sites most in need of transformative actions.

Michael W. Apple
John Bascom Professor Emeritus of
Curriculum and Instruction
and
Educational Policy Studies
University of Wisconsin, Madison

References

Alexander, M. (2012). *The new Jim Crow: Mass incarceration in the age of colorblindness*. New York: The New Press.
Apple, M. W. (2013). *Can education change society?* New York: Routledge.
Apple, M. W., Gandin, L. A., Liu, S., Meshulam, A., & Schirmer, E. (2018). *The struggle for democracy in education: Lessons from social realities*. New York: Routledge.
Baldridge, B. J. (2019). *Reclaiming community: Race and the uncertain future of youth work*. Palo Alto: Stanford University Press.
Burch, P. (2021). *Hidden markets: Public policy and the push to privatize education* (2nd ed.). New York: Routledge.
Farooq, U. (2012). Books over bars. *The Nation*, February 20, p. 5.

1
SYSTEM FAILURE
Policy in the School-to-Prison Pipeline

Patricia Burch

> In these days, it is doubtful that any child may reasonably be expected to succeed in life if he is denied the opportunities of an education. Such an opportunity, where the state has undertaken to provide it, is a right that must be made available on equal terms.
>
> *Chief Judge Warren, Brown v. Board of Education of Topeka,*
> *347 U.S. 483 (1954)*

The United States has an unconscionable history of racism that is firmly embedded in its education policies. Addressing racism in every aspect of our school system is the central task in making public education more equitable. This includes education provided within the walls of the U.S. juvenile justice system, which has a known history of disproportionately confining racially minoritized students and students with disabilities, due to patterns of discriminatory policies and practices related to school discipline, policing, arrests, and sentencing. This system functions as a critical point in the "school-to-prison pipeline," through which students, disproportionately racially minoritized students, and students with disabilities are funneled out of public education and toward the adult criminal justice system (Erevelles, 2014; Redfield & Nance, 2016; Wald & Losen, 2003; Wallace et al., 2008).

Existing policy research on the school-to-prison pipeline has drawn attention to the role of school-level discipline policies as tools for pushing Black and Brown youth out of regular school through suspension and expulsion through metal detectors, how these practices are disproportionately inflicted on students of color (Kupchik & Ward, 2014), and how these practices contribute to increased contact with the justice system (c.f. Noguera, 2003; Skiba et al., 2002, 2014). There has been less work on the role of education policies and practices originating "outside of schools" – for example, in and through the actions of school board members, police and community actors at the district level, federal agencies, teacher education programs, curriculum vendors, and in the courts. This book brings together new evidence of the consequences of these hidden "outside of school" policy dynamics on the educational trajectories of youth, specifically youth of color. The papers individually and collectively speak both to the explicit aims of policy and to policy silences – what happens when things are left "unsaid" or unnamed. Taken together, the chapters offer practical pathways for reimagining policy.

The purpose of this chapter is to provide an introduction to these ideas. I begin with an overview of research to date in understanding the policy problem in the school-to-prison pipeline. I chart key developments in federal policy, including policy efforts specifically aimed at improving the quality of education in prison schools. Prison schools are a central "link" in the school-to-prison pipeline as students arrive there because of harsh disciplinary practices and racist pedagogies. While prison schools should be abolished, as long as they remain, they must be placed where incarcerated students have a right to a quality public education. Much policy aimed at improving learning conditions within prison schools is a failure. It has aspects, following Schneider and Ingraham (1997) of degenerative policies, which send signals that the intended beneficiaries (incarcerated youth) remain the real policy problem. I end with a discussion of the specific contributions of the chapters in illuminating these dynamics and by identifying ways to address system failure as part of a broader effort to abolish the school-to-prison pipeline.

Existing Perspectives

There has been much good work on the school-to-prison pipeline. This work has drawn attention to the role of school discipline policies as tools for pushing Black and Brown youth out of regular school with suspension and expulsion through metal detectors, how these practices are disproportionately inflicted on students of color (Kupchik & Ward, 2014), and how these practices contribute to increased contact with the juvenile system (c.f. Noguera, 2003; Skiba et al., 2002, 2014). From this perspective (rooted in part in implicit bias theory), a largely white and female teaching force view Black and Brown students as violent and risky and enact these biases inside of classrooms in the form of low expectations, repeated in-school suspensions, and expulsions. Implicit bias theory refers to practices whereby individuals act on existing stereotypes rather than facts or reality. These exclusionary practices (rooted in part in labeling theory in which individuals enact the stereotypes placed on them) lead youth toward chronic absenteeism, truancy in and outside of school, and dropping out of school. Students who are perceived as criminals start to behave differently, more generally as "bad kids" and are labeled as making other students uncomfortable; so, they start to do things that will keep them out of the settings where they are treated as unequal, such as schools (Hirschfield, 2008; Noguera, 2003).

Work informed by a critical race theory perspective has argued that the behavior of teachers and others is rooted in school policies that racialized codes of conduct (Crawley & Hirschfield, 2018). For example, Skiba, Michael, Nardo, and Peterson (2002) found that Black and Latinx students were more likely to be disciplined for disrespect, talking loudly or minor threats. This work shows how categories of discipline, codified in school codes, such as insubordination and willful defiance created the conditions for Black and Latinx students to be disciplined and pushed toward incarceration.

Through the lens of these theories, scholars have argued that the incarceration of youth of color correlates with racist policies and practices *inside of schools*. The empirical evidence suggests that the rise of harsh disciplinary policies enacted by racist educators and administrators within schools correlate with increased incarceration rates among these youth. The other side of the school-to-prison pipeline argument is that when harsh disciplinary policies and practices are addressed and replaced, for example, by less punitive approaches to discipline, incarceration rates among the populations decline (c.f., CPSV, 2008; APA, 2006).

From this perspective, the school-to-prison pipeline is created by and through the micro level actions of school staff who draw on broader and often institutionalized understandings in society about who deserves to be in school, what it means to be a good student, how schools should regulate and manage youth while in school, understandings that take the form of broad cultural repertoires that educators enact, sometimes without reflection. The criminal justice system sees youth as schools tragically have and inflicts harsh and long sentencing practices, typically for minor violations. The youth are placed in short- or long-term juvenile detention centers where they are further othered, deprived of social ties and social capital (Rios, 2011), go on to become repeat offenders, and move on a track toward lifetime incarceration.

The second conceptual wave, which builds on the first in its integration of political economy perspectives and Critical Race Theory, argues the importance of a wider lens on the sources of these behaviors (c.f., Hirschfield, 2012; Meiners, 2010; Turner, et al., 2021). This work locates harsh disciplinary practices at a societal relational level. For example, Hirschfield (2008) has examined the relationship between carceral policies in society and school policy. One instance of this dynamic is the political benefits that legislators accrue with the expansion of the prison system in the form of population-based political benefits (e.g., representation) and economic benefits in the form of revenue and jobs to their jurisdiction. This creates a dynamic whereby schools get less funds and prisons get more (Hirschfield, 2008).

From this perspective, the logics of harsh discipline and zero tolerance is just one of the many manifestations of a broader set of societal logics. These broader discourses include dominant ideologies of white privilege and racial capitalism whereby systems are structured to make it easier for whites to get and stay ahead, without explicit forms of racism, but instead with rules and practices that seem race neutral on the face but that have disproportionate consequences for Black and Latinx youth.

School discipline policies that invoke generalized ideas of school safety draw on historically rooted racism and property rights (Harris, 1993), and assume the form of new jobs or expanded surveillance in schools in the form of school safety officers (Turner and Beneke, this volume). These ideas circulate through behavior inside of schools and the criminal justice system, but also in and through many other segments of society, including social and popular media (Meiners, 2010). "Mass media sutures the transition between schools and jails with hyperbolic representation of youth of color in need of management" (ibid., p. 26). The ideas are constantly in motion – manifest through practices and behavior, through written texts but also through other "literacies" such as television shows where African Americans or Latinx are portrayed as criminals and where youth violence of any sort is sensationalized.

Through the discourse and discursive lens, scholars have examined whether and how policies of harsh school discipline intersect with racial capitalism; how the disciplining of youth serves a larger narrative that keeps students of color out of schools and pushes them into low wage, low-skilled jobs that whites feel are beneath whites. It has looked at how television executives distribute and naturalize ideas of mass incarceration of youth of color through the roles they assign Black actors, their portrayal of Black individuals in films and in advertisements about behavior in schools. This work views the school-to-prison pipeline as historically situated and as reproduced and reinforced in political systems of the 1970s and 1980s (when good governance became associated with being tough on crime and became a popular political platform). It understands the school-to-prison pipeline less as pipeline and more as a nexus. Work that attends to the intersection between racial capitalism and the school-to-prison pipeline acknowledges historically situated intersections between school funding and the school-to-prison pipeline (Kim, McCarter, & Logan-Greene, 2020; Turner et al., 2021). Redlining (especially during the Roosevelt era via the Federal Housing Authority) did not allow people of color to obtain loans for housing, and as a result, those practices did not allow people of color to own houses in certain areas These housing policies and practices excluded people of color from getting homes in certain areas and pushed them toward neighborhoods with lower property taxes and low-quality schools. Most students of color attend these low-resourced schools where funds tend to be spent on security and surveillance over school counselors.

In contrast to the idea of a unidirectional pipeline, a nexus implies a multi-directional complex landscape (school policy, housing policy) with overlapping motives from various actors – a set of discourses (including both formal and informal policy) that legitimate the relationship between schools and incarceration. Policy research and designs that attend to the nexus also examine policies and practices in the interstices of the pipeline in the probation phase (Crumé et al., 2021).

Both perspectives are useful; the first draws attention to how the daily actions of staff within and across schools and the criminal justice system exclude youth from school, send them to prison for life, and deny them basic educational and human rights. The second draws attention to how micro practices gain legitimacy from broader discourse as produced and disseminated in policy, in media, and in scholarship. Why, then, another book on the school-to-prison pipeline given decades of powerful research on how the prevalence of school practices, particularly punitive discipline, correlates with incarceration rates? Why, another book, given persuasive arguments that the behaviors we see in schools and the criminal justice system are the result of broader discourse, specifically racism, anti-Blackness, and the role of schools in the socialization and sorting of students?

The answer is this. First, despite over a decade of intense policy and public attention to the school-to-prison pipeline, it persists, and its existence disproportionately harms youth of color. Over the past three decades, out-of-school suspensions have increased, despite dropping slightly (10%) since 2004. Black students are most likely to be expelled or suspended. Students with disabilities are twice as likely to be suspended than students without disabilities, and students with disabilities are more likely to be students of color (Hill, 2017; US Department of Education, 2015). In addition, while the overall number of incarcerated young people has declined, Black youth are still more likely to be incarcerated than white or Latinx youth, and the proportion of Black youth in prison has stayed relatively constant over the past decade. Well-intended policy is being passed. In some instances, it is making matters worse. Rather than the solution, policy is the problem in the school-to-prison nexus.

Second, abolishing the pipeline requires a wider lens on policy. There has been considerable focus on policies inside of schools, less on the role of education policies outside of schools. And let's be clear; it's not just the mass media or housing policies that are the problem here. Education policies are part of the equation. The book expands scrutiny of policies to school boards, to for-profit education vendors, to probation officers, to schools of education, and to prison schools. While typically not considered as such, these outside of school policies are CENTRAL LINKS in the very school-to-prison pipeline that needs to be abolished. The failures and structural racism of these settings (racist pedagogy, watered-down learning opportunities, unfair sentencing practices, etc.) work to MAINTAIN the school-to-prison pipeline. These settings need to be scrutinized and reformed (or abolished) as part of any serious effort to abolish the school-to-prison pipeline. They are part of the system that is failing youth.

One of the larger concerns of the book is to look at conditions of policy failure that contribute to the school-to-prison nexus. By policy design failures, I mean following in the tradition of Schneider and Ingraham (1997), policies intended to benefit individuals viewed by society as deviant. Beneficial policies aimed at groups viewed as deviant such as those who become labeled as juvenile offenders are focused on changing the micro level behavior of individuals and organizations through rules and sanctions rather than attacking the structural failures, such as poverty and racism. Policy failures are those that delay systemic, structural change, are based on the perspective that a clearer statement of the problem is needed, or more data is needed, or more alternatives (typically those that don't put groups with more political power such as whites at a disadvantage). Policy failures are those that are silent about issues of structural racism while being framed in the language of equal opportunity. Color blindness, or what some have termed race evasive policies, manifest or exemplify these kinds of policy failures. Policy failures are also those that claim universal benefits of policy while constructing those with less power as deviant. The framing is important, as Schneider and Ingraham have argued.

> In spite of strenuous efforts by educators to claim that education is a fundamental basis for economic viability, and in spite of the logic of this position) political leaders tend to ignore this justification because it would require massive shifts of expenditures, On the other hand if education is justified in terms of providing equal opportunities, then there is less pressure from the public to insist on improvements in the quality of education.
> *(Ibid, p. 134)*

Beneficial policies for disadvantaged groups may focus on rehabilitation of criminals or rehabilitation of the system. But these policies rarely work because they don't get at the larger social construction of groups positioned as deviant, such as youth in the juvenile justice system, who are perceived as guilty at some level and in need of rehabilitation rather than potential contributors to our economy.

Policy Designs to Address Problem of School-to-Prison Pipeline

Policy matters in the abolition of the school-to-prison pipeline because policy defines who is seen as deserving (or deviant and labeled an offender), who gets benefits, who is denied basic rights (fair discipline, educational opportunities while incarcerated), and whose expertise (agency directors, private experts) is sought in reform (for example, juvenile detention centers). It's easy to read increased policy activity (more well-intended policies) as an indicator that the problem is getting better. At least people are paying attention. This is dangerous thinking. In recent years, the quality of education services provided in juvenile residential placement facilities has received significant federal policy attention in the form of national task forces, reports, legislation, and guidelines. In the next section, I describe the trajectory of some of these policies at the federal level, before considering evidence of how they are failing the very youth they are intended to help and how they maintain white privilege.

Early Efforts at Reform

Over the past half century, significant policy and research attention has been focused on the reform of the juvenile justice program. The 1960s and 1970s focused on juvenile offender "rehabilitation" with the Juvenile Justice Delinquency Prevention Act (JJDPA) of 1974 as the hallmark legislation. The JJDPA offered formula grants to states and local districts. It established the Office of JJDP, which was intended to serve as a hub of research and evaluation, develop national standards, and coordinate federal activities related to the improvement of conditions. In the 1980s and 1990s, states across the country overturned or revised rehabilitative policies, reflecting a more "get tough" orientation. This included passing laws that lowered the minimum age for which youth could be tried as adults or in the case of a few states, removing the minimum age all together. There was also loosening of restrictions on when youth offenders could be transferred to the adult system. At the federal level, the turn away from the rehabilitative orientation was less pronounced with continued emphasis on ensuring states' compliance with JJDPA mandates. The get-tough orientation appeared to soften somewhat beginning in the early 2000s. Some states repealed laws of the 1980s and 1990s, raising the minimum age, where youth could be tried as adults and transferred from juvenile to adult facilities.

Federal policy emphasis on alternatives to juvenile lock-up, and greater state and local accountability for reducing disproportionate impact of juvenile justice system on Black and Latinx youth, continued with the reauthorization of the Juvenile Justice Reform Act (JJRA) in 2018. Under Title II, the JJRA introduced several core provisions, including strengthening protections for youth who commit a status offense, such as a traffic violation where motive is not a consideration in determining guilt. Among other provisions, the bill directed states and localities to plan and implement data-driven approaches to ensure fairness and reduce racial and ethnic disparities, to set measurable objectives for disparity reduction, and to publicly report such efforts. The bill promoted community-based alternatives to detention and encouraged family engagement in design and delivery of treatment and services. It also promoted; improved screening, diversion, assessment, and treatment for mental health and substance abuse needs; and strengthened incentives for investment in evidence-based practices. The bill also strengthened provisions to promote interventions with demonstrated impacts on reducing recidivism, based on research that showed that community-based alternatives can produce better outcomes for youth and protect public safety at less cost. Additionally, the bill called for states to develop policies and procedures to eliminate the use of dangerous practices and the unreasonable use of restraints and isolation using alternative behavior management techniques.

Recent Policy Attention to Issue of Education

Federal policy attention to the problem of improving educational quality in juvenile residential placement facilities is more recent, given that state law has been focused on the provision of education. State laws set the fundamental legal framework for many basic education requirements. State regulations specify the minimum age for compulsory education, the length of the school day, school year, sequence and range of courses offered, and graduation requirements; these requirements extend to justice-involved youth. As part of the Every Student Succeeds Act (ESSA), which is the 2014 reauthorization of the Elementary and Secondary Education Act of 1965, state agencies must establish opportunities for youth to earn credits through coursework, including high school, post-secondary education, and career and technical education. State agencies must also establish procedures to ensure timely reenrollment of students in secondary schools and to ensure that their credits earned while incarcerated will transfer. The ESSA also supports targeted evidence-based services for youth and calls for better coordination across agencies and systems to minimize disruption to students' education, for example, through credit transfer.

Students' rights to education in juvenile justice contexts are further protected by several federal laws. Under Title VI of the Civil Rights Act, students in juvenile residential facilities that receive federal financial assistance cannot be discriminated against on the basis of race, color, or national origin. Title IX of the Education Amendments of 1972 prohibits discrimination based on sex, and Section 504 of the Rehabilitation Act of 1973 (Section 504) and Title II of the Americans with Disabilities Act of 1990 (Title II) both prohibit discrimination based on disability, the former by recipients of federal financial assistance and the latter by public entities regardless of whether they receive public funds. Additionally, per the Individuals with Disabilities Education Act of 1990, all students with disabilities must be educated in the least restrictive environment and be afforded a non-discriminatory evaluation process that applies to any education provided in juvenile residential facilities. Parents and caregivers of students with disabilities in the court system also retain due process rights regarding their children's education plan. Furthermore, under Title VI of the Civil Rights Act of 1964 (Title VI) and the Equal Educational Opportunities Act of 1974 (EEOA), public schools must ensure that English learner (EL) students can participate meaningfully and equally in educational programs. This includes having procedures in place to identify EL students, including a thorough, valid, and reliable test that assesses student proficiency, and provide appropriate language support services so EL students can participate meaningfully in educational programs.

In 2014, the U.S. Department of Education and the U.S. Department of Justice issued further guidance that focused on five general civil rights principles, which included creating safe and healthy learning environments, adequate funding to support improved educational services, high-quality teaching, and standards alignment. These criteria were identified as supplementing 2006 guidance focused on the following: (a) making sure students with disabilities had appropriate services, (b) strengthening services for English Language Learners, (c) safeguarding students from unnecessary restraints and lockdown, (d) aligning curriculum programs with state standards, and (e) improving the transfer of credits upon students' return to community schools.

That same year, the Secretary of Education and U.S. Attorney General sent all 50 state superintendents of schools and state attorneys general a joint letter stressing the importance of improving the quality of teaching and learning in juvenile residential facilities. The JJRA of 2018 requires annual reports that include information on how many children have contact with the juvenile justice system due to an offense committed on school grounds, at a school-sponsored event off campus, or via a school official's referral.

The ESSA requires that states hold all schools accountable for providing a high-quality education to their students and to develop a plan that describes state-wide accountability to identify schools in need of support or improvement. As part of this effort, states have the opportunity to ensure that accountability systems are inclusive of students in alternative education settings. However, states vary in terms of whether and how they include youth in juvenile programs in their accountability plans and the measures they use. These measures must, at the minimum, include participation in required state assessments for eligible students, but some states have taken more expansive approaches to include: (a) growth measures (credit recovery, pre/post-assessment scores, grade-level reading growth), (b) participation in assessments of English proficiency, and (c) measures related to career and technical education, workforce, and outcomes and other measures of school quality (American Youth Policy Forum, 2018).

However, most states do not include data from youth in juvenile facilities in their assessment or reporting systems, making it critical for federal agencies to push for enforcement of education accountability measures in juvenile justice settings. Some see current accountability systems as contributing to the school-prison pipeline by pushing out youth rather than providing accountability and improvement of education. The enforcement of education accountability measures in juvenile justice is framed by its advocates as a different kind of accountability (inclusion as opposed in the case of school discipline).

In summary, in the past two decades, there has been considerable policy activity aimed at juvenile justice system reform. The first of these policies were designed to move juvenile justice centers toward a more rehabilitative orientation. Federal policies emphasized alternatives to juvenile lock-up, and greater state and local accountability for reducing disproportionate impact of the juvenile justice system on Black and Latinx youth.

A later generation of policies focused on improving educational opportunities within juvenile justice facilities. These policies were focused on creating better learning environments for youth while incarcerated in part by making sure that records were transferred, that students' educational needs were evaluated in a timely matter, and there was effort to transfer records to the school to which the student returned.

This decades-long wave of policy activity may be interpreted as an indication of rising awareness of the school-to-prison pipeline. This activity however occurs in a larger context of public policymaking in the United States organized around the political power of advantaged groups to set the policy agenda, set the rules, and determine the mechanism for who gets what (Schneider and Ingraham, 1997). There are elements of this degenerative context or policy failure at work. Much of the policy described above focuses on the reform of individuals (rehabilitative programs) or of agencies (requirements for inter-agency exchange or educational records, requirements regarding reporting of data). The rights of youth to a free and quality public education is understood, in the policy waves, as a long-term problem, that derives largely from changes in the organization of juvenile residential facilities. Addressing the problem is understood in terms of equal educational opportunity rather than broader societal benefits. The basic premise of the policy – that the public needs to be protected from youth in juvenile residential facilities and they are offenders – remains unquestioned. The policies use gentle tools to goad agencies into changing their behavior, which contrasts sharply with the coercive demands for information and harsh sanctions (school expulsion/incarceration) levied on those youth named as intended beneficiaries of the policy.

The messages sent by these policies, I argue, may contribute to limited will and "disinterest and passivity" (Schneider and Ingraham, 1997, p. 13) in the part of those agency personnel and school personnel responsible for implementation. I consider indicators of that passivity and disinterest next, through a longitudinal examination of census data collected from juvenile residential facilities. The policies aimed at ensuring the continued inclusion of youth in a free and quality public education are silent about structural racism, about the fact that Black and Latinx youth have endured years of structural racism at the hands of harsh discipline and in every sector of society outside of schools. Government-funded data collected from youth and their support systems on educational and other conditions is virtually non-existent and rarely collected.

Persistence of the Problem

There are numerous indicators that even with considerable policy activity toward supporting the educational rights of incarcerated youth at the federal level, the system persists, much as it did before the policies were introduced. I review some of these indicators next. This analysis builds on the work of scholars who have drawn on census data to describe national patterns in the characteristics of residential facilities and the youth population. I extend this work through new empirical analysis of ten years of census data on learning conditions within short- and long-term residential placement facilities (youth jails). The data makes clear that structural racism and racist pedagogies *work in and through* the very federal policies aimed at improving the education rights of youth of color. This is not a side bar to the data (or additional data point) as some reports have suggested; it is the main and only story.

1. Even though the number of incarcerated youth has decreased, there are slight increases in percentages of incarcerated Black and Latinx youth, while percentages of incarcerated youth who are white and Asian have decreased (Tables 1.1 and 1.2).

TABLE 1.1 Racial/ethnic distribution of juveniles in residential placement facilities in 2003 and 2017

	2003 (%)	2017 (%)
White	38.6	32.6
Black	38.1	40.9
Latinx	19.1	21.0
American Indian	1.8	1.7
Asian	1.2	0.5
Pacific Islander	0.3	0.3
Other Race	0.9	2.9
Total	100	100★

★ The database from which this data originates computed the total percentage as 100%.
Note: The "Latinx" category includes persons of Latin American or other Spanish culture or origin regardless of race. These persons are not included in the other race/ethnicity categories.
Source: Sickmund, Sladky, Kang, & Puzzanchera (2019)

TABLE 1.2 Racial/ethnic distribution of juveniles in residential placement facilities in 2017 by category of facility operation

	State Facilities (%)	Local Facilities (%)	Private Facilities (%)	All Facilities (%)
White	32.0	27.6	39.8	32.6
Black	44.4	39.4	39.0	40.9
Latinx	18.2	27.9	15.1	21.0
American Indian	1.8	1.8	1.6	1.7
Asian	0.4	0.7	0.3	0.5
Pacific Islander	0.5	0.3	0.2	0.3
Other Race	2.7	2.2	3.9	2.9
Total	100	100★	100★	100★

★ The database from which this data originates computed the total percentage as 100%.
Note: The "Latinx" category includes persons of Latin American or other Spanish culture or origin regardless of race. These persons are not included in the other race/ethnicity categories.
Source: Sickmund, Sladky, Kang, & Puzzanchera (2019)

The Census of Juveniles in Residential Placement (CJRP) was administered for the first time in 1997 by the Bureau of the Census for the Office of Juvenile Justice and Delinquency Prevention (OJJDP). The CJRP replaced the Census of Public and Private Juvenile Detention, Correctional, and Shelter Facilities, also known as the Children in Custody (CIC) census, which had been conducted since the early 1970s. The CJRP, which is repeated biennially, collects data from close to 3,100 facilities and asks juvenile residential facilities in the United Staes to describe each youth assigned a bed in the facility on the census reference date.

Even though the number of incarcerated youth has decreased, the incarceration rates of Black and Latinx youth have increased slightly. Students confined in residential facilities tend to include an overrepresentation of students of color (particularly Black and Latinx male youth). In 2017, as reflected in Table 1, Black youth made up the largest percentage of youth in residential facilities. Between 2003 and 2017, the percentage of white youth in juvenile residential placements declined slightly while the percentage of Black and Latinx youth increased. The small percentage of American Indians, Pacific Islanders, and those identified as "Other Race" stayed relatively constant over the same time period (Sickmund et al., 2019).

2. Even with considerable federal policy activity, incarcerated youth (who again are disproportionately Black and Latinx) are being denied their basic rights to public education while in detention (Figures 1.1 and 1.2).

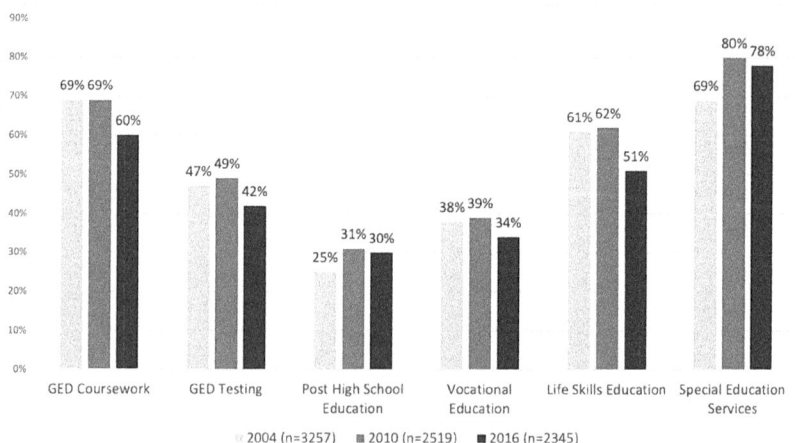

FIGURE 1.1 Curricular opportunities and special education services provided in residential placement facilities in 2004, 2010, and 2016.
Source: OJJDP Juvenile Residential Facility Census (2004, 2010, & 2016)

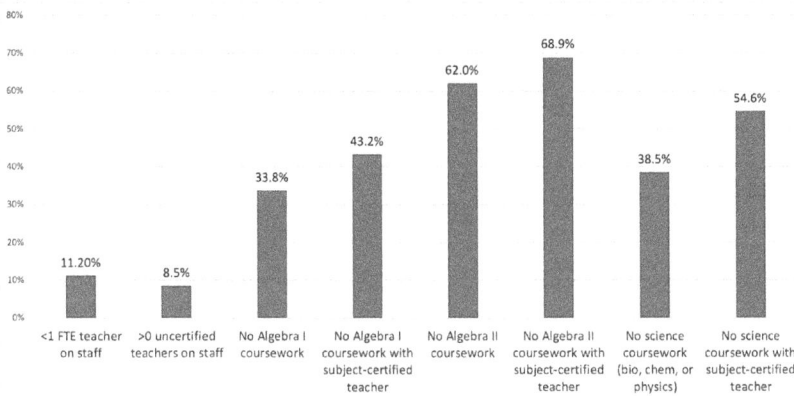

FIGURE 1.2 Percentage of agencies offering graduation-aligned coursework in residential placement facilities that reported serving at least one high school grade level in 2015–2016 (grades 9–12; n = 553).
Source: Civil Rights Data Collection (2015–2016)

There are two major national data sets that speak directly to learning opportunities for incarcerated youth. The Juvenile Residential Facilities Census (JRFC), hosted by the Office of Juvenile Justice and Delinquency Prevention, is a biennial survey of public and private residential facilities in every state. The JRFC began in 2000 and asks questions about facility ownership and operation, security, capacity, injuries and fatalities, as well as supplementary information on specific kinds of services including education (as of 2004), mental health, substance abuse, and physical health. The JRFC includes most, but not all, facilities who hold juvenile offenders except for facilities where treatment focuses exclusively on mental health or substance abuse treatment. The facilities included in this survey also may hold adults (over 18) and youth for non-offense reasons such as foster care. But to be included in the census, the facility needs to have at least one juvenile offender on the census date.

The second source is the Civil Rights Data Collection (CRDC). CRDC is a biennial survey required by the Office of Civil Rights since 1968. It collects data on indicators of civil rights that are related to the access and barriers to educational opportunity from early childhood through grade 12. The data is intended to inform investigations of complaints alleging discrimination and non-compliance for acute and/or nationwide civil rights issues. The data includes public local education agencies, including juvenile facilities, charter schools and alternative schools, and schools primarily serving students with disabilities. Juvenile facilities have been included in the survey since 2009–2010.

To contextualize these data, let's remember that students in residential facilities are disproportionately Black and Latinx, and many are eligible for special education services. A significant number of them (taking into account problems of under-reporting) are English learners. Most of them are not in custody for major offenses, but instead for drug offenses, violation of parole or property offenses. They tend to be performing below expected grade level academically, and an overwhelming majority (93%) aspire to continue their education after high school.

3. Many residential placement facilities (40%) do not provide incarcerated students with access to any public schooling, violating their rights to continue their education despite the fact that facilities draw operational revenue from public education funds. Despite new laws against the school-to-prison pipeline, the condition of education for incarcerated students and their access to basic education is getting worse.

By law, youth placed in residential facilities have the right to continue their public education while they are living in these facilities. However, since 2004, some students have continued to be restricted from attending school. Indeed, there is evidence that the problem of unequal access has increased. In 2004, approximately 25% of students in overnight juvenile facilities did not have access to public school. In 2016, that number had increased to 40%.

Youth attending school in juvenile residential facilities receive approximately the same hours of instruction as students in regular public school. In 2014, a typical reported school day in a juvenile residential facility was six hours long (30 hours per week), which would seem to meet or exceed most state-specified minimums (National Center for Education Statistics, 2018) but it is not clear from the data whether this time includes any breaks (such as lunch or physical activity). Furthermore, by students' report, time spent on instruction is much less than reported by facilities. In 2005, less than half of all youth offenders reported spending at least six hours a day in school. It is also not clear whether the six hours reported by facilities includes time spent in transportation to and from school (16% of facilities that report students attend school off site). There is also evidence suggesting the culture and goals of "safety" in facilities can take precedence over education. In 2016, for example, nearly 95% of all facilities reported using lockdowns, with 10% of all facilities reporting regularly locking students in their cells for a part of each day.

4. As of 2016, 30% do not provide incarcerated students with access to any special education services.

By law, students with disabilities must continue to receive their required accommodations while they are in juvenile facilities. There is a robust research base on the risk factors connecting youth with disabilities to the juvenile system, such as the lack of appropriate diagnoses and services at school that can contribute to students' arrests (c.f. Quinn et al., 2005; Rutherford & Nelson, 2005). However, compliance around this issue has been a serious problem, as evidenced in the number of court cases charging denial of services to students in facilities. The JRFC data provides further indication of the problem. Between 2004 and 2016, the percentage of facilities providing ANY special education services to eligible youth increased from 48 to 70%.

5. Many residential placement facilities (30%) do not provide students with any form of educational assessment upon intake. This suggests incarcerated students are often getting instruction and curriculum that is well above or below their actual grade level.

The timely review of educational records, including each student's academic records, English learner status, special education status, and most recent Individualized Education Plan (IEP) and/or Section 504 plan, are critical for ensuring the continuation of required education accommodations and services in the context of a transfer across different facilities and from regular public schools to juvenile residential facility schools. Despite federal policies requiring timely and appropriate assessment and placement upon entry, spotty assessment and placement practices in residential placement facilities have persisted, remaining relatively unchanged since 2003. While a majority of facilities report conducting the evaluation between 24 hours and seven days of receiving a student, 30% of all facilities report that some students in their facility are never evaluated. There has been some "progress" in area of timeliness of evaluation. Only 4% of facilities reported that they evaluate after seven days in 2016, as opposed to 13% in 2004. It is important to point out that these data refer only to grade level evaluation, as opposed to review or identification of English learner status or special education status, which require supplementary forms of assessment and evaluation by qualified staff.

Since 2004, approximately 50% of facilities that do assess students for grade level report using tests to determine students' needs. A slightly higher number (64–69%) report using students' academic records. In-person evaluations by an educational specialist are less common. In 2016, 43% of facilities used education specialists, including teachers, while 51% reported using other staff, including guidance counselors and intake counselors.

Once a student transfers to a new facility or is released to public school, juvenile residential facilities have a responsibility to transfer student records in a timely manner, again by federal law. This requires, at the minimum, that education records are created initially upon intake and updated through an evaluation when students have been in the facility for more than a short duration. In 2016, one out of two facilities did not evaluate students' needs at the point in which they left the facility; even though, as noted above, a significant percentage of these facilities had youth in custody for over a year. Despite that fact, a majority of the students within their care planned to return to regular public school after leaving the facility. A significant percentage (66%) of facilities did report they shared some form of academic records with the appropriate agency, whether it be a school, community school or juvenile or adult facility; however, this still indicates that one-third of facilities are not providing schools with any updated information about transferring students' education status or progress.

6. Students who have fallen behind in credits before entering the facility are not guaranteed access to opportunities to make progress on graduation-aligned coursework while committed, which only worsens their position upon their return to school.

Since 2004, juvenile facilities consistently have been more likely to offer high school and middle school curriculum than elementary-level curriculum. Given evidence presented earlier that many students entering facilities are well below grade level, many students do not have access to appropriate grade level curriculum that would help facilitate their continued progress toward graduation or a GED diploma, which represents a direct violation of their right to continued access to public education during confinement. As reflected in Figure 1.1, despite explicit federal policy requirements, nearly half of all facilities in 2014 did not offer youth any form of GED prep (40%), GED testing (60%), post-high school options (73%), vocational/technical curriculum (68%), and life skills (50%).

Students' equal access to a graduation-aligned and "career and college ready" curriculum is further compromised by limited math and science offerings (Figure 1.2). Certain subjects, among them Algebra I, Algebra II and, a science (e.g., chemistry, biology, physics) are critical not only for making progress toward a diploma in most states, but also important for college access. In 2015, 40% of facilities did not offer Algebra I, 60% did not offer Algebra II, and 60% did not offer any science as part of their curriculum.

7. Incarcerated students are placed in overcrowded classrooms and sometimes with teachers who lack appropriate expertise. This ensures that incarcerated youth are kept at an educational disadvantage and leave jails (if they do) more behind than when they entered.

While there is little available data on teacher characteristics in juvenile facilities, we can estimate the average class size and rough teacher qualifications based on the CRDB. The average class size (20 students) in juvenile facilities appears to be similar to that of regular public schools and approximately in line with most state requirements for maximum class size. However, in 20% of schools, class sizes are larger than 20 students and are likely exceeding state regulations. The tendency toward larger class sizes is notable considering the known wide variation in student grade level and learning needs among students entering juvenile facilities. Large class sizes seem to indicate that students of varying ages, grade levels, and academic progress are being taught in the same classroom by a single teacher for the duration of their residential placement.

Recognizing this trend as a structural barrier in many juvenile residential facilities, guidance issued jointly by the U.S. Department of Justice and U.S. Department of Education in 2014 called for high-quality teachers who can manage the needs of diverse learners simultaneously and "should be able to teach across multiple subject areas in a given class period while ensuring that students master core subject matter content" (p. 3). However, 10% of juvenile facility schools report utilizing uncertified teachers in classrooms, although only 2% of school reported staff in their first or second year of teaching. Additionally, approximately 20% of schools do not employ a full-time teacher at all, even though the size of the facilities indicates that they are responsible for an average of 51 students, or a minimum of three classes (median 30 students, or a minimum of two classes) who are required to receive education from a qualified teacher for at least five hours per day.

8. Private ownership and management of juvenile residential facilities varies by type of facility, and disproportionately impacts youth of color. However, there are no apparent differences in students' access to basic educational services across public and private facilities.

The expanding privatization of the criminal "justice" system has been a topic of national concern. Research on the public contracting of education services to private firms suggests that public versus private operation can determine educational quality and access (Burch, 2009, 2014; Heinrich et al., 2014). From the JRFC data, we know that since 2004, nearly half of all juvenile residential facilities in the United States have been privately owned and operated. Most of these are operating as not-for-profits (93–96%), with only a very small percentage (4%) registered as for-profit businesses.

Notably, public money follows juveniles into the facility. When youth are in private detention facilities, the private organization operating the facility will often charge the cost of other services (e.g., daily room and board) to the government agency that referred and/or is charged with oversight for the youth. Additionally, whether public or private, the organization operating the facility might choose to contract with an outside agency to provide education services. While private agencies might in some cases contract with a local school district or county education service, the more common arrangement is for public facilities to contract with private agencies to provide education services to youth. In a case where a private agency (facility or third-party education service) is providing education services, the agency can charge back for any public education services, up to the amount that state dollars allocate.

Between 2004 and 2016, the percentage of publicly owned facilities increased only slightly (7%). Certain types of facilities are more likely to be privately versus publicly owned. In 2017, 77% of group homes and 69% of runaway/homeless shelters were privately owned. In contrast, the majority (81%) of reception/

diagnostic centers were publicly owned as were approximately 50% of ranch/ wilderness campuses. Between 2003 and 2017, the percentage of Black students held in private facilities more than doubled, as compared to local and state facilities, which saw decreases (local) or slight increases (state). During the same time period, the percentage of Latinx students in private facilities also more than doubled, compared to declines over the same time period in local facilities. The percentage of privately operated facilities with more than 201 residents increased between 2003 and 2017. While the percentage of students in custody in the facility for more than one year decreased in public facilities, over the same time period, the percentage of long-term residents in private facilities nearly doubled.

The problem of access to high-quality education is both a public and a private problem. Privately owned and operated facilities draw on federal, state, and local funds to run their companies and organizations. Whether a student is incarcerated in a public facility or a privately operated facility does not affect their educational access. It is equally limited. Public and private facilities report offering approximately the same hours of instruction per week and months per year. There also were no substantive differences in the length of school day and school year in public versus private facilities. These patterns held in agencies' reported responses to other aspects of educational services. For example, a little over half of all public agencies reported evaluating students in the time frame of one day to under a week. The same was true when it came to privately operated agencies. Public and private agencies were as likely to report both reviewing students records and having the student interviewed by a specialist as part of educational evaluation. They were equally as likely to conduct educational evaluations; and within three or four percentage points, to make sure that youth received an educational evaluation upon discharge and that assessment of grade level needs as part of that discharge. It is important to interpret this data with caution, as it is self-reported data. In these and other analyses, privately operated centers and privately owned centers were examined separately. On nearly every indicator, 100% of privately owned centers (a very small percentage of the population <5%) reported following the law and engaging in best practices with regards to educational evaluation. This number (100% on every single indicator) suggests inflated results. More work is needed to examine these patterns.

I interpret this very preliminary data as another challenge to the repeated claim that private operation of schooling has benefits for students, including instructional improvements and expanded curriculum. However, the data also suggests the danger of assuming government-run agencies are somehow better and more ethical than privately run agencies. When judged in terms of students' educational rights, publicly run juvenile detention centers are equally culpable and equally bad (Table 1.3).

Even if the data doesn't point to glaring differences, we know from other research (Vaught, 2011), the privatization process removes accountability from the public sphere and can mask inequities. For example, while district and state

TABLE 1.3 Educational evaluation: public and private

	Private (%)	Public (%)
Evaluated <7 days?	52	56
Review of Records?	54	49
Evaluation by Specialist?	50	53
All Receive Ed Evaluation?	51	51
Ed Eval on Discharge?	43	46
Grade Level Needs Evaluated on Discharge?	54	48

Responding Yes: Source JJRF Census 2010.
Percent represents % of all private (or % of all public) agencies reporting that provide the service.

operated programs are required to make sure that all teachers are highly qualified (though data indicates this requirement is not always met in practice), the same standards do not apply to privately operated facilities that don't count federal funds as revenue. There is no available data to compare the characteristics of the teaching force in public versus private agencies, assess class-teacher ratios, and the services provided for students who qualify for special education services or for English learners.

In summary, in spite of a decade of federal policy requirements and guidance, as of 2016, slightly under half (40%) of residential placement facilities do not provide incarcerated youth with access to ANY public schooling while in custody, despite the fact that these facilities draw operational revenue from public education funds at the federal, state, and local level. Despite laws and general push against the school-to-prison pipeline, the condition of education for incarcerated students and their access to basic education is getting worse. Where students with disabilities and with language differences have access to public schooling, they may not have access to the appropriate accommodations that are required by federal law to enable more equitable access to learning. There are still some facilities that fail to provide ANY form of educational assessment when students arrive at their facility. Given what we already know about problems in the transfer of records from schools, this suggests the likelihood that while in custody, students are getting instruction and curriculum that is well above or below their actual grade levels, making it difficult for students to make any educational progress while in custody. Privately operated and owned centers are still a significant part of the youth prison landscape. While there are no substantive public and private differences in the quality of education provided to incarcerated youth, Black and Latinx youth are more likely to be incarcerated in privately owned and operated youth prisons. Here is a chilling example of policy failure, where white financial interests are protected *at the expense of Black and Latinx youth*.

Despite the prevalence of students who report their intention to pursue a high school diploma, college enrollment, and/or GED, many incarcerated youth will have to wait until they leave the facility to take the math and science coursework required to pursue these goals. In addition, students who have fallen behind in credits before entering the facility are not guaranteed access to opportunities to make progress on graduation-aligned coursework while committed, which unjustly halts their academic progression and only worsens their position upon their return to school. Among other risk factors, youth in these facilities may find themselves in a school without a full-time teacher and/or an inexperienced teacher. Thus, while education in these facilities is provided under the argument that it will help address recidivism, these programs contribute to or fail to disrupt the conditions of under-education that produce the school-to-prison pipeline.

The problems that created challenges for juveniles in regular public school (e.g., large class sizes) only continue or are compounded when they are in custody. These patterns have persisted over time in spite of the known disproportionate impact on Black and Latinx youth, English learners, and students with disabilities. Further, these problems cannot be explained primarily as a government/or public mismanagement given that they appear to be as prevalent among privately operated agencies. Whether conscious or not, decisions to focus on individuals and limited elements of agency operation – while often framed as equitable – can contribute to the school-to-prison pipeline and the injustices it facilitates and represents.

Goals of Book and Overview of Chapters

The premise of this book is that policies inside and outside of regular school settings naturalize and legitimate the school-to-prison pipeline, including those that are taken up in the name of incarcerated youth. The research and arguments presented in the book are intended to help show how this happens and to better reveal where tolerance for the school-to-prison pipeline starts, how it spreads through education policies outside of schools and that on the face of it seem well intentioned.

In Chapter 2, Erica O. Turner and Abigail Beneke examine how racial neoliberalism intersects with city policies to expand the School Resource Officers (SRO) program in its high schools. The discourse that pushed for keeping the SROs argued that individual officers provided necessary care and support for "at-risk," low-income students of color and filled a gap in what public school employees could provide. Despite concerns about its deleterious effects on students of color, in and through the actions of school board members, police and community actors at the district level, investment in SROs is maintained through policies and by the actions of white parents claiming progressive education values.

In Chapter 3, Jennifer Darling-Aduana, Kathy Villalón, and Annalee Good examine the policies and practices of curriculum vendors in online courses targeting educationally disenfranchised youth. Even before the pandemic, online courses had emerged as a popular mode of curriculum used in alternative schools for "drop-outs," credit recovery programs, and virtual charter schools. The authors examine the extent to which four widely used online high school courses were culturally relevant and responsive. They argue that online lessons reflected a culture of power, emphasizing normative cultural narratives, retreating to symbolic use versus application, and presenting neoliberal ideologies as fact. Their work underscores the importance of looking at how the school-to-prison pipeline can be reproduced in curriculum policy intended to offer youth an "alternative" curriculum in settings such as community schools (also see Chapter 6).

In Chapter 4, "Redirecting the Teacher's Gaze: Teacher Education, Youth Surveillance, and the School-to-Prison Pipeline," John Raible and Jason Irrizary consider the unexamined role of teacher education policy and practice in orienting teachers to play a surveillance role in schools. They argue that dismantling the school-to-prison pipeline requires helping teachers interrogate their "inherited professional roles in the surveillance and disciplining of youth." Their work is instructive in naming teacher education policy as directly shaping the surveillance behaviors of classroom teachers.

In Chapter 5, Bo-Kyung Elizabeth Kim and associates argue that juvenile justice-involved youth with special education eligibility may have distinct needs from other justice-involved youth that place them at higher risk of re-offending. The study examines the extent to which the comorbidity of risk factors, such as school challenges and mental and emotional health problems, are related to recidivism among probation youth with a diagnosis eligible for special education. Despite the decline in the number of youth involved in the juvenile justice system over the recent years, youth of color, especially African American youth, continue to be disproportionately represented in the system. The authors assess the difference in mental health and school problems (e.g., suspension/expulsion history) between those with and without special-education status in future recidivism. The findings of the study illuminate important factors for continued justice involvement as well as insights into service and treatment planning for African American youth serving probation in the community, especially for those who are eligible for special education.

The final two book chapters (Chapter 6 and 7) shift the discussion away from formal policy problems and how youth draw on strategies, cultures or ingenuity toward policy change and resistance. In Chapter 6, Adrian H. Huerta and Cecilia Rios-Aguilar consider how gang-associated Latinx males use knowledge derived from gang participation to navigate their urban schools and communities. The work brings the reader inside the subcultures and settings largely ignored in the school-to-prison pipeline debates. It challenges deficit thinking common in these debates and articulates the ways in which gangs provide support to youth ignored or othered in school. In Chapter 7, Kcybo Wyze Carillo with Patricia Burch narrate a young man's journey out of the school-to-prison pipeline and the role of creativity in his successful resistance. The story also illuminates how accountability policy failures contributed to a fundamental denial of a young man's educational rights.

Implications for Policy Design

The task of strengthening policy to abolish the school-to-prison pipeline could not be more politically urgent. In 2018, President Trump convened the Federal Commission on School Safety to review, among other items, guidance issued by the Obama administration in 2014 that named disproportionate harsh school discipline policies as a violation of the Civil Rights Act of 1964 (U.S. Department of Justice and U.S. Department of Education, 2014). The commission ultimately recommended elimination of the Obama guidance under the rhetoric of strengthening school safety (DeVos et al., 2018). Here is degenerative policymaking at its worst. What can be done?

Together, the chapters offer the following perspectives on educational policy designs that reinforce the school-to-prison pipeline. These can include do-gooder policies taken up on behalf of youth and Black and Latinx youth, in particular. These policies circulate inside of regular school systems and in the criminal justice system. However, educational policies that reinforce the school-to-prison pipeline also circulate outside of "regular school settings" in organizations that are often touchpoints for youth in the system – online credit recovery programs, community schools and in the decisions of policymakers not typically associated with the school-to-prison pipeline such as school board members, sentencing groups, and teacher education programs. These are the warning signs.

Anti-School-to-Prison Pipeline Policies That Are Race Neutral Have Racialized Impacts

Policy advanced in the name of education reform can and has served to strengthen the school-to-prison pipeline. One particularly egregious example is the Safe Schools Act of 1994 that provided financial incentives for school codes rooted in a zero-tolerance framework and harsh discipline. Another example is the No Child Left Behind Act, which punished students and schools serving these students for failing standardized tests. Note that both policies were advanced under seemingly "neutral" reform principles – safe schools and greater educational equality.

Race conscious policies to address the school-to-prison pipeline are policies that name and address racial discrimination by recognizing and addressing the structural barriers that have denied youth of color full participation in the education system (Kim, McCarter, & Logan-Greene, 2020). This includes policies that address residential segregation, that dismantle unequal funding systems that underfund schools attended by students of color. Policies are never race neutral, but they can be race evasive and when they are, they serve to reproduce the very practices that they claim are abhorrent and further harm the very students they name as intended beneficiaries. One current example of race evasive policies are city-wide ordinances (as described in Chapter 2) to keep police officers in schools even when there is evidence that their presence contributes to a surveillance culture and to othering of youth of color. At the federal level, race evasive policies invest in collecting organizational level data on educational conditions within youth prisons without collecting systematic data to assess the disproportionate impacts of these very policies.

Anti-School-to-Prison Pipeline Policies That Are Not Located in a Civil Rights and Racial Justice Policy Framework Are Ineffective and Have Racialized Impacts

Policies that are not located in racial justice policy framework are policies that, as noted, do not address the underlying conditions, such as underfunded schools, that fuel the school-to-prison pipeline. Policies that are not located in a civil rights framework are policies that fail to leverage the resources and mandates of civil rights legislation, including the Americans with Disabilities Act and Individuals with Disabilities Education Act. For example, as discussed above and in Chapter 5, students of color are disproportionately represented as students with disabilities. Harsh school discipline policies disproportionately effect students of color and students with disabilities (Kim et al., in press). If you are a student of color, and a student with disabilities, you are doubly crossed. Disabilities diagnoses are racialized. Disabilities law specifically IDEA nevertheless has strong protections that can address discrimination for youth labeled as juvenile offenders. The IDEA requires students with disabilities provided with educational services to help them learn and limits the schools' ability to exclude students with disabilities from school, including through disciplinary action. While not without its problems, one example of policy that leans toward these intersections is the promotion of evidenced-based Positive Behavioral Intervention Services (PBIS) by the U.S. Department of Education's Office of Special Education. PBIS programs are aimed at providing states and school districts with additional resources to train staff working with students with disabilities in positive, non-punitive responses including culturally responsive interventions that are responsive to different ways of learning. There is an emerging research base that the PBIS model contributes to reducing suspension and dropout rates (Horner et al., 2010).

Policy Design Failures Are Not Just a Public Problem: They Are a Public/Private Problem. In a Way, They Are a Solution for Private Actors Seeking Profit and Markets for Their Goods

Existing research on the school-to-prison pipeline has powerfully documented the role of the prison industrial complex in the perpetuation of the school-to-prison pipeline (McGrew, 2016; Meiners, 2010). This work, much of which draws on theories of political economy, has demonstrated how broader policy networks within and outside of education benefit politically and financially from the expansion of prisons and youth jails. Much of this work draws usefully from theories of political economy in mapping links between larger political and economic processes and the prison industrial complex and describes the network of economic and political elites who draw power and wealth from the expansion of prisons.

However, the policies of the Prison Industrial Complex also manifest in more hidden forms of neoliberalism – the hidden markets (Burch, 2009) – that gain revenue whenever schools or programs feel pressure (direct or indirect) to buy solutions to social problems. These agencies operate more under the radar than the prison companies and corrupt politicians appropriately called out in the media. These organizations can include credit recovery programs, online schools or curriculum content providers, among others. They include the thousands of organizations that are hired and paid by the government to manage youth prisons (even if they don't own them) by installing and providing security services or transportation to schools or by hiring security staff. These second layer industrial complexes also include the vast network of consultants hired for exorbitant fees to make presentations in youth prisons – to youth and staff.

The sums paid to these organizations, particularly when the organizations are private, are difficult to track down. The protection of these private, corporate actors from surveillance is particularly ironic given the presence of policies that require youth to disclose everything (records of suspension, detention, incarceration) for their entire lives when they apply for a job or for public housing.

As in Chapter 3, the curricular policies of these vendors, if left uninterrogated, can do real harm to youth. Rather than restorative or asset based, the alternative curricula can expose youth of color to a curriculum rooted in norms of white privilege and racialized hierarchies. Current accountability policies including the Elementary and Secondary Education Act do not go far enough in regulating and tracking the practices, outcomes and profits of private vendors (for profit and not-for-profit) that benefit from the school-to-prison pipeline. For example, the No Child Left Behind Act, a market-based federal policy, limited the abilities of public agencies to hold outside vendors accountable for equal opportunities to learn, insisting instead on limited regulation even as they demanded more transparency and indeed more surveillance of students and the schools serving them. These vendors are not "the problem" per se, as evidenced in Chapter 3; government agencies can and do engage productively with vendors to strengthen vendor accountability. But they remain, as in much of educational policy, a protected category of citizen, required to report the minimum while they draw on public funds to operate their programs.

Policies That Are Disconnected from the Informal Ecosystems That Support Youth Are Incomplete and Often Deficit Based

Anti- school-to-prison pipeline policies can make claims that they want to eliminate the criminalization of youth in schools. But the mechanism and assumptions behind these policies can send powerful signals that incarcerated youth are underserving of a quality public education (Harper, 2005). These signals can be present in policy (as argued in this chapter) and in policies of school-based prevention programs, targeting gang-related youth, which rely solely on a universalized negative construction of the role of gangs. They are present in policies that dismiss the informal forms of education (that help youth survive and resist the pipeline) and that minimize all aspects of their culture and language. Youth are treated as the targets of the policies with little power or capacity to contribute to solutions; their voices and experiences largely excluded from systematic efforts to assess the problem. When they offer their views and advocate for alternatives, as demonstrated in Chapter 2, they may be dismissed or ignored. They are othered, and in the omission of their experiences to inform public policy design, constructed as deviants.

School-to-prison pipeline policies that break with these policy failures are linked to social justice and social movements (Perera, 2020) – and identify these curricular opportunities as having equal importance with say, vocational training or GED programs, which federal policy ruled must be present in curricular opportunities for jailed youth. School-to-prison pipeline policies that break with these policy failures also recognize the different systems that incarcerated youth encounter, including the child welfare system (Johnson, 2020) and the ways in which these systems intersect and reinforce (or if reformed help dismantle) the school-to-prison pipeline.

Policies that center youth strengths and assets reject the idea that as Hirschfield (2012) has argued, the pipeline is indeterminate and universal. Students "enter" the pipeline with unique histories. They are pushed deeper into it at different points – whether it be the drop out credit recovery program that is school in name only – the diversion program that fails to keep track, or the detention center that puts them in solitary confinement and restricts access to the education that is their right. Policies connected to youth ecosystems of support are based on "funds of knowledge" that are, in turn, based on students' experiences in the school-to-prison pipeline, as opposed to the idea about "the pipeline" imposed by outside researchers. Policies connected to youth ecosystems also recognize and promote the use of students' peer groups, families, and communities as necessary experts in transforming educational practice.

Conclusion

Whether the school to-prison pipeline is abolished in the near future depends fundamentally on the design of policies undertaken in the name of youth caught in the system. Policy analysis that contributes to the abolition of the pipeline needs to name and interrogate "degenerative characteristics" of policy (Schneider and Ingraham, 1997, p. 206), exposing where possible, how racism and white privilege come to be embedded in designs, and how do-gooder education policies maintain the pipeline and protect white interests. Policy analysis to abolish the school-to-prison pipeline needs to move away from the binary of seeing policies as either for or against the school-to-prison pipeline, and to examine how ableism (as in Chapter 4), and anti-Blackness inhabits policies purportedly aimed at better supporting incarcerated youth. Policy analysis to abolish the school-to-prison pipeline needs to provide a better vision of how to advance the full citizenship and rights of incarcerated youth by involving them and their communities in the design of policy solutions. The chapters that follow help to understand the policy designs and processes that are central to regeneration and renewal, and taken together, contribute to a framework on which future policy can be built.

Bibliography

Alemán, E. (2007). Situating Texas school finance policy in a CRT framework: How "substantially equal" yields racial inequity. *Educational Administration Quarterly: EAQ*, *43*(5), 525–558.

American Psychological Association. (2006). *Are zero tolerance policies effective in the schools? An evidentiary review and recommendations.* Washington, DC: APA.

American Youth Policy Forum. (2018). *Leveraging the every student succeeds act to improve educational services in juvenile justice facilities.* https://www.aypf.org/wp-content/uploads/2018/01/Leveraging-ESSA-to-Improve-Outcomes-for-Youth-in-Juvenile-Justice-Facilities.pdf

Americans With Disabilities Act of 1990, Pub. L. 101–336, 104 Stat. 328 (1990).

Annamma, S. A. (2018). *The pedagogy of pathologization: Disabled girls of color in the school-prison Nexus* (1st ed.). New York: Routledge.

Benner, G. J., Zeng, S., Armstrong, A. L., Anderson, C., & Carpenter, E. (2016). *Strengthening education in short-term juvenile detention centers: Final technical report.* https://www.ncjrs.gov/pdffiles1/ojjdp/grants/251118.pdf

Bishop, D. M. (2005). The role of race and ethnicity in juvenile justice processing. In D. Hawkins & K. Kempf-Leonard (Eds.), *Our children, their children: Confronting racial and ethnic differences in American juvenile justice* (pp. 23–82). Chicago: University of Chicago Press.

Bishop, D., & Leiber, M. (2011). Race, ethnicity, and juvenile justice: Racial and ethnic differences in delinquency and justice system responses. In D. Bishop & B. Feld (Eds.), *Juvenile justice* (pp. 445–484). New York: Oxford University Press.

Boundy, K. B., & Karger, J. (2011). The right to a quality education for children and youth in the juvenile justice system. In F. T. Sherman & F. H. Jacobs (Eds.), *Juvenile justice: Advancing research, policy, and practice* (pp. 286–309). New Jersey: John Wiley & Sons, Inc.

Brown v. Bd. of Education of Topeka, 347 U.S. 483 (1954).

Brunson, R. K., & Weitzer, R. (2009). Police relations with black and white youths in different urban neighborhoods. *Urban Affairs Review, 44*(6), 858–885.

Burch, P. (2009). *Hidden markets: The new education privatization.* New York: Routledge.

Caldwell, S. L. (2010). *The effects of a self-management procedure on the on-task behavior, academic productivity, and academic accuracy of female students with disabilities in a juvenile correctional high school setting.* (Doctoral dissertation, The Ohio State University). https://search.proquest.com/docview/902550107?accountid=14749

Civil Rights Act of 1964, Pub. L. 88-352, 78 Stat. 241 (1964).

Crawley, K., & Hirschfield, P. (2018). Examining the school-to-prison pipeline metaphor. In *Oxford research encyclopedia of criminology and criminal justice*. Oxford, UK: Oxford University Press.

Crumé, H. J., Nurius, P. S., Kim, B. K. E., & Logan-Greene, P. (2021). School engagement among youth entering probation. *Journal of Youth and Adolescence, 50*(6), 1098–1113.

Development Services Group, Inc. (2019). *Education for youth under formal supervision of the juvenile justice system: Literature review*. Office of Juvenile Justice and Delinquency Prevention (U.S. Department of Justice).

DeVos, B., Nielsen, K. M., Azar II, A. M., & Whitaker, M. (2018). *Final report of the federal commission on school safety*. Washington, DC: US Department of Education, Department of Homeland Security, Department of Health and Human Service, and Department of Justice. https://www2.ed.gov/documents/school-safety/school-safetyreport.pdf

Education Amendments of 1972, Pub. L. 92-318, 86 Stat. 235 (1972).

Engen, R. L., Steen, S., & Bridges, G. S. (2002). Racial disparities in the punishment of youth: A theoretical and empirical assessment of the literature. *Social Problems, 49*(2), 194–220.

Equal Educational Opportunities Act of 1974, Pub L. 93–380, 88 Stat. 515 (1974).

Erevelles, N. (2014). Crippin' Jim Crow: Disability, dis-location, and the school-to-prison pipeline. In *Disability incarcerated* (pp. 81–99). New York: Palgrave Macmillan.

Every Student Succeeds Act, 20 U.S.C. § 6301 (2015). https://www.congress.gov/bill/114th-congress/senate-bill/1177

Fabelo, T., Thompson, M. D., Plotkin, M., Carmichael, D., Marchbanks, M. P., & Booth, E. A. (2011). *Breaking schools' rules: A statewide study of how school discipline relates to students' success and juvenile justice involvement*. New York: Council of State Governments Justice Center.

Forman Jr, J., & Domenici, D. (2011). What it takes to transform a school inside a juvenile justice facility: The story of the maya angelou academy. In N. Dowd (Ed.), *Justice for kids: Keeping kids out of the juvenile justice system* (pp. 283–306). New York: New York University Press.

Gagnon, J. C., Haydon, T., & Maccini, P. (2010). Juvenile correctional schools: Assessment and accountability policies and practices. *Journal of Correctional Education, 61*(1), 23–45.

Geib, C. F., Chapman, J. F., D'Amaddio, A. H., & Grigorenko, E. L. (2011). The education of juveniles in detention: Policy considerations and infrastructure development. *Learning and Individual Differences, 21*(1), 3–11.

Harper, S. (2005). Success in these schools: Visual counter narratives of young men of color and urban high schools they attend. *Urban Education, 50*(2), 139–169.

Harris, C. I. (1993). Whiteness as property. *Harvard Law Review, 106*(8), 1707.

Hill, E. (2017). The school-to-prison pipeline at the intersection of race and disability testimony of Eve L. Hill before the U.S. commission on civil rights. https://inclusivity.consulting/2017/12/08/school-prison-pipeline-intersection-race-disability. First retrieved April 1, 2020.

Hirschfield, P. J. (2008). Preparing for prison? The criminalization of school discipline in the USA. *Theoretical Criminology, 12*(1), 79–101.

Hirschfield, P. J. (2012). A critical assessment of theory and research on the 'school-to-prison pipeline'. *American Society of Criminology 2012 Meeting*, Chicago, IL.

Horner, R. H., Sugai, G., & Anderson, C. M. (2010). Examining the evidence base for school-wide positive behavior support. *Focus on Exceptional Children, 42*(8), 1–14.

Individuals with Disabilities Education Act of 1990, Pub. L. 101-476, 104 Stat. 1142 (1990).
Juvenile Justice and Delinquency Prevention (JJDP) Act, 42 U.S.C. § 5601 (1974).
Karger, J., & Currie-Rubin, R. (2013). Addressing the educational needs of incarcerated youth: Universal design for learning as a transformative framework. *Journal of Special Education Leadership, 26*(2), 106–116.
Kim, B. K. E., Johnson, J., Rhinehart, L., Logan-Greene, P. B., Lomeli, J., & Nurius, P. S. (in press). The school-to-prison pipeline for probation youth with special education needs. *American Journal of Orthopsychiatry, 91*(3), 375–385. https://psycnet.apa.org/doi/10.1037/ort0000538
Kim, B. K. E., McCarter, S., & Logan-Greene, P. (2020). *Achieving equal opportunity and justice in juvenile justice* (Grand Challenges for Social Work Initiative Working Paper No. 25). Grand Challenges for Social Work website: https://grandchallengesforsocialwork.org/wp-content/uploads/2020/06/Achieving-Equal-Opportunity-and-Justice-in-Juvenile-Justice-3.pdf
Korman, H. T. N., Marchitello, M., & Brand, A. (2019). *Patterns and trends in educational opportunity for students in juvenile justice schools: Updates and new insights*. Washington: Bellweather Education Partners. https://bellwethereducation.org
Koyama, P. R. (2012). The status of education in pre-trial juvenile detention. *Journal of Correctional Education (1974), 63*(1), 35–68.
Kupchik, A., & Ward, G. (2014). Race, poverty, and exclusionary school security: An empirical analysis of U.S. elementary, middle, and high schools. *Youth Violence and Juvenile Justice, 12*(4), 332–354. https://doi.org/10.1177/1541204013503890
Leone, P. E., & Meisel, S. (1997). Improving education services for students in detention and confinement facilities. *Children's Legal Rights Journal, 17*, 1–12.
Leone, P. E., & Wruble, P. C. (2015). Education services in juvenile corrections: 40 years of litigation and reform. *Education & Treatment of Children.* https://muse.jhu.edu/article/597975/summary
McGrew, K. (2016). The dangers of pipeline thinking: How the school-to-prison pipeline metaphor squeezes out complexity. *Educational Theory, 66*(3), 341–367.
Meiners, E. (2010). *Right to be hostile: Schools, prisons, and the making of public enemies*. New York: Routledge.
Mulcahy, C. A., & Leone, P. E. (2012). Ensuring that they learn. *Handbook of Juvenile Forensic Psychology.* https://link.springer.com/chapter/10.1007/978-1-4614-0905-2_34
National Forum on Educational Statistics. (2016). *Forum guide to collecting and using disaggregated data on racial/ethnic subgroups*. Washington, DC: National Forum on Educational Statistics.
National Research Council. (2013). *Reforming juvenile justice: A developmental approach*. National Academies Press.
Noguera, P. A. (2003). Schools, prisons, and social implications of punishment: Rethinking disciplinary practices. *Theory into Practice, 42*(4), 341–350.
Office for Civil Rights. (2016). *Civil rights data collection, 2015–2016*. U.S. Department of Education. https://ocrdata.ed.gov/
Office of Juvenile Justice and Delinquency Prevention. (2000). *Juvenile residential facility census, 2000*. United States Department of Justice. https://www.ojjdp.gov/ojstatbb/publications/statbb.asp?ID=T35
Office of Juvenile Justice and Delinquency Prevention. (2002). *Juvenile residential facility census, 2002*. United States Department of Justice. https://www.ojjdp.gov/ojstatbb/publications/statbb.asp?ID=T35

Office of Juvenile Justice and Delinquency Prevention. (2004). *Juvenile residential facility census, 2004*. United States Department of Justice. https://www.ojjdp.gov/ojstatbb/publications/statbb.asp?ID=T35

Office of Juvenile Justice and Delinquency Prevention. (2006). *Juvenile residential facility census, 2006*. United States Department of Justice. https://www.ojjdp.gov/ojstatbb/publications/statbb.asp?ID=T35

Office of Juvenile Justice and Delinquency Prevention. (2008). *Juvenile residential facility census, 2008*. United States Department of Justice. https://www.ojjdp.gov/ojstatbb/publications/statbb.asp?ID=T35

Office of Juvenile Justice and Delinquency Prevention. (2010). *Juvenile residential facility census, 2010*. United States Department of Justice. https://www.ojjdp.gov/ojstatbb/publications/statbb.asp?ID=T35

Office of Juvenile Justice and Delinquency Prevention. (2012). *Juvenile residential facility census, 2012*. United States Department of Justice. https://www.ojjdp.gov/ojstatbb/publications/statbb.asp?ID=T35

Office of Juvenile Justice and Delinquency Prevention. (2014). *Juvenile residential facility census, 2014*. United States Department of Justice. https://www.ojjdp.gov/ojstatbb/publications/statbb.asp?ID=T35

Office of Juvenile Justice and Delinquency Prevention. (2016). *Juvenile residential facility census, 2016*. United States Department of Justice. https://www.ojjdp.gov/ojstatbb/publications/statbb.asp?ID=T35

Perera, J. (September 2020). *How black working class youth are criminalized and excluded in the public school system: A London case study*. London: Institute on Race Relations.

Read, N., & O'Cummings, M. (2010). *Fact sheet: Juvenile justice facilities*. National Evaluation and Technical Assistance Center for the Education of Children and Youth Who Are Neglected, Delinquent, or At Risk (NDTAC). http://www.neglected-delinquent.org/nd/docs/factSheet_facilities.pdf

Redfield, S. E., & Nance, J. P. (2016). *The American bar association joint task force on reversing the school-to-prison pipeline preliminary report*. American Bar Association Coalition on Racial and Ethnic Justice, Criminal Justice Section, and Council for Racial & Ethnic Diversity in the Educational Pipeline. University of Florida Levin College of Law Research Paper No. 16-44. doi:10.2139/ssrn.2736323

Reed, D. K., & Wexler, J. (2014). "Our teachers … don't give us no help, no nothin'": Juvenile offenders' perceptions of academic support. *Residential Treatment for Children & Youth, 31*(3), 188–218.

Rehabilitation Act of 1973, Pub.L. 93–112, 87 Stat. 355 (1973).

Rios, V. M. (2006). The hyper-criminalization of black and Latino male youth in the era of mass incarceration. *Souls, 8*(2), 40–54.

Rios, V. M. (2011). *Punished: Policing the lives of black and Latino boys*. New York: New York University Press.

Rodriguez, N. (2010). The cumulative effect of race and ethnicity in juvenile court outcomes and why preadjudication detention matters. *Journal of Research in Crime and Delinquency, 47*(3), 391–413.

Rutherford, R. B., & Nelson, C. M. (2005). Disability and involvement with the juvenile delinquency system: Knowing versus doing. *Exceptionality, 13*(2), 65–67.

Schneider and Ingraham. (1997). *Policy design for democracy*. University of Kansas.

Sedlak, A. J. (2016). *Survey of youth in residential placement: Conditions of confinement*. SYRP Report. Rockville, MD: Westat. https://www.ncjrs.gov/pdffiles1/ojjdp/grants/250754.pdf

Sedlak, A. J., & Bruce, C. (2016). *Survey of youth in residential placement: Youth's characteristics and backgrounds*. SYRP Report. Rockville, MD: Westat. https://www.ncjrs.gov/pdffiles1/ojjdp/grants/250753.pdf

Sedlak, A. J., & McPherson, K. (2010). *Survey of youth in residential placement: Youth's needs and services*. SYRP Report. Rockville, MD: Westat. https://www.ncjrs.gov/pdffiles1/ojjdp/grants/227660.pdf

Sickmund, M., Sladky, T. J., Kang, W., & Puzzanchera, C. (2019). Easy access to the census of juveniles in residential placement. https://www.ojjdp.gov/ojstatbb/ezacjrp/

Skiba, R. J., Arredondo, M. I., & Williams, N. T. (2014). More than a metaphor: The contribution of exclusionary discipline to a school-to-prison pipeline. *Equity & Excellence in Education, 47*(4), 546–564.

Skiba, R. J., Michael, R. S., Nardo, A. C., & Peterson, R. L. (2002). The color of discipline: Sources of racial and gender disproportionality in school punishment. *Urban Review, 34*(4), 81–97.

Teplin, L. A., Abram, K. M., McClelland, G. M., Dulcan, M. K., & Mericle, A. A. (2002). Psychiatric disorders in youth in juvenile detention. *Archives of General Psychiatry, 59*(12), 1133–1143.

The Urban Institute. (2010). *The U.S. juvenile justice policy landscape*. https://www.urban.org/research/publication/us-juvenile-justice-policy-landscape

Turner, E. O., Beneke, A. J., Velazquez, M, & Timberlake, R. (2021). The politics of the school-prison nexus: Racial capitalism and possibilities for transformation in schools and beyond. In A. Welton & S. Diem (Eds.), *Strengthening Anti-Racist School Leaders*. Bloomsbury Press.

U.S. Department of Education, Office of Elementary and Secondary Education, Rethink School Discipline: Resource Guide for Superintendent Action (July 2015), at 10. https://www2.ed.gov/policy/gen/guid/school-discipline/rethink-discipline-resource-guide-supt-action.pdf.

US Department of Justice and US Department of Education. 2014. *Dear colleague letter on the nondiscriminatory administration of school discipline*. Washington, DC: Civil Rights Division of the Department of Justice and Office for Civil Rights of the Department of Education. https://www2.ed.gov/about/offices/list/ocr/letters/colleague201401-title-vi.pdf

Vaught, S. E. (2011). Juvenile prison schooling and reentry: Disciplining young men of color. In F. T. Sherman & F. H. Jacobs (Eds.), *Juvenile justice: Advancing research, policy, and practice* (pp. 239–264). John Wiley & Sons, Inc.

Wald, J., & Losen, D. J. (2003). Defining and redirecting a school-to-prison pipeline. *New Directions for Youth Development, 2003*(99), 9–15.

Wallace, J. M., Goodkind, S., Wallace, C. M., & Bachman, J. G. (2008). Racial, ethnic, and gender differences in school discipline among U.S. high school students: 1991–2005. *The Negro Educational Review, 59*(1–2), 47–62.

Wexler, J., Pyle, N., Flower, A., Williams, J. L., & Cole, H. (2014). A synthesis of academic interventions for incarcerated adolescents. *Review of Educational Research, 84*(1), 3–46.

Williams, J. L., Wexler, J., Roberts, G., & Carpenter, C. (2011). Intensive reading instruction in juvenile correctional settings. *Exceptionality, 19*(4), 238–251.

Youth Law Center. (2016). *Educational injustice*. https://ylc.org/wp-content/uploads/2019/05/EDUCATIONAL-INJUSTICE.pdf

Zimmerman, E. B., Woolf, S. H., & Haley, A. Population health: Behavioral and social science insights: Understanding the relationship between education and health. U.S. Dept. of Health and Human Services, Agency for Healthcare Research and Quality. https://www.ahrq.gov/professionals/education/curriculum-tools/population-health/zimmerman.html

2
'SOFTENING' SCHOOL RESOURCE OFFICERS

The Extension of Police Presence in Schools in an Era of Black Lives Matter, School Shootings, and Rising Inequality

Erica O. Turner and Abigail J. Beneke

Introduction

School Resource Officer (SRO) programs that place police officers in public schools serve a well-documented role in the web of interwoven punitive threads that shape marginalized students' lives and connect schools and prisons, also known as the 'school to jail nexus' (Meiners, 2007; Meiners & Winn, 2010), and, therefore, schools to the carceral state (Sojoyner, 2013; Vaught, 2017). SRO programs are predictive of school officials referring students to law enforcement for low-level offenses (Nance, 2015), are related to an increase in arrests for non-serious violent crime (Na & Gottfredson, 2013), and are correlated with higher rates of suspension and expulsion, which leads to lost class time (Fisher & Hennessy, 2016). Furthermore, these programs reproduce and exacerbate racial inequalities in school discipline and student entanglement with the penal system (James & McCallion, 2013; Javdani, 2019; Nance, 2015). Despite these problems and little to no evidence of their effectiveness, SRO programs are increasingly implemented in the name of ensuring safe school environments (Hirschfield, 2018; Kupchik, Brent, & Mowen, 2015; Petrosino, Guckenburg, & Fronius, 2012).

The adoption and expansion of SROs in schools is an interesting case of how policies that have no research base supporting their effectiveness, and in fact have been shown to increase racial disparities and strengthen the school to jail nexus, are nonetheless promulgated, even in 'progressive' places. Although city- and school district-level processes are key sites for decision-making about school discipline policy, research has not typically examined how and why polices come to be adopted, implemented, or expanded at this level. This study examines how and why, over the past two years, a US city known nationally for its political

DOI: 10.4324/9781003262077-2

progressivism has continuously reaffirmed its decision to maintain and expand the presence of SROs in its comprehensive high schools.

We emphasize the connections among the school to jail nexus, the carceral state, and the broader constellation of racial capitalism. The framing of the school to jail nexus illuminates 'the tentacles *in policies, practices, and informal knowledges* that support, naturalize, and extend relationships between incarceration and schools' (Meiners, 2007, 4, italics in original). This framing is powerful for understanding the linkages between schools, the racialized patterns of the prison industrial complex, and the carceral state. However, this framing can make it difficult to understand how shifting and contradictory recent trends such as restorative justice, anti-gun control measures, and a shortage of teachers of color in schools, which are not typically considered part of the school to jail nexus, but nevertheless can play a role in its expansion.

To capture this broader landscape, we situate this study in a racial capitalist framework. Racial capitalism is a term developed to describe the current world system, in which racism and capitalism are deeply interdependent means of organizing bodies (Robinson, 2000). Such a perspective emphasizes that race is not simply a justification for capitalism; rather, racism has always played a role in sustaining liberal-capitalist systems (Spence, 2012). In this study, elements of racial capitalism included racialized poverty and trauma, declining and inadequate education funding and social provision, policy responses to school shootings, and racism in schools.

We show how a constellation of discourses, policies, debates, groups, and practices related to racialized poverty and trauma, declining and inadequate state funding and social provision in and out of schools, efforts to address racial disparities in school discipline, state policy response to mass school shootings, and racism in schools from the national to school levels, intersect to contribute to the expansion of the school to jail nexus in this city. Two primary discourses emerged to make sense of how minoritized students' experiences of trauma, 'disruptive' student behavior, racially disproportionate school discipline data, and SROs should be understood: (a) a race radical discourse, which argued that SROs enacted harm and racism against low-income students of color, especially Black students, and should be removed from schools, and was largely disregarded by committee members charged with making recommendations about the SRO program and (b) a neoliberal therapeutic discourse, which argued that individual SROs benefitted low-income students of color by providing care and challenging school racism to justify the extension of the SRO program in the district, and which dominated the committee's decision-making process. We argue that SROs became an 'easy' fix to racial capitalism in the school district and city.

Racial Capitalism and Police in Schools

Major US cities began stationing police in their schools in the 1960s and 1970s and by 1972, school districts in 40 states had adopted some form of school-police partnership (ACLU, 2017). Today, there are sworn police officers in an estimated 48% of US schools (Diliberti, Jackson, & Kemp, 2017). The discourse and developments that have pressed forward punitive school discipline policies, including SRO programs and the broader bundle of zero-tolerance practices (e.g. metal detectors, surveillance cameras), illuminate how racial capitalism drives the expansion of the school to jail nexus.

The origins of policing in US schools date back to the late 1940s as Black migration to major cities was occurring and Black students were entering white schools. Kafka (2011) describes how Los Angeles teachers responded to school overcrowding, an increasingly racially and socioeconomically diverse student population, and moral panics about juvenile delinquency by attributing discipline problems to individual students' behavior and advocating for the Board of Education to adopt 'therapeutic services beyond the *educational* expertise of a regular classroom teacher' (55), a shift from viewing discipline as an educational matter and the teacher's responsibility to a criminal matter that is the responsibility of specialists. Sojoyner (2013), who also studied Los Angeles, found that school policing also 'developed in an attempt to suppress assertions of Black culture, Black autonomy, and Black liberation movements within schools' (245) (see also Schnyder, 2010). Together, this research suggests that the abdication of teacher authority and an active effort to control Black youth led to the rise of school policing.

Yet, formal SRO programs, launched in the 1960s and 1970s, were often explained as essential to forming positive relationships between police, students, and communities (ACLU, 2017). In practice, in most partnerships, school districts paid police departments to take over school disciplinary practices. After the Columbine High School shooting in 1999, US schools saw a spike in school-police partnerships, along with other penalizing measures, such as the installation of metal detectors and school security cameras (Advancement Project, 2010; Krueger, 2010). New neoliberal discourses have played a key role in promulgating SRO programs by positioning gun violence as inevitable and situating school policing as the only solution to 'assuage (largely White) fears and social security' (Nolan, 2015, p. 904). By 2013, there were 20,000 to 30,000 police officers patrolling US schools (James & McCallion, 2013).

The call for additional police in schools again circulated nationwide after the 2018 school shooting in Parkland, Florida. In the state where this study takes place, thousands of people, spurred by the Parkland shooting, marched as part of a national protest for gun control. Two days later, the governor signed a law providing school safety grants to school districts and requiring school staff to report serious and imminent threats of school violence directly to police, but the governor denied that gun violence was a problem. In this example of racial capitalism, the threat of school shootings committed primarily by white boys and men has triggered policies that double-down on 'school safety' while targeting Black and Latinx students (Triplett, Allen, & Lewis, 2014), a national trend that was mirrored in our study site. In this way, SROs operate as part of a larger neoliberal structure that renders youth of color more vulnerable to increasingly precarious situations (Turner, 2020).

The effects of SRO programs appear to be racialized, as well. While most research on SROs has not centered race (Javdani, 2019), research on school discipline and on the juvenile justice system indicates that minoritized students are more likely to receive frequent, harsh treatment by educators than their white peers (Skiba, Eckes, & Brown, 2009/10), and that children of color who become involved with law enforcement have higher rates of subsequent arrest and conviction (Soler, Shoenberg, & Schindler, 2009). Black and Latinx boys are more likely to face jail time as a result of contact with police, and to be subjected to low-level penal management (Nolan, 2011). While a large body of research has focused on the disproportionate punishment of Black and Latinx boys (Ferguson, 2000; Rios, 2011), Morris (2016) found that Black girls are disproportionately punished and pushed out of schools due to their perceived 'bad attitudes', the criminalization of their appearance, and punitive school practices like zero-tolerance policies. State-level discipline data in the state echo these findings. Black, Latinx, and Native American students across gender categories are significantly overrepresented in the exclusionary discipline in the state.

SROs are not new in the state but, beyond the adoption of the state law noted above, there are little data or research on SROs in the state. We do know that Black high school students in this state are suspended at a higher rate than anywhere else in the US, while the white suspension rate is one of the lowest in the country. State-level data beyond the schoolhouse walls suggest connections between policing and racial capitalism. For example, the state leads in the US in incarceration rates for Black and Native American adults. State sentencing and policing laws disproportionately affect Black people and have contributed to skyrocketing incarceration rates and prison construction, often in white rural locales seeking jobs. The state now spends more on incarceration than on higher education, which has faced significant budget cuts.[1]

Overall, research on SROs illuminates the importance of racial capitalism in school discipline policy and specifically school policing, but leaves unexplored policymaking in action. In this study, we examine the contested discourses at play in a debate about one SRO program as a way to understand how—through these discourses—racial capitalism works to *expand* the school to jail nexus.

Viewing Racial Capitalism through Racial Projects

Theories of racial formation and racial projects help explain the shifting and contested discourses and forms that racial capitalism has taken over time. Racial formation highlights race as a socially constructed and historically situated process that is always intertwined with class, gender, sexuality, and other systems of oppression. The concept of racial projects 'capture[s] the simultaneous and co-constitutive ways that racial meanings are translated into social structures and become racially signified' (Omi & Winant, 2015, p. 109). The notion of a racial project connects particular racial ideologies, representations, and identities with efforts to '*organize and distribute resources (economic, political, cultural) along particular racial lines*' (125, italics in original). Racial projects come in many forms, including macro policy and everyday practice, making the concept useful for denoting the different amalgams of official texts, discourses, processes, and practices that may play roles in the school to jail nexus, including SRO policy.

White supremacy is the foundational racial project in the United States. US custom, law, and institutions such as citizenship, slavery, segregation, and other public policies were all justified by explicit white supremacist ideologies designed to exclude people of color from full social, economic, and political rights (Harris, 1995). Today, racism is a fundamental characteristic of education policy and practices (Gillborn, 2005). Yet, racial projects are continually created, changed, coopted, and merged.

Since the post-World War II era, many racial projects have sutured together the language of racial equity and civil rights with policies that maintain raced and classed social order. These racial projects reflect 'official anti-racisms' (Melamed, 2011); they signal that they oppose racism but do little to challenge racism's ideologies or structures. In particular, beginning around the 1990s, racial projects of neoliberal multiculturalism (Melamed, 2011) and color-blind managerialism (Turner, 2020) emerged in relation to racial capitalism's current instantiation: racial neoliberalism. Racial neoliberalism in the US elevates market-based ideologies; emphasizes individual and private responsibility for self- and community-improvement; stifles notions of public responsibility and impulses for democratic and collective, political action; depoliticizes structural inequities; and has contributed to policies that have dramatically cut social spending, dismantled public sector social supports (e.g. schools, health) (Apple, 2006; Harvey, 2007; Spence, 2012). The carceral state (including punitive school discipline and SROs) has expanded to accommodate the legal and extra-legal racialized violence required under this system (Meiners, 2007; Melamed, 2011). These developments have had disproportionately negative effects on poor people and communities of color and have contributed to growing inequality and poverty. Yet, '[F]ar from eschewing race, [the neoliberal project] recruits familiar racial imaginations for its ideological and policy agendas' (Dumas, 2016, p. 96). Current racial projects mis-read or co-opt anti-racist notions to legitimize education policies that expand or protect racial neoliberalism (e.g. Stern & Hussain, 2015). In this article, we identify a *neoliberal therapeutic discourse* as an official anti-racism that justifies the extension of SRO presence in schools and thus racial capitalism.

White supremacy has always been contested by anti-racists. Marginalized and oppressed groups have challenged dominant racial projects and put forward emancipatory racial projects (Robinson, 2000). Mass movements and intellectuals in the Black radical, or race radical tradition,[2] have pressed for 'antiracist thinking, struggle and politics that reckon precisely with those aspects of racialization that official liberal antiracisms screen off', including inequities and harm that result from racial capitalism (Melamed, 2011, p. 47). They call for a complete rejection of enslavement and racism, communitarian and radical democratic commitments (rather than individualized ones), and distinguish moral from political action (Robinson, 2000). Race radical projects thus provide a new ethical critique and alternative vision for society. In this study, we identify a *race radical discourse* that challenged dominant discourses and offered an alternative to policing in schools.

Through these theories, we can more fully understand the decision to maintain and expand the presence of SROs in a city known nationally for its political progressivism. Attention to racial projects illuminates the neoliberal therapeutic discourse as an official anti-racism that reinforces SRO policy, and the race radical discourse challenging that dominant discourse, and thus racial neoliberalism in schools. Finally, in connecting racial projects to racial capitalism, we analyze SRO policy as interwoven with policies and structures related to racial neoliberalism and offer a way to understand how—through local debate and discourses—racial capitalism works to expand the school to jail nexus.

Methods and Context

This study draws on data from a qualitative case study of policymaking and community advocacy in one midwestern city. The findings are based on three years (2015–2018) of ethnographic data, including field notes of school board, SRO committee, and community meetings; 33 semi-structured interviews with diverse educational advocates (e.g. youth activists of color, a conservative commentator), members of the SRO committee, and school board members; and documents (e.g. reports, news coverage).

To examine the discourses invoked in the SRO debate, their underlying ideological implications, and the contexts shaping these positions, we engaged in analytic memoing about themes and concepts from the data (Corbin & Strauss, 2008), developed a codebook using both inductive and deductive codes, systematically coded data, and created data displays identifying themes participants used in discussing the SRO program (Miles & Huberman, 1994).

The debate about SRO policy unfolded in the context of ongoing shootings of unarmed Black people, the rise of the Movement for Black Lives, and unprecedented attention to racially disproportionate school discipline in the US (Green, 2018; Loveless, 2017). Although the city in which this research was conducted is widely conceived of as a liberal enclave in a purple state,[3] racial inequities have plagued the city and its schools for decades. Locally, there was considerable attention to and protest against the lethal shooting in 2015 of an unarmed Black youth, a recent graduate of the school district. Partly in response to racially disproportionate discipline data, the district had recently adopted a new discipline policy that called for 'progressive' discipline aimed at avoiding zero-tolerance practices whenever possible and moved toward implementing district-wide restorative practices. As Winn (2018) notes, 'restorative practices' are a promising direction, but can reflect a focus on method rather than the deep, transformative commitment and change that is required of restorative justice.

In this context, several community groups began organizing to end the school district's SRO contract with the police department. While the contract was renewed in October 2016, the school board subsequently established a committee to evaluate and make recommendations to improve the SRO program. The SRO committee was composed of three school board members (all of whom identified as white) and nine board-appointed community members, including a high school teacher, a former SRO, a developmental psychologist, a director of a community development organization, a social worker, a criminal defense attorney, a city council member, an outreach coordinator for a non-profit, and a retired corporate executive. Three committee members were Black, one committee member was Latinx, and one committee member was Asian; however, their views were moderate when compared to the Black- and Southeast Asian-led organization Transformative Justice and the predominantly white organization Racial Justice Allies, the race radical community organizations opposing the SRO program.

Nevertheless, the committee was ostensibly committed to challenging inequities perpetuated by the SRO program. At the first meeting, a school board member suggested it was a 'possibility and perhaps a necessity' to consider whether they should continue to have SROs at all. Another school board member on the committee suggested that the committee could reduce the number of students who enter the prison system by reconsidering the SRO program.

In the 2018–2019 school year, the school district paid over $350,000 to employ SROs, three of whom were people of color and one was white.

Findings

Amidst a variety of views, two contending discourses shaped the debate about the SRO program in the school district: a race radical argument and a neoliberal therapeutic argument. These discourses proffered dramatically different notions of what it means to care for minoritized students exhibiting non-sanctioned behavior and who in schools should be responsible for that work. Taken together, elements of racial neoliberalism, including a state policy that overdetermined the extension of police presence in the school district, reemerge within the neoliberal therapeutic discourse such that it counters race radical logics that challenge SROs in schools. Thus, our findings demonstrate how and why it is possible that research evidence, the history of racist policing, disproportionate discipline data, and testimony of low-income families and students of color, can all be dismissed and/or reincorporated into the school to jail nexus and allow for the continuation and extension of an SRO program.

The Race Radical View of SROs

Race radicals critiqued the placement of police officers in schools and viewed SROs—like police officers more broadly—as agents of state violence and part of a system that harms and criminalizes youth of color, particularly Black youth. Working-class Black and Southeast Asian youth activists who organized together through Transformative Justice, a local organization aligned with the national Movement for Black Lives, and Racial Justice Allies, a predominantly white group aimed at disrupting white supremacy in the local schools and in this midwestern community, both argued for the removal of SROs from schools and community control over school discipline. Consistent with a tradition of Black radical thought, race radicals emphasized anti-racist and anti-capitalist themes, including a rejection of racism experienced by people of color and a focus on systemic or institutional change, redistribution of resources and recognition, and radical democratic structures.

The race radical discourse centered on eliminating the racism and injustice that contributed to and was caused by the school to jail nexus. Throughout the three years of research, race radicals consistently pointed to the fear and harm to youth of color that came from police presence in schools. They offered news and social media accounts of SRO violence against Black students, and they testified as Black and Southeast Asian youth to their own and others' stories of fear and physical harm in interactions with SROs. For example, after saying he does not understand how SROs can be resources to students, given statistics on disproportionate policies, Jason, a Black student activist, related to the committee:

> I came to school late, walking to the classroom. The officer asks why I'm skipping class. I told him the reason: I was studying for the math test and going through depression. The cop told me I have a warning. If I skip again, I would be cited. This is putting students of color into more danger, making us feel uncomfortable in schools. It's the prison pipeline.

Race radical discourses highlighted the police role in criminalizing Black youth and families for racialized, non-criminal behavior like speaking in their native tongue or being stopped by police who said that they dressed suspiciously or assumed they were carrying drugs and weapons. Linda, a Southeast Asian youth organizer and high school student, admitted, 'I do get in trouble with cops here and there'. She explained: 'I hold teachers accountable for saying messed up shit. If I wear a hoodie, I have a teacher who is going to tell me to put it down'. From her perspective, interactions with SROs were linked to racist teachers (i.e. teachers who espoused Eurocentric views and who targeted her for her clothing) handing their discipline concerns over to SROs.

The race radical discourse recognized school discipline issues and the entanglements that students of color experienced with SROs as associated with poverty, homelessness, racism, and ongoing traumatic experiences, as indicated in some earlier quotes. However, in contrast to common views of trauma that treat it as a result of individual pathology, race radicals were careful to articulate minoritized students' entanglements with SROs as rooted in socio-economic and political structures of poverty and racism. The discourse was never only about SROs or even the school to jail nexus. Rather, race radical discourses positioned their opposition to SROs in schools as part of a broader struggle to end harm to students of color, particularly Black youth, in all realms.

Race radicals advocated for systemic or institutional change, redistribution, and recognition for low-income students of color, and radical democratic structures to transform schools and society. In public testimony to the SRO committee, a Black student and organizer, Nia, articulated Transformative Justice's demands as: 'Take cops out of schools. We don't need them to be involved in Restorative Justice', demands that were met with snaps of approval from a member of Racial Justice Allies. Reflecting race radical anti-racist and anti-capitalist commitments, she also demanded investment in community-based organizations that support the youth of color and greater cultural relevancy and self-determination over school curriculum.

Race radical discourse emphasized transformative institutional changes to schools and policing rather than individualized forms of change. For example, activists argued that individual SROs were part of a larger system that was organized to police and criminalize youth of color and link them to incarceration. At an SRO committee meeting in the fall of 2017, a Southeast Asian student, Carlton, testified in opposition to cops in schools, saying: 'Even though we have cops creating relationships, their job is to criminalize and dehumanize. Not creating opportunities for students of color, only making incarceration accessible'. In this statement, he emphasized that the institution of policing was the problem. He concluded with a demand for system change, saying: 'We want community control over school discipline'. Carlton and other race radicals proposed ending police patrol of schools and replacing existing systems with ones that are controlled by communities of color. These proposals focused on changing government institutions rather than individualized solutions.

Other race radical suggestions included redistributing resources and recognizing the history, knowledge, and care of communities of color. Race radicals argued for food, housing, and transportation for families living in poverty. They suggested redistributing funds away from the SRO program to school counselors and social workers, a solution that contributes to improved student outcomes and school safety (ACLU, 2019). For months, they reiterated proposals to shift the funds allocated to the SRO program to other uses. For example, they issued calls to the committee to 'Terminate the [SRO] contract. Use the money for things that would help low-income students, like healthier food, teachers of color, and transportation'. Race radicals also advocated for hiring teachers of color and instituting culturally relevant curriculum to address students' alienation and experiences with racism in schools. Furthermore, they proposed radical democratic experiments, like community control of school discipline, as a way to create institutional change in school discipline. Linda insisted:

> We know what's best for us. If a fight were to happen, and a student brings a weapon to school, that's why you hire youth advocates. If I were to get in trouble for a fight again, I would want those who care about me to hold me accountable, and not the cops.

From this perspective, appropriate care for students who were experiencing trauma, poverty, and racism met students' basic needs, recognized and tackled racism in schools, and came from within communities of color.

In the context of racial neoliberalism, race radical groups consistently articulated key themes of anti-racism, institutional or systemic change, redistribution, and recognitional responses, and radical democratic decision-making in their public testimony to the SRO committee. Their perspectives provided a counter to the neoliberal therapeutic view of SROs, but race radicals had little ideological opening to be heard and SRO committee members largely dismissed their points.

The Neoliberal Therapeutic View of SROs

The neoliberal therapeutic discourse framed SROs as mentors or counselors to troubled students and likened them to social workers who provided an alternative to punitive discipline even as they still held police powers. Through their counseling, mentoring, and social work, SROs, who were often Black men, were held up as individuals who were valiantly, and directly, addressing the trauma and school racism that impacted low-income students of color and contributed to racial disparities in discipline. This discourse emphasized themes of trauma; privatized responsibility for social welfare; therapeutic and relational Black male police 'care' for minoritized students; and the inevitable need for force.

Neoliberal therapeutic discourse drew on an already circulating discourse about students suffering from trauma or mental health challenges. Teachers and others argued that such students were not receiving the services they needed, placing greater burdens on teachers and schools, and making it difficult to carry out the district's new 'progressive' discipline plan. In testimony before the SRO committee, Sherry, a Black social worker, explained:

> A lot of our students go through trauma. A lot of adults in the school building don't know how to deal with it. All of our staff needs to learn to respond as if all of our students have had trauma.

This discourse suggested that learning to respond to trauma (e.g. through counseling) was something that communities and schools did not know, nor were they adequately staffed, to do. Discussions of trauma can reflect assumptions of individual or group pathology and be a refreshed version of old cultural deficit narratives, or they can speak to the harm caused by societal conditions and structural poverty. The neoliberal therapeutic discourse can absorb both of these explanations of trauma. But, to the extent that trauma was associated with social and structural factors, it was connected to poverty rather than racism and disconnected to these through its color blindness and solutions that did not address the societal and structural causes of trauma.

Central to the neoliberal therapeutic discourse was the notion of private individual or community responsibility for social welfare. SROs are employees of the state but, as suggested by the quotes below, the neoliberal therapeutic discourse positioned individual SROs as the solution to poverty, trauma, and racism. This notion was captured in the narratives about SROs espoused by SRO advocates and by committee members who regularly singled out and praised SROs as exceptional, virtuous practitioners. For example, a high school principal testified about a former SRO:

> Jerome Hill bought students lunch and breakfast, helped parents find a student who refused to come home, dealt with a student who choked another student (could have been a battery charge). He made a follow-up conversation with that student to counsel him through that. What could have happened if there was another police officer who didn't know him as well?…I like to think of Jerome as 80% teacher coach and mentor, 15% more of a secondary social worker, psychologist even, and 5% police officer.

These statements highlight aspects of Officer Hill's work that were of his own initiative and involved his personal funds or sacrifice. The rehabilitation that traumatized youth was seen to need should come through individual SROs who 'personify the responsibilizing and saving work that the population needed' (Schept, 2014, p. 51) and focused on the relational work of a social worker, teacher or coach, rather than the punitive work of a police officer.

That SROs, who were often Black men, were cast as individually responsible for intervening in the lives of predominantly Black male youth illustrate what Dumas (2016) identifies as a racialized neoliberal push to privatize care for Black boys and proclaim 'Black responsibility for managing Black communal affairs without economic support from the state' (99). The framing of SROs as solutions to racial disparities in discipline echoes a broader tendency to position Black men as 'supernegroes' who will 'save' Black children (Baldridge, 2017) and offer the firm discipline that Black and Latinx boys, who are positioned as hypermasculine, need (Ferguson, 2000; Rios, 2011). Black males become white teachers' 'dumping grounds' for students of color whom they cannot control (Brockenbrough, 2014).

SROs were cast as individuals who could challenge racism in schools and compensate for poverty and a lack of social welfare provision through their individual counseling, mentoring, and caring relationships; work connecting students to resources and support; and restorative disciplinary practices. From the beginning, committee members discussed the importance of preserving SROs' positive relationships with students. As predominantly Black men, SROs held particular potential to be role models to Black students and were recognized as having developed strong relationships with Black students, who were most likely to get caught up in disciplinary nets (Irby, 2014).

SROs were described in contrast to teachers and racist school cultures. According to a Black staff member:

> We have teachers that don't give a damn about our kids. They don't understand where we're coming from.... The issue is about color. It's not about a police officer.... The issue is, we don't sit down and learn from our kids.... We were bragging a couple years ago at [his high school] that we had 85% students of color graduating on time when 5% were reading at a college level. That's BS.

Saying 'the issue is about color' and pointing to teachers who are racist or who do not understand students of color, this staff member argued that police officers were not the real problem. What was needed were people who 'give a damn about our kids' and want to 'sit down and learn from our kids'. Everyday racism in schools helped frame SROs, who were often Black, as an important corrective to racism in schools. Furthermore, the fact that SROs were some of the only adults of color working in high school buildings that made it possible for them to also be imagined as building relationships with students of color and as countering racism in schools. This assumed that any Black police officer would build relationships with students of color and counter racism, and that it was impossible for Black officers to enact racist practices. Such assumptions belie the heterogeneity among Black people and the structural racism tied up in policing, regardless of an individual police officer's racial identity. That SROs could be positioned as a solution to racism and as compensating for a lack of teachers of color, despite research evidence and minoritized students' testimony about the harm caused by the presence of SROs in schools, speaks to larger problems of racism in the schools.

In the neoliberal therapeutic discourse, SROs also served as boundary spanners (Honig, 2006) who helped school staff learn about students' lives outside of schools and connect students with needed resources. SROs were seen as helping to address the disconnect between school staff and poor or working-class students and families who were on police radars. Indeed, police officers by virtue of their policing roles had sources of information that were not available to school staff. In response to questions from committee members, SRO Pederson, a white man, explained:

> The other thing you're going to miss without an SRO, is it is not uncommon for a social worker to ask you what happened in the community. It happens if there's a runaway…who refuses to come home. Information on students getting suicidal at home. So, when we talk about police, we talk about arrests. The vast majority of my time is digging up that stuff, telling the right person at the school…

Officer Pederson downplayed typical police functions like arrests, classifying his work as more about connecting home and school. The idea that SROs connect students' home lives to school and to social services appeared to resonate. The 'Monday phone call', which notified school staff of incidents in the community, became emblematic of this connection. A school board member on the SRO committee reiterated the importance of the Monday phone call. 'It's a sharing of information between police, social service, and school people. And, I want to make sure that this [set of recommendations] does not preclude that communication', he said. Officers could also refer students to Youth Court and help students access social services in ways that school staff could not. With a shortage of school social workers and limited access to social services, SROs were seen as playing an important role in connecting students to resources or counseling during difficult moments in their lives.

Finally, SROs' work was framed as engaging in 'restorative' roles and practices rather than punitive ones, thus distinguishing them from neighborhood police officers. SROs were described as central to trauma-informed and restorative practices in schools and the district's newly adopted discipline policy. School staff also argued that SROs prevented disciplinary problems from developing and reduced or postponed student contact with the penal system. A white teacher on the SRO committee, Mark, argued that SROs gave schools the chance to 'deal with behavior issues internally'. This, he believed, might prevent a student from entering the criminal justice system earlier than needed. Similarly, Sherry told the SRO committee that 'Officer[s] Tenuta or Hill are our number one referrers for restorative justice', and she emphasized their role in diverting students they ticketed to Youth Court so that students would avoid a juvenile record. Rather than points in the school to jail nexus, SROs were recast as countervailing forces who kept students from the nexus.

Even as SROs were admired for their work in non-punitive discipline, there was still something alluring or seemingly necessary about police powers. As Nolan (2015) has argued, school policing is frequently framed as a 'best practice' (900) or necessary response, particularly in contexts with large populations of students of color. In a committee meeting, Officer Pederson spoke eloquently about choosing to be an SRO, explaining, 'My goal is to keep the kids in school. I try to keep them more engaged in school. I hate when I actually have to act, it's difficult' but he added shortly thereafter, 'The other thing, too, if something were to go horribly wrong.... As an SRO, I'm always at the school'. Even as they touted the care SROs offered, SRO proponents also allowed that it was still good to have police officers in the school buildings, because someday the force they represented might be necessary, too.

Rather than proposing social investment and hiring additional social workers, teachers, or community and culturally sensitive counselors to carry out therapeutic work (as race radicals suggested), the neoliberal therapeutic logic identified SROs as a kind of social workers-plus—individuals who offered counseling and relationships to students of color, and linked students to schools and to much-needed social services; individuals who could, by virtue of their identity, address racism in the school system, all with the added bonus of being agents empowered by the carceral state to take action when needed.

By framing SROs, particularly police of color, as an extension of the city and district's social welfare policies, anti-racist commitment, and overall ethos, committee members and school staff interjected school police into the broader narrative of social services and a liberal, anti-racist, benevolent city and school district (see Schept, 2014). Taken together, these circumstances made it seem like common sense that SROs fill the role of counselor or social worker that they could be a safeguard against racism in schools and society, and that SROs were, in fact, a desirable presence in schools.

State Policy and the Hardening of Debate on SROs

Relatively absent from local actors' discussions about SROs was tough on crime discourse that has justified zero-tolerance policy nationally. A local conservative figure, some school district staff, and one school board member did occasionally evoke this discourse, but it did not have much resonance in this progressive city. For example, when a committee member declared that students in schools without SROs were 'sitting ducks', several other committee members pointed to research and recent examples of school shootings and soundly rejected the idea that stationing police in school was effective protection against school shootings. A committee member of color responded immediately: 'At every school there's been a shooting at, there has been police'. Nevertheless, a school safety law signed by the governor just a month after the 2018 school shooting in Parkland, Florida,[4] is an example of how powerful policy overdetermined the outcomes of SRO committee work. In particular, as we show below, by requiring school staff to report any serious and imminent threats of school violence directly to police, the state law made the continued placement of SROs in schools seem eminently logical, even in the face of community protests and disconfirming data.

In a June 2018 meeting, news of the law was just trickling into committee discussions. However, it had an almost immediate effect of hardening the committee stance on SROs. The neoliberal discourse of the inevitable need for policing in schools was back. No one questioned that there would be threats to safety which would require contacting police officers under the law, and SROs were understood as preferable to having neighborhood officers in schools. Officer Pederson expressed:

> I guess I'm concerned about what our other options are. Without an SRO in the school, you have another officer.... Not every officer likes working with juveniles.... With an SRO, you know what you get.

Officer Pederson suggested that without SROs on campus, teachers and staff would have to call neighborhood police officers every time there was a concern. Sherry, the school social worker argued:

> At certain points, police officers are going to have to be called. Our police officers in our building know our students, they know our students in special education who may have severe behavior responses. If it was someone with an extreme behavior, another officer might take him to the ground. He's able to help de-escalate.

The assumptions, reflected in the quotes above, that the two groups of officers were meaningfully different and that calling neighborhood police officers was undesirable were only questioned by two individuals. Much like white teachers with whom SROs had also been compared and viewed favorably, SROs were viewed as preferable to neighborhood police officers who were associated with police brutality and excessive force against people of color, both locally and nationally.

As the conversation about the need for SROs was hardening, a conversation about different options for softening SROs was also building. The idea of 'softening' SROs gained steam among committee members who expressed concern or skepticism about having armed law enforcement in the schools. The committee explored ways to minimize or eliminate the parts of SROs that contribute to 'the school-to-prison pipeline', as the committee chair said. They discussed having unarmed or ununiformed police officers, placing SROs outside the building, replacing SROs with a police 'liaison' position, and putting SROs through additional training, including restorative justice training. Such proposals are not uncommon. Nineteen states have proposed or passed legislation to train SROs in areas like 'youth development, positive behavioral interventions, de-escalation techniques, mental and behavioral health, and trauma-informed care' (Finkel, 2018). But there was a protest; for example, in one exchange, a school board-committee member asked the district's former Director of Safety: 'Would you feel safe if officers were not in uniforms, didn't carry weapons, and didn't have the ability to give arrests and tickets? …'. This board member tentatively floated the question of 'softening' SROs. The former-school district official replied:

> [A]s a former police officer, if you want police officers in our school without badges, without guns, no one is going to support that. If you want to take that track, you might as well say we don't want SROs in our schools.

In multiple cases, ideas about softening SROs were immediately shot down as unacceptable to police officers.

The committee did enthusiastically pursue the idea of providing SROs with additional training. A committee member commented 'we're hearing over and over…that restorative practices seem to work…. [W]hy don't we significantly increase restorative practice staff training?' But, it turned out that the district was already giving restorative practices and discipline policy training to SROs and security assistants. Additional training represented more of a continuation of what was already happening rather than the pursuit of a new direction. Overall, the debate about whether or not there should be SROs had hardened, and alternatives to 'soften' the existing SRO arrangements were largely rejected.

Thus, while a tough on crime approach was scorned discursively by most committee members and members of the public who testified at meetings, state policy that reflected this sentiment nonetheless played an influential role in local decision-making. State policy did not structurally change much. Police officers could still be stationed in or out of schools and the law did not specify how officers in schools should be dressed, equipped, or supervised. Many of the alternatives the committee considered for softening SROs could still reasonably be adopted (e.g. community control, un-uniformed, unarmed). It was not inevitable, but policy overdetermined the continuation of SROs in the school district. Questions of how to soften SROs and provide a response to structures of inequality and racism, both of which had previously been proposed as alternatives to SROs, were sidelined and SROs were retained without much change. Certainly, the racial neoliberal nexus that had shaped both the race radical and neoliberal therapeutic discourses remained very much the same.

Discussion: The Official Anti-racism of SROs

Almost a year and a half after the committee began its work, the committee issued its final report. It contained a unanimous recommendation that the school district maintain SRO presence in the city's four comprehensive high schools. Sixteen months after the committee was first convened, SROs had come to be understood as a positive element in schools: a solution to the 'undesirable' behavior of youth of color who were experiencing trauma, mental health problems, and insecurity in food, transportation, and housing—and thus as a form of anti-racism.

The neoliberal therapeutic perspective prevailed, as is evident in the committee's recommendation for additional professional development:

> We recommend that SROs should be required to complete training and demonstrate competency, within a reasonable time from their selection, in all areas of de-escalation; trauma informed interventions, adolescent brain development; trauma response, discipline, security measures, [the new discipline policy] and classroom Code of Conduct.

Though there was an effort to officially add training in trauma-informed care to SRO's skill set, the punitive authority over students and the potential for violence remained in place. The final recommendation allowed for SROs to continue to be in schools, to wear uniforms, to carry their weapons and to arrest or cite students—all things that had been under question as the committee debated its recommendations. Other recommendations included measures intended to make SROs more accountable to the school district, such as a veto over officer assignments to district high schools and the establishment of a district complaint process. This provided additional oversight of SROs by district leadership but did not change the police role or practices in schools. Moreover, this recommendation did not provide for the community control or radical democratic oversight that race radicals demanded.

It may appear that not much had changed after 16 months of conflict and deliberation. However, the committee's recommendation was not simply more of the same. Rather, the recommendation strengthened the role of SROs in restorative practices and involvement in education teams and thus *extended* SROs' involvement in students' lives and the educational mission of schools. The perceived ability for these SROs, predominantly men of color, to provide care, community connection, and social services for low-income students of color, while insulating these students from harsher and more punitive engagement with non-SRO police officers provided a 'progressive' officially anti-racist justification of their presence and positioned them as central to the work of schools in serving students of color.

Furthermore, while committee members seemed to believe that their recommendations would improve the SRO program and benefit youth of color, their decision to proceed in contradiction to race radical students' voices—students who, as low-income youth of color, were those most likely to be impacted by the discipline policy and the school to jail nexus—reveals the degree to which the committee process and ultimate decision fell short of truly remaking school discipline in a restorative justice model and schools in democratic or anti-racist ways. Instead, their decision reflected the continued effort to control students of color and continued exclusion of communities of color from schools and from real decision-making power.

The contradictions of the situation were captured by one committee member who said she wanted to make 'one final statement' as the Board of Education accepted the committee's recommendations:

> It's been clear to me that we're very afraid to push back against [the police department]....These are youth whose lives are being impacted. The recommendations, I stand by all of them. I just want to strongly recommend that the renewal of the contract be contingent on some oversight....Since a lot of fundamental issues has [sic] to do with a sense of not mattering, [it] could send a strong message to students: "Hey, you can show up and adults will listen, and we care about you being safe."

These comments brought the conversation from the relatively narrow concerns of the SRO program, to the wider concerns of how low-income students of color were treated in the district. Like the race radicals, she situated the SRO program within a broader struggle for youth of color. Yet, the recommendations the committee unanimously endorsed addressed few of the elements of racial neoliberalism that had driven their thinking. The committee had not proposed a systemic, communal, radically democratic, social welfare solution to the racism that students of color experienced, but rather a vision of neoliberal privatization and the individualized responsibility of four SROs for the trauma, poverty, racism, and inequality in the lives and school experiences of low-income students of color.

Conclusion

With growing attention to racial disparities in school discipline, mounting critiques of zero-tolerance discipline, police brutality and killings of Black people, and a spike in school shootings, many school districts are turning to SROs to prevent school violence while forming positive relationships with school communities (Weiler & Cray, 2011). Though research shows that SRO programs reproduce and exacerbate racial inequalities in school discipline and student entanglement with the penal system (James & McCallion, 2013; Javdani, 2019; Nance, 2015), advocates suggest that they may also play a role in positive school discipline. This study of the decision to maintain the presence of SROs in one politically liberal school district suggests the multiple perspectives and challenges related to discipline policy and SROs that are likely to ensue in many locales, particularly in more progressive places.

In examining the politics of SROs in one school district, our study contributes to a better understanding of the local negotiation, and extension, of the school to jail nexus, and the role of neoliberal logics therein. In particular, in connecting the school to jail nexus to a broader constellation of racial neoliberalism, particularly broader neoliberal discourse, we show how the official anti-racism of neoliberal therapeutic discourse works with and responds to white supremacy and neoliberalism to perpetuate the placement of SROs in schools and thus the school to jail nexus. In addition, in highlighting the role of state policy in overdetermining policymaking outcomes, we point to how tough on crime policy becomes incorporated into a context where the school to jail nexus and zero-tolerance policy are explicitly, discursively rejected. Finally, we illuminate the official anti-racism of SRO policy, as racism was used to justify SRO presence in schools, and SROs were presented as a remedy to this racism. Thus, this study builds upon previous scholarship demonstrating the centrality of color-blind and color-mute language in district policymaking (e.g. Turner, 2015, 2020) by illustrating how and why anti-racism becomes a justification for the racist policy, and how neoliberal logics help to structure this outcome. Acknowledging racism did not preclude racism; in fact, neoliberal logics greatly allowed for this.

This work suggests potential alternatives and political considerations. Though they were not all taken up in this city, measures that committee member proposed, including careful vetting of potential SROs; requiring unarmed and plain-clothed officers; and training SROs in trauma-informed and restorative practices might be attractive to those interested in mitigating the negative effects of SROs in schools. However, such reforms, in and of themselves, are not ultimately a solution to the school to jail nexus. We want to be clear that it is only to the extent that such measures push people to imagine an end to the presence of SROs in schools and to adopt alternatives—such as those that youth activists imagined—to policing in schools, that they represent a step forward for just schools and justice in the lives of all children (Meiners, 2011).

This study also highlights the political challenge of community groups that ostensibly wanted the same thing (i.e. ending harm to students of color and the school to prison nexus), but whose 'solutions' are likely to result in substantial differences in practice. Youth activists proposed alternatives to policing and to the poverty and racism underlying disparities in school discipline, including community control over school discipline, additional funding for social services and basic needs, and a switch from SROs to counselors. Committee members advocated keeping SROs (rather than neighborhood police officers) in schools. There was a certain 'good sense' in the committee stance (Apple, 2006). SROs in these sites seemed to represent important distinctions from neighborhood police officers, even though they were still a police presence in schools. Moreover, the committee recognized the potential that new state policy might increase the in-school presence of police officers in schools who had no relationships with students. Nevertheless, recommendations to maintain SROs in schools continued and extended the logics of punitive discipline and zero-tolerance and had greater potential to harm students in practice. Navigating differing community approaches to ostensibly similar concerns requires being mindful of the likely implementation of these alternatives and the ultimate goals these solutions can achieve (i.e. better trained police officers in schools v. dismantling structures that criminalize students and building more democratic schools).

Furthermore, as long as state and federal policy takes a tough on crime and pro-policing approach, both of which are instantiations of racial neoliberalism, the race radical viewpoint is extremely disadvantaged. Even in relatively liberal locales, advocates seeking to end the school to jail nexus will need to address these policies and the structural origins of the nexus. This will require developing broad political power at the city and state levels. In this study, a school board election which became, in part, a referendum on SROs, resulted in the election of two candidates who explicitly opposed SROs in schools and potentially shifted institutional power in powerful ways. But the next steps remain to be seen. A distinct possibility remains that SROs will displace efforts to create meaningful change in the school to jail nexus and liberals will become further complicit in racial neoliberalism.

Notes

1 We do not cite specific research or reporting in order to maintain the anonymity of study participants.
2 We recognize the specificity of Black experiences and the intellectual origins of this thought tradition in Black mass movements. We use 'race radical' (Melamed, 2011) because those most closely associated with race radicalism in this study identified themselves as Black and Southeast Asian, followed by white.
3 In the US, a 'purple state', also known as a 'battleground' or 'swing' state, is a state where neither the Democratic Party (blue) nor the Republican Party (red) dominates election outcomes.
4 This state policy was in line with the STOP School Violence Act, approved by Congress in 2015 (Ujifusa, 2018), and the Trump Administration's repeal of Obama-era guidance to reduce racial disparities in discipline (Binkley, 2018). Both shifted funding and focus toward policing and away from ending punitive discipline in schools.

References

ACLU. (2017). Bullies in blue: The origins and consequences of school policing. https://www.aclu.org/report/bullies-blue-origins-and-consequences-school-policing

ACLU. (2019). Cops and no counselors. https://www.aclu.org/issues/juvenile justice/school-prison-pipeline/cops-and-no-counselors

Advancement Project. (2010). *Test, punish, and push out: How zero tolerance and high stakes testing funnel youth into the school-to-prison-pipeline*. Los Angeles: Advancement Project.

Apple, M.W. (2006). *Educating the right way: Markets, standards, god, and inequality*. New York: Routledge.

Baldridge, B. J. (2017). "It's like this myth of the Supernegro": Resisting narratives of damage and struggle in the neoliberal educational policy context. *Race Ethnicity and Education*, 20(6), 781–795. doi:10.1080/13613324.2016.1248819

Binkley, C. (2018). Trump cancels Obama-era policy on school discipline. *U.S. News & World Report*. https://www.usnews.com/news/politics/articles/2018-12-21/trump-officials-cancel-obama-era-policy-on-school-discipline

Brockenbrough, E. (2014). "The discipline stop": Black male teachers and the politics of urban school discipline. *Education and Urban Society*, *47*(5), 499–522. doi:10.1177/0013124514530154

Corbin, J., & Strauss, A. L. (2008). *Basics of qualitative research: Grounded theory procedures and techniques*. Thousand Oaks, CA: Sage Publications.

Diliberti, M., Jackson, M., & Kemp, J. (2017). *Crime, violence, discipline, and safety in U.S. public schools: Findings from the school survey on crime and safety: 2015–16* (NCES 2017-122). Washington, DC: U.S. Department of Education, National Center for Education Statistics.

Dumas, M. J. (2016). My brother as 'problem': Neoliberal governmentality and interventions for black young men and boys. *Educational Policy*, *30*(1), 94–113. doi:10.1177/0895904815616487

Ferguson, A. (2000). *Bad boys: Public schools in the making of black masculinity*. Ann Arbor: University of Michigan Press.

Finkel, E. (2018). The softer side of patrolling schools. *Spotlight on Poverty & Opportunity*, September 26. https://spotlightonpoverty.org/spotlight-exclusives/the-softer-side-of-patrolling-schools/

Fisher, B. W., & Hennessy, E. A. (2016). School resource officers and exclusionary discipline in US high schools: A A-analysis. *Adolescent Research Review*, *1*, 217–233. doi:10.1007/s40894-015-0006-8

Gillborn, D. (2005). Education policy as an act of white supremacy: Whiteness, critical race theory and education reform. *Journal of Education Policy*, *20*(4), 485–505. doi:10.1080/02680930500132346

Green, E. (2018). Government watchdog finds racial bias in school discipline. *The New York Times*, April 4. https://www.nytimes.com/2018/04/04/us/politics/racial-bias-school-discipline-policies.html

Harris, C. I. (1995). Whiteness as property. In K. Crenshaw, N. Gotanda, G. Peller, & K. Thomas (Eds.), *Critical race theory: The key writings that formed the movement* (pp. 276–291). New York: The New Press.

Harvey, D. (2007). *A brief history of neoliberalism*. Oxford: Oxford University Press.

Hirschfield, P. J. (2018). Schools and crime. *Annual Review of Criminology*, *1*, 149–169.

Honig, M. I. (2006). Street-level bureaucracy revisited: Frontline district central-office administrators as boundary spanners in education policy implementation. *Educational Evaluation and Policy Analysis*, *28*(4), 357–383. doi:10.3102/01623737028004357

Irby, D. J. (2014). Trouble at school: Understanding school discipline systems as nets of social control. *Equity & Excellence in Education*, *47*(4), 513–530. doi:10.1080/10665684.2014.958963

James, N., & McCallion, G. (2013). *School resource officers: Law enforcement officers in schools* (Report No. 7-5700). Washington, DC: Congressional Research Service.

Javdani, S. (2019). Policing education: An empirical review of the work of school police officers. *American Journal of Community Psychology*, *63*(3–4), 253–269. doi:10.1002/ajcp.12306

Kafka, J. (2011). *The history of "zero tolerance" in American public schooling*. New York: Palgrave Macmillan US.

Krueger, P. (2010). It's not just a method!: The epistemic and political work of young people's lifeworlds at the school-prison nexus. *Race Ethnicity and Education*, *13*(3), 383–408. doi:10.1080/13613324.2010.500846

Kupchik, A., Brent, J., & Mowen, T. (2015). The aftermath of Newtown: More of the same. *The British Journal of Criminology*, *55*(6), 1115–1130. doi:10.1093/bjc/azv049

Loveless, T. (2017). Racial disparities in school suspensions. *The Brookings Institute.* https://www.brookings.edu/blog/brown-center-chalkboard/2017/03/24/racial-disparities-in-school-suspensions/

Meiners, E. R. (2007). *Right to be hostile: Schools, prisons, and the making of public enemies.* New York: Routledge.

Meiners, E. R. (2011). Ending the school-to-prison pipeline/building abolition futures. *The Urban Review, 43*(4), 547. doi:10.1007/s11256-011-0187-9.

Meiners, E. R., & Winn, M. T. (2010). Resisting the school to prison pipeline: The practice to build abolition democracies. *Race Ethnicity and Education, 13*(3), 271–276. doi:10.1080/13613324.2010.500832

Melamed, J. (2011). *Represent and destroy: Rationalizing violence in the new racial capitalism.* Minneapolis: University of Minnesota Press.

Miles, M. B., & Huberman, A. M. (1994). *Qualitative data analysis: An expanded sourcebook.* Thousand Oaks, CA: Sage Publications.

Morris, M. W. (2016). *Pushout: The criminalization of black girls in schools.* New York: The New Press.

Na, C., & Gottfredson, D. C. (2013). Police officers in schools: Effects on school crime and the processing of offending behaviors. *Justice Quarterly, 30,* 619–650. doi:10.1080/07418825.2011.615754

Nance, J. (2015). Students, police, and the school-to-prison pipeline. *Washington University Law Review, 93*(4), 919–987.

Nolan, K. (2011). *Police in the hallways: Discipline in an urban high school.* Minneapolis: University of Minnesota Press.

Nolan, K. (2015). Neoliberal common sense and race-neutral discourses: A critique of 'evidence-based' policy-making in school policing. *Discourse, 36*(6), 894–907.

Omi, M., & Winant, H. (2015). *Racial formation in the United States.* New York: Routledge.

Petrosino, A., Guckenburg, S., & Fronius, T. (2012). Policing schools' strategies: A review of the evaluation evidence. *Journal of Multidisciplinary Evaluation, 8*(17), 80–101.

Rios, V. (2011). *Punished: Policing the lives of black and Latino boys.* New York: New York University Press.

Robinson, C. J. (2000). *Black marxism: The making of the black radical tradition.* Chapel Hill: University of North Carolina Press.

Schept, J. (2014). "Keep local kids local": Departed capital, derelict land, and (neo) liberal detention. *Social Justice, 414*(138), 40–61.

Schnyder, D. (2010). Enclosures abound: Black cultural autonomy, prison regime and public education. *Race Ethnicity and Education, 13*(3), 349–365.

Skiba, R. J., Eckes, S. E., & Brown, K. (2009/10). African American disproportionality in school discipline: The divide between best evidence and legal remedy. *New York Law School Review, 54,* 1071–1112.

Sojoyner, D. M. (2013). Black radicals make for bad citizens: Undoing the myth of the school to prison pipeline. *Berkeley Review of Education, 4*(2). doi:10.5070/B84110021

Soler, M., Shoenberg, D., & Schindler, M. (2009). Juvenile justice: Lessons for a new era. *Georgetown Journal on Poverty Law & Policy, 16,* 483–541.

Spence, L. K. (2012). The neoliberal turn in black politics. *Souls, 14*(3–4), 139–159. doi:10.1080/10999949.2012.763682

Stern, M., & Hussain, K. (2015). On the charter question: Black marxism and black nationalism. *Race, Ethnicity and Education, 18*(1), 61–88. doi:10.1080/13613324.2014.946490

Triplett, N., Allen, A., & Lewis, C. (2014). Zero tolerance, school shootings, and the post-brown quest for equity in discipline policy: An examination of how urban minorities are punished for white suburban violence. *The Journal of Negro Education*, *83*(3), 352–370. doi:10.7709/jnegroeducation.83.3.0352

Turner, E. O. (2015). Districts' responses to demographic change: Making sense of race, class, and immigration in political and organizational context. *American Educational Research Journal*, *52*(1), 4–39. doi:10.3102/0002831214561469

Turner, E. O. (2020). *Suddenly diverse: How school districts manage race and inequality*. Chicago: University of Chicago Press.

Ujifusa, A. (2018). President trump signs spending bill that includes billions more for education. *Education Week*, March 23. http://blogs.edweek.org/edweek/campaign-k-12/2018/03/president_trump_signs_spending_bill_increases_education_money_billions.html

Vaught, S. E. (2017). *Compulsory: Education and the dispossession of youth in a prison school*. Minneapolis: University of Minnesota Press.

Weiler, S. C., & Cray, M. (2011). Police at school: A brief history and current status of school resource officers. *The Clearing House: A Journal of Educational Strategies, Issues and Ideas*, *84*, 160–163. doi:10.1080/00098655.2011.564986

Winn, M. T. (2018). *Justice on both sides: Transforming education through restorative justice*. Cambridge, MA: Harvard Education Press.

3

THE CULTURE OF POWER ONLINE

Cultural Responsiveness and Relevance in Vendor-Developed Online Courses

Jennifer Darling-Aduana, Kathy Villalón, and Annalee Good

The Culture of Power Online: Cultural Responsiveness and Relevance in Vendor-Developed Online Courses

In recent years, around 14 percent of secondary public school students in the United States received instruction online (Gemin et al., 2015). This percentage is expected to increase in future years due to increased familiarity with the learning medium and infrastructure investments made during the COVID-19 era of emergency virtual schooling (Goldstein et al., 2020). Accordingly, the online education marketplace was valued at over 250 million dollars in 2020 and is forecasted to grow over 20 percent by 2027.[1] Several large, for-profit companies dominate the K-12 online education marketplace (Gemin et al., 2015). These companies are responsible for developing and delivering courses to millions of students each year, giving a small number of corporations substantial control over not just content development but also the instructional core of schooling (Boninger et al., 2017; Gemin et al., 2015). At the same time, the carceral system creates a huge profit margin via the exploitation of marginalized communities. In similar ways, alternative educational programming runs parallel to carceral systems. By outsourcing curriculum, in this case online credit recovery programs, learners in public schools are commoditized creating profit for private online learning companies (Boninger et al., 2017; Molnar, 2013).

Despite this, online courses represent an understudied trend in the education sector. More specifically, the curriculum in these online courses remains a "black box" for teachers, administrators, parents, and policymakers. This mixed method study expands understanding of the ramifications of this outsourcing of educational content through an examination of the curriculum integrated in four asynchronous, online high school courses. Findings establish the extent

DOI: 10.4324/9781003262077-3

to which the courses studied perpetuate privilege by reinforcing the culture of power online.

The culture of power includes the ideas, attitudes, and activities that are regarded as normal or conventional and are often aligned with (and advantage) the cultural norms and practices of the social groups in power (Apple, 2018; Apple et al., 2009; Delpit, 1995; McLaren, 2015). The School-to-Prison Pipeline is one means by which the culture of power is realized and reinforces the status quo. By assigning seemly objective (but truly normative) labels like "at-risk" or "behavioral issues" to students belonging to marginalized groups, schools legitimate exclusionary and self-fulfilling practices (Fine, 1991; Tyson, 2011). These practices are further reinforced through classroom curriculum and instruction through (often default, normative) choices such as what knowledge and ways of being are valued (Oakes, 2008; Tyson, 2011). These systems of marginalization are well documented in traditional, face-to-face classroom settings (Fine, 1991; Tyson, 2011; Valenzuela, 1999). Yet, there is relatively little understanding of how these same punitive systems occur (and are potentially magnified) within online learning environments.

Accordingly, we examined how social messages related to the culture of power are perpetuated, acknowledged, or disrupted in a fully online instructional environment through an in-depth analysis of curriculum in online learning spaces. This allowed us to identify in what ways students' identities and experiences were (or were not) recognized, validated, and embedded as central to learning processes online (Ladson-Billings, 1995, 2014; Paris, 2012; Paris & Alim, 2014). Through this research, we push back against the trend toward increasingly standardized and limited community connection prevalent in the most popular asynchronous online course systems that reinforce a monocultural narrative, fail to engage students in critical reflection, alienate students belonging to groups marginalized by systemic inequalities, and limit opportunities for students to learn the cultural flexibility necessary to succeed in an increasingly globalized world (Ladson-Billings, 1995, 2014; Paris, 2012; Paris & Alim, 2014).

Further examination of this topic is critical from an equity perspective, as students from marginalized backgrounds are disproportionately exposed to vendor-develop online curriculum and other educational services (Apple, 2018; Heinrich et al., 2019). Due to systemic funding disparities and subsequent limited financial resources, school districts serving marginalized populations are more likely to offer the types of large-scale, online course-taking options that often lack enriching, truly culturally sustaining instruction (Heinrich et al., 2019). Despite lower costs for online courses, schools often receive the same state funding per pupil, increasing profitability (Molnar, 2013). Secondly, within schools, online course-taking are most often used for credit recovery (i.e., the opportunity to take a previously failed course over again to earn the course credits required for high school graduation) (Darling-Aduana, 2020; Heinrich et al., 2019; Powell et al., 2015). Educators also report reassigning students to online course-taking to reduce behavioral disturbances in face-to-face classroom settings (Heinrich et al., 2019). These factors, combined with institutionalized societal inequities, result in the disproportionate assignment of students from marginalized groups – including students belonging to minoritized racial/ethnic groups and/or with a prior track record of academic failure or disciplinary referrals – to online course-taking.

We believe this is the first study to examine Culturally Relevant Pedagogy (CRP) within an asynchronous, online learning context from an explicitly critical lens, allowing us to establish the degree to which the generally standardized, plug and play structure of online courses and cultural responsiveness are compatible. As such, we examine the following research questions:

1. What is the nature of cultural responsiveness and relevance in the online courses, specifically the extent to which they perpetuate, acknowledge, and/or disrupt the culture of power?
2. Where are the places where cultural responsiveness and relevance are and could be better integrated in asynchronous, online courses?

This study builds upon the potential of CRP to transform the educational experiences and outcomes of students, particularly those from historically marginalized groups (Au, 2012; Dee & Penner, 2017, 2019). We apply knowledge gained from traditional, face-to-face classroom settings to map the types of cultural responsiveness and relevance observed within the enacted curriculum developed by one of the largest online course vendors in the United States. In doing so, we document the inherent limitations and leverage points for integrating CRP within a standardized, online course structure employed by an *urban emergent* school district located in a large (but not major) city that operates with a scarcity of resources and serves predominately students of color and from lower socioeconomic backgrounds (Milner, 2012). We conclude with a discussion of the systems and structures that perpetuate the culture of power within the online courses and recommendations on how to facilitate disruption of the culture of power in these and similar courses.

The Context of an Expanding Private Sector in K-12 Curriculum and Instruction

Current neoliberal education policies emphasize the importance of privatization, such as through the incursion of online course vendors into the curriculum design and delivery space (Burch & Good, 2014; Lipman, 2013). Neoliberal ideology emphasizes the role of free markets in forcing companies to meet consumer's needs while perpetuating claims such as false neutrality (i.e., the false notion that one can ever be unbiased or neutral) and color blindness (i.e., the belief that it is possible to "not see race," which reinforces the racial status quo) (Bonilla-Silva, 2006; Lipman, 2013). Researchers caution that by allowing for-profit companies to provide direct instruction to students, children have become commodities (Boninger et al., 2017; Molnar, 2013). This is particularly true for students residing in urban centers who are disproportionately targeted for the educational services provided by for-profit companies (Apple, 2018).

Further, there is growing evidence that high school students learning in asynchronous, online environments may learn at slower rates than similar students engaged in traditional, face-to-face instruction (Ahn & McEachin, 2017; Heppen et al., 2017). The declines in learning appear to be disproportionately experienced by students from historically marginalized groups (Ahn & McEachin, 2017; Heinrich et al., 2019). Due to the incentives for online course vendors to provide highly standardized products, succeeding in online courses often rewards conformity and discipline valued in working-class jobs over the proactivity and assertiveness that support post-secondary success (Anyon, 2006; Apple, 2004; Bowles & Gintis, 1976/2011; Darling-Aduana, 2021; Darling-Aduana et al., 2019; Karp & Bork, 2014). In this way, online course-taking may represent a new form of tracking, providing students belonging to marginalized groups differential access to essential knowledge and skills.

Online courses are particularly vulnerable to the neoliberal policy landscape because of their potential to increase educational productivity through instructional efficiencies, reduced operational costs, and economics of scale (Bakia et al., 2012). The modularized, asynchronous, "absorb and assess" type online courses that are most profitable epitomize the neoliberal conceptualization of education as interchangeable inputs and outputs that fail to consider or adapt to local contexts or students (McLaren, 2015). At the same time, the continued emphasis on profits among for-profit vendors disincentivizes high-quality and responsive curriculum and instruction, which often require greater financial investments and reduces the potential for scalability (Burch & Good, 2014; Boninger et al., 2017). These incentives appear consistent with trends among the online courses provided by large-scale, third-party vendors, which are often distinguished by an overemphasis on memorization, alignment of content with dominant cultural norms and values, and little state oversight of curricular content (Molnar, 2013).

In other words, the structure of many online course systems perpetuates privilege through the enactment of the hidden curriculum by exposing students disproportionately from minoritized and lower-income backgrounds and in urban centers to educational experiences that require them to recite and remember (Apple, 2004, 2018; Bowles & Gintis, 1976/2011; Darling-Aduana, 2021; Darling-Aduana et al., 2019; Karp & Bork, 2014). This combined with the prioritization of scalability through standardization among many low-cost online course providers has the potential to exacerbate the emphasis on normative values, assumptions, and expectations, resulting in disparate educational experiences and subsequent alienation by student identity (Apple, 2018; McLaren, 2015).

Applying a Critical Lens to Online Learning

To examine these concerns, we apply two frameworks to guide our examination of online learning: critical curriculum studies and culturally relevant pedagogy. We discuss each below.

Critical Curriculum Studies

Critical curriculum studies identify ways in which the official knowledge contained in school curricula is a subjective collection of truths, often from the perspective of dominant social groups designed to support and provide legitimacy to the status quo (Apple, 2018; Ladson-Billings, 1995; McLaren, 2015). The dichotomy between the official, explicit curriculum established by state standards and this *hidden curriculum* – "the teaching of norms, values, and dispositions that goes on simply by… living in and coping with the institutional expectations and routines of school" (Apple, 2004, p.13) – results in students and communities belonging to non-dominant groups encountering curricular content and instruction that do not reflect or validate their lived realities (Apple, 2018; Au, 2012; McLaren, 2015). Student interactions with the instructional core of schools can either perpetuate or disrupt inequities based on the extent to which cultural hegemony is accepted versus identified and questioned (Apple, 2018; Apple et al., 2009; Ladson-Billings, 1995; McLaren, 2015).

Implicit and explicit bias and assumptions around life experiences, frames of references, and values in educational materials and curricula contribute to the alienation of students from historically marginalized populations (Au, 2012; Gay, 2010; Kohli et al., 2017; Ladson-Billings, 1995). In aggregate, the normative frames represented in most curricular content results in differential access to educational experiences that resonate with students based on their cultural background (Gay, 2010). Normative frames include the ideas, attitudes, and activities that appear conventional due to their alignment with dominant cultural norms (Apple, 2018). For instance, curriculum developers may believe a word problem about the incline of a ski slope may be interesting to students but depending on their background students may struggle with the problem because they may not have lived experience with skiing to construct the necessary equations to solve the problem. In this way through continual negative micro-interactional processes, social constructs are transformed into real disparities through mechanisms such as a decreased sense of belonging, learned helplessness, stereotype threat, and internalized oppression (Steele & Aronson, 1995; Tappan, 2006). These interactions are compounded and reinforced by instances of overt prejudice and explicit bias enacted in the classroom (Kohli et al., 2017; Seale, 2019).

While these patterns are present in traditional, face-to-face classrooms, the increased standardization and automation facilitated by the technology sector, as well as the lack of diverse voices at these tables, often contributes to greater transmission of dominant social norms and assumptions (Benjamin, 2019). Further, the material highlighted in an asynchronous, online course potentially has increased weight because there are fewer means for student-teacher interactions to adapt content to local contexts or make meaning of the content together (Au, 2012; Bondy et al., 2015). The type of online credit recovery courses studied effectively place students in solitary learning environments (offering few chances to engage in meaningful or interactive learning) with the potential threat of further marginalization (Darling-Aduana, 2021). Therefore, perhaps to a greater extent than in traditional, face-to-face classrooms, content and delivery also shape how students interact with their teachers and engage in online standardized content.

Culturally Relevant Pedagogy

In response to the hegemonic patterns in curricula described above, which may be exacerbated in but are not limited to online courses, researchers have proposed several institutional changes to curricular content, instructional tasks, and teaching styles to provide equal access to quality educational experiences and success to students from historically marginalized groups (Banks, 1993; Gay, 2010; Ladson-Billings, 1995, 2014). Importantly, CRP was designed to first acknowledge and then disrupt the culture of power present in schools as a social institution (Ladson-Billings, 1995; Gay, 2010). CRP is based on the premise that students learn best when taught within their cultural frame of reference (Delpit, 1995; Gay, 2010; Ladson-Billings, 1995). In culturally responsive instruction, teachers scaffold the knowledge, skills, and behaviors students will need to be successful upon a base of mutual respect and effective communication (Gay, 2010; Gamoran, 2009; Ladson-Billings, 1995). The goal of this form of teaching is for students to learn how to navigate both community and dominant cultural norms, without attaching greater value to one culture (Delpit, 1995; Gay, 2010; Gamoran, 2009; Ladson-Billings, 1995).

The goals of CRP require first an acknowledgment of the culture of power, followed by the active disruption of institutional and structural inequalities that reinforce the status quo (Gay, 2010; Ladson-Billings, 2014). Teachers have addressed this need by incorporating multicultural content within a critical framework to help students take an active role in understanding race, culture, and systemic inequalities in their communities (i.e., Dee & Penner, 2017; Gutstein, 2006; Ladson-Billings, 1995). Integrating CRP online often requires instructional strategies not commonly found in asynchronous courses including feedback from the instructor, connections with peers, and opportunities to establish trust, build relationships, and form community, and feel cared for (Bondy et al., 2015; Frye et al., 2010; Hsiao, 2015; Shevalier & McKenzie, 2012; Ukpokodu, 2008).

Students – particularly those from historically marginalized groups – are less likely to be alienated from instruction when teachers integrate CRP (Aronson & Laughter, 2016; Gay, 2010). Studies have identified improved student engagement

(Christianakis, 2011; Dee & Penner, 2019; Milner, 2011), psychological empowerment (Hipolito-Delgado & Zion, 2017), and deeper, more meaningful learning (Gutstein, 2006; Laughter & Adams, 2012; Morales-Doyle, 2017). Specific to achievement, students assigned to an ethnic studies course just below the threshold for assignment earned GPAs 1.4 points higher than students just above the threshold who were not enrolled (Dee & Penner, 2017). Students identified as Black and Latinx scored higher on standardized test scores in mathematics and demonstrated enhanced mathematical knowledge when lessons integrated history and content that acknowledged the socioeconomic realities of their daily lives (Langlie, 2008; Martin, 2010). Similarly, students demonstrated improved reading comprehension when teachers integrated familiar cultural references and culturally relevant texts (Clark, 2017; Lee, 2007), while Latinx students in Arizona outperformed White peers when taught using a Mexican American Studies focused, social justice-oriented curriculum (Cammarota & Romero, 2009).

Methods

Data and Sample

Our findings draw on data from a multi-year, mixed methods study on the use of digital educational tools. All data were collected within an urban emergent district in the Midwest that contracted with one of the largest online course vendors in the country (Milner, 2012). This district operates with a scarcity of resources due to decades of city-wide disinvestment like that experienced in other Rust Belt cities and serves a population consisting predominately of students of color and from lower socioeconomic backgrounds who experience marginalization due to inequitable institutional structures and systemic inequalities (Paris, 2012; Milner, 2012). Although individuals experience structural inequalities for many reasons, including sexual orientation, language, and disability status, our study focuses on cultural identity tied to racial/ethnic background, socioeconomic status, and gender. We centered these identities as they appeared most salient to students and educators in the district studied. Further, we took care to not equate sharing the same sociodemographic characteristics with identity or culture, basing wherever possible assertions of shared assumptions, norms, and experiences on data collected through interviews, observations, and conversations (Paris & Alim, 2014).

Data collection occurred during the 2014–15 through 2018–19 school years. We analyzed data collected from qualitative and quantitative coding of online course videos, activities, and assessments supplemented with findings from classroom observations. Online course-takers made up 23 percent of the sample with qualitatively similar student populations enrolled and not enrolled online. Exceptions included increased likelihood of online course enrollment among 11th and 12th grade students and those with lower scores on standardized assessments, which reflects the predominant use of online course-taking in the district for credit recovery. Across the district, 83 percent of students identified as either Black or Hispanic, and 78 percent of students qualified for free or reduced priced lunch.

The district studied provides a salient setting for considering how the nature of online courses intersects with the dynamics of the School-to-Prison Pipeline in schools. Despite working with the U.S. Department of Education to address racial disparities in suspensions and expulsions in recent years, students identified as Black (who represent around half of the district student population) represented 81 percent of suspensions during the 2019–20 school year and 80 percent of other disciplinary referrals.[2] In total, 23,000 students (in a district serving around 78,000 students) received suspensions or expulsions during the same school. During the study period, approximately 108 youth were incarcerated on any given day in the county the school district served.[3] This context had particular relevance to our study, for example, teachers and administrators in the district shared in interviews that the online courses studied were often used to help students recover course credit after leaving the juvenile justice system (Heinrich et al., 2019).

The district provided researchers access to all third-party, vendor-developed online course content. We focused our analysis on the most frequently assigned course in each of the four core content areas: algebra 1, English/language arts (ELA) 9, citizenship, and physical science. We focused on these courses due to the large number of students enrolled and because we wanted to document differences across subjects. Within the district, these courses represented approximately 15 percent of all online sessions logged. We also relied on 200 classroom observations collected during the larger study.

Data Collection

We developed the Online Curricular Responsiveness and Relevance Protocol based on previous rubrics developed to evaluate CRP (i.e., Fiedler et al., 2008; Frye et al., 2010; Griner & Stewart, 2013; Hsiao, 2015; Siwatu, 2007). We kept items related to curricular content, structure, instructional strategies, and assessment, removing those related to relationship building or group belonging, which Hsiao (2015) identified as separate factors. Next, we divided the remaining items into three categories: elements that could never be facilitated by a standardized online course structure, elements that were always facilitated by the online course structure, and elements that varied by lesson. Although we summarized findings that emerged from course elements that were either always or never facilitated by the online course structure, we focused the observation protocol on those elements that varied. After adapting items to the online context, we distributed the observation protocol for expert review by eight scholars and educators with experience in online learning and/or CRP. We made revisions, additions, and deletions based on their feedback. The final protocol asked observers to rate the frequency that they observed key elements of curricular content, instructional tasks, and assessment strategies within each lesson. In addition to the rating scale items, observers also provided a detailed, written description.

The curricular content section focused on what was taught. For instance, items asked raters to evaluate the extent to which the module used normative examples – or those drawing from dominant narratives of White, male authority, and power – versus ones reflecting multiple cultural backgrounds. Thus, these items quantified the extent to which the topics covered acknowledged or disrupted the culture of power. The second section focused on how content was taught. Sample items asked the rater to evaluate the extent to which the instructor used a variety of teaching methods to meet different learning needs or how often students were asked to apply their learning to an issue, context, or problem beyond school. These types of instructional tasks designed to encourage higher-order thinking and application are a core component of attempts to support academic attainment and development of a critical consciousness. The third section focused on how students demonstrated understanding. For instance, did the module assess student learning using various types of assessment or integrate assessment strategies that incorporated culturally diverse content. Because assessments evaluate students' performance, any assumptions regarding student background or worldview may result in differential performance that does not accurately capture differences in comprehension. The assessment strategies employed also communicate expectations and values to students that may influence how they interact with lesson content and perform instructional tasks.

We established interrater reliability through two training sessions where all raters observed and completed the observation protocol for the same lesson followed by a discussion and reconciliation of ratings. Members of the research team then individually coded each of the 29 to 37 lessons per course using the protocol. For each lesson, we reviewed the approximately 20-minute video-based lecture component, practice problems, assessment questions, and any supplemental assignments. All of the five research team members earned or are working toward a Ph.D. in an education field, and all but one team member had previous classroom teaching experience. We assigned raters to courses based on content-level expertise. We also facilitated reliability discussions during meetings held throughout the analytic process.

Observations in the school-based computer labs and classrooms where students had access to work on these online courses during the school day were collected using a research-based, well-tested observation instrument that enabled observers to evaluate the extent to which the integration of educational technology into an instructional session facilitated quality learning opportunities for students (Heinrich et al., 2019). Dimensions covered included the physical environment, technology and digital tools, curricular content and structure, instructional model and tasks, interactions, digital citizenship, student engagement, instructor engagement, and assessment/feedback.

Analytic Strategy

Informed by our theoretical framework, we coded in Dedoose all narrative descriptions gathered using our observation protocol. During an analytic process, the research team agreed upon initial thematic codes that were updated and refined through the coding process. We wrote analytic memos around content and strategies that either perpetuated, acknowledged, or disrupted the culture of power. Subsequent qualitative and quantitative analyses were then used to corroborate the validity and reliability of the resulting analytic themes across lessons. For instance, we used descriptive statistics of rating scale distributions to confirm our perceptions of the frequency of various curricular content and instructional activities across and within courses. We also used rating scale items to identify lessons that reflected either typical or exceptional alignment with CRP.

Positionality Statement

Our research team is composed of five education researchers specializing in education policy and digital learning. All members are cisgender, non-disabled women of various racial and ethnic backgrounds. Further, all but one research team member has previous experience as a K-12 classroom teacher. We believe the experiences gained through membership in and identification with these groups informs our interpretation of the world and our data. As researchers, we apply theoretical frameworks that acknowledge and explain how individual expectations, interactions, and norms are shaped by and contribute to larger social forces. In acknowledgment that any social science research is influenced by the lenses and biases researchers bring to the work, we actively worked to acknowledge and question how our interpretations were informed by our cultural identities, lived experiences, and community contexts. We confirmed the prevalence of themes by triangulating data across sources and methods. We also held analytic meetings where we discussed alternative interpretations and explanations that ultimately led to an agreement of themes across members of the research team.

Setting the Classroom Context: What Did the Online Course Labs Look Like?

In the district studied, students were assigned to a computer lab classroom for one or more periods a day, which were staffed by one or more certified teachers; students could also choose to logon and complete lessons outside the school day. Teachers in the school-based labs primarily managed the logistics of the online courses (e.g., enrollment, unlocking tests), student behavior (e.g., keeping students on task), and technical challenges (e.g., internet access, headphones). Teachers also occasionally offered instructional support, most often in the form of tracking student progress and giving assistance on which quiz questions students needed to redo. In these classrooms, instruction occurred primarily through student interactions with the online platform, with the average student receiving fewer than one minute of instructional assistance from a live instructor.

The curriculum was highly structured and sequenced by the online course vendor with standardized content and structure delivered to each student. Content was completely housed and determined by the software. Each lesson consisted of the lecture video(s) followed by predominately multiple-choice-based assessments or practice problems. While there were limitations to the type of interactions students could have with online course content given its structure, we occasionally observed students engaging more actively with course content. Examples of active learning tasks included virtual science labs and scaffolded math problems, where the remote instructor worked through a new technical skill with a student that students then applied on their own before proceeding. Students also completed extended reading and writing exercises as part of the ELA course.

After observing students interact with the online course interface, and particularly considering low rates of academic engagement, we grew interested in the actual course content being presented to students (see Darling-Aduana et al., 2019; Heinrich et al., 2019). Interviews with district teachers overseeing the online credit recovery labs and an initial review of course lectures raised concerns regarding the cultural responsivity and relevance of lesson content. Although we focused this study primarily on what is feasible within an online structure to disrupt the culture of power, we first briefly discuss the inherent strengths and limitations of the online instructional environment.

Culturally Responsive-Aligned Features Facilitated by the Online Course System

In developing the observation protocol, we identified course features that were either always or never present within the online course system. For instance, the online course system collected information on student comprehension of course content through frequent practice problems and quizzes, which might facilitate some element of differentiation. However, instructional modifications based on student responses were not accommodated within the online course framework, and most questions only required students to remember lecture content versus demonstrate deeper understanding or apply content. As a function of the standardized and asynchronous structure of the course, the remote instructors communicated the same expectations of success to all students. Expectations regarding appropriate classroom behaviors and what students needed to do to be academically successful were explicitly communicated. However, these expectations rarely exemplified the high academic standards stressed as part of CRP and were not responsive to students' needs or cultural backgrounds.

The list of core culturally responsive and relevant components that the online course system could not facilitate was much longer. Courses were designed to be completed independently and did not facilitate collaboration. This limited the extent to which the online system could support the development of a community of learners. Courses did not gather information on students' learning preferences, home lives, or cultural backgrounds, and there were no mechanisms to make adaptations based on this information. In sum, our review of these online learning environments suggests there are barriers to CRP embedded into the very *structure* of standardized, asynchronous digital learning platforms. The following sections examine the extent to which the course *content* was culturally relevant or responsive.

Perpetuating the Culture of Power: What Does It Look Like Inside the Online Courses?

Within the constraints of the online course system structure, we next examined the extent to which course content perpetuated the culture of power – the ideas, attitudes, and activities of cultural groups in power that are often regarded as common sense and rewarded in a way that perpetuates social reproduction (Delpit, 1995). Although the online course provider developed and delivered the curriculum for each student, elements such as cultural relevance varied by content area and lesson. Out of the four courses studied, the ninth grade ELA course integrated culturally relevant and responsive content most often, such as when encouraging deep dives into the lifestyles and values of Haida, Mao, and Massai societies through an examination of their mythologies. Instructional tasks only rarely required critical reflection. However, raters noted occasional lessons within the ELA 9 and physical science courses that integrated these practices. Among CRP-aligned instructional techniques identified in our protocol, the online course system most often provided opportunities for students to use prior knowledge, prioritized depth over breadth, and used a variety of teaching methods. In contrast, course content was least likely to make the culture of power explicit or provide skills to function within the culture of power. Low ratings on these items indicated that online course content rarely acknowledged or disrupted the presentation of normative academic knowledge.

We also identified several emergent themes in the narrative comments about each lesson that we confirmed using rating scale data. Normative values, perspectives, and visual representations were identified in 49 percent of citizenship lessons, 35 percent of algebra 1 lessons, 21 percent of ELA 9 lessons, and 17 percent of physical science lessons. In these instances, instructors presented dominant cultural narratives as facts without opportunities for critical reflection. Similarly, "real world" applications in word problems and other examples often assumed a White, middle-class life experience, such as receiving a new car upon turning 16 or experiencing positive police-community relations. The prevalence of this theme was also documented on rating scale items, with raters identifying only 29 percent of lessons where "the module use(d) content examples from multiple cultural backgrounds" *sometimes* or *often*. In addition, raters only identified the use of "examples that are taken from a diverse representation of everyday life" *sometimes* or *often* in 28 percent of lessons.

Qualitative analysis of online lesson content also documented positivist perspectives and an emphasis on abstract or symbolic versus applied understanding. A positivist framework assumes everything has rational explanations proven through narrowly defined concepts of evidence and knowledge. We identified similar trends in rating scale data, with only 24 percent of lessons *sometimes* or *often* incorporating "tasks that require students to apply their learning to an issue, context or problem beyond school." We also observed a neoliberal bias to lecture examples. This content was characterized by an assumption and privileging of free-market capitalism. Additionally, content was coded as explicitly offensive in over 10 percent of citizenship lessons. As these themes emerged inductively from qualitative analysis, we did not have corresponding rating scale items to triangulate the prevalence of these themes across methods. The way each of these elements perpetuated the culture of power is discussed in greater detail below.

Normative Cultural Narratives

The most prevalent theme that emerged included failing to challenge dominant cultural narratives in course content, including ignoring the experiences of individuals other than White men. This was reflected through microaggressions in the instructional delivery of content. Many of these comments reinforced the narrative of American exceptionalism and the White male experience as both normative and the only one of importance. The following description of a representative citizenship lesson demonstrates how these concerns were realized:

> When talking about the Constitutional Convention the teacher said, "The convention was a gathering of great men. Thomas Jefferson called them `a gathering of demigods.'" The instructor repeated this at the wrap up of the section with no counter-narrative of how many of these same "demigods" also owned slaves and argued to keep certain rights (voting, owning property, running for office) from entire groups of people based on their race, gender or class. The instructor referred to Washington numerous times as the "Father of the United States" and Madison as the "Father of the Constitution." While talking about the Connecticut Compromise, there was a bullet on the "number of members based on free inhabitants plus 3/5 of the slave population," which was described in mechanical terms, but not in terms of the ethical and moral implications this compromise represented. At the end, the instructor asked [paraphrased] How would your lives be changed if the compromises hadn't happened, including would we still

have slavery. In the same lesson, the Missouri Compromise was invoked. The instructor said it caused peace for a while without any discussion of for whom the Missouri Compromise caused peace and for whom it did not.

As noted within the lesson description, without any acknowledgment of his perspective or privilege, the instructor (who was a White man) presented a version of United States history based only on the experience of White men. His language conjured patriarchal imagery with repeated use of phrases such as "great men" and "Father of the United States." The use of "demigods" to describe members of the Constitutional Convention represents a theme observed throughout the lesson of American exceptionalism and the presentation of history as founding myths versus facts that require critical reflection and analysis. Further, the emphasis on and lauding of White men within this lesson minimized the sociopolitical realities of centuries of slavery and the disenfranchisement of African Americans. Mentioning the Connecticut and Missouri Compromises without discussing the ethical implications of those decisions further marginalized the ancestral experiences of many Americans and failed to support students from dominant cultural groups in understanding how they continue to benefit from the same structural conditions that shaped these decisions.

Similarly, the following lesson presented dominant cultural narratives about taking land from Native Americans and internment camps in an insensitive way without critical reflection:

> In talking about the Worcester v. Georgia decision, the instructor referred to the federal government as "giving" land to Native Americans in treaties. On a slide regarding the Korematsu v. U.S. decision and Japanese internment, the instructor said, "Now they're not concentration camps, we weren't hurting or harming the Japanese Americans. We're treating them very, very well, but they are detainment camps."

The use of the word "giving" to describe the seizure of Native American lands avoids challenging normative assumptions about American exceptionalism and morality. To describe what happened in Japanese internment camps as not harming or hurting human beings is inaccurate and ahistorical. In both instances, the instructor described a Supreme Court decision without reflection on the unethical and ultimately unconstitutional elements in that decision, while the use of pronouns ("we") situated Japanese Americans as the other. Other examples of normative cultural narratives included the instructor describing post-Hurricane Katrina clean up as an example of a community coming together with no recognition of the long-lasting devastation experienced by marginalized populations in the Mississippi Delta.

Many examples of failing to challenge dominant cultural narratives were generated from the citizenship course, but there were a handful of excerpts from other courses as well. In science specifically, excerpts described science and reasoning as something done only by scientists (who are presented within text and images as all White men). In these excerpts, White men were presented as the center of enlightened policy, scientific discovery, and historical importance, as shown in the following excerpt:

> Within the lesson, all images (Rodin sculpture of The Thinker, paintings behind the Enlightenment discussion) were White men. The instructor framed the entire lesson by saying "Every institution is based on the theories of those that came before us" but then only included Greek, Roman, and European philosophers.

Not only does the content above perpetuate that White men are solely responsible for scientific thought and reasoning, but the exclusion of individuals from other cultural groups limits the diversity of thought presented to students and fails to leverage the higher-order thinking that the presentation of alternative systems of thought could encourage. In a similar light and with similar ramifications, when summarizing characteristics of an epic hero on an epic journey in ELA, the only epic heroes highlighted were European.

Positivism and Abstraction

While the previous examples presented decontextualized facts or white-washed narratives, other lessons completely avoided potentially sociopolitically relevant connections through the presentation of content as absolute truth. This positivist presentation was accompanied by comfortable or abstract examples. These instances reinforced the culture of power by failing to acknowledge its role in what is identified as academic knowledge and not preparing students to apply these skills to better understand and challenge the culture of power. In addition to not showing application to the lives of students from minoritized groups by avoiding potentially controversial (or sociopolitically relevant) content, these strategies also protect students belonging to dominant groups from recognizing their privilege or learning how to navigate in an increasingly multicultural world (Paris & Alim, 2014). For instance, problems required students to analyze polling data on students' favorite sports instead of using real-world data on topics such as voting, immigration, and health care. These occurrences were apparent most often in the physical science and algebra 1 courses (noted in 21 and 19 percent of lessons respectively).

Neoliberal Bias

We also identified a neoliberal bias in course content, particularly in the citizenship course but also observed in physical science and algebra 1 lessons. For instance, the discussion of budget deficits in one lesson was one-sided, attributing war, economic crises, and events such as oil spills as "something that happens" or acts of God, as opposed to acknowledging human or corporate culpability.

> The lecture lists several reasons why a budget deficit may be necessary such as a war, economic crisis, or natural disaster (earthquakes, oil spills). The instructor explains wars as "something that happens" and oil spills as a natural disaster... The advantages of a balanced budget listed are that it helps the economy by lowering taxes. This is not necessarily true, and lower taxes may result in an unbalanced budget. Disadvantages of an unbalanced budget are emphasized, including that an unbalanced budget "raises taxes and reduces government aid programs," which again is misleadingly simple. There is also an emphasis on international competition, that a balanced budget makes the dollar worth more against foreign currencies by stabilizing interest rates and inflation, lowering the price of imported goods, and increasing the value of government bonds.

The assessment questions in this lesson continue the emphasis on how deficits could negatively affect student's daily lives (i.e., interest rates, inflation, price of imported goods), avoiding asking students to wrestle with the complexity of national budgeting. Other questions required students to indicate a pro-corporation stance to select the "right" answer when other options were technically correct. For instance, to answer one question correctly, a student needed to identify that offering corporations tax breaks could lead to increased property taxes in the long run as the tax breaks expire but the businesses stay (despite the possibility that businesses will not stay or will negotiate additional tax breaks in the future). Further, many word problems and assessment questions in math were related to consumerism, including buying products or other forms of economic participation.

Application of math and science to social, political, or historical problems was comparatively rare, and the environmental impacts of industry were overlooked, resulting in false neutrality in content consistent with neoliberal ideologies. For instance, one sample response to an assessment question required students to write something like "producing plastics benefits the economy by employing workers and helps the economy of every state by spending billions of dollars on shipping plastics products." In the lesson proceeding this assessment question, the instructor did not discuss counterpoints, such as toxicity to humans or the environment, instead focusing on the "large quantity/low cost" ideology of consumption. The entire discussion of the "plastics economy" makes assumptions about the value of plastics and who it benefits. The emphasis on neoliberal thought and consumerism in these lessons, particularly in assessment questions, would likely lead to lower quiz grades among students with opposing perspectives and might actively alienate these students as well. Additionally, the decontextualization of facts represents a missed opportunity for students from both dominant and marginalized populations to grapple with conflicting facts and to demonstrate the real-life relevance of course content.

Discriminatory Content

Lastly, we highlighted particularly egregious content specific to the citizenship course. Many of these included the discussion of diversity or immigrants in a negative, assimilationist light and the perpetuation of racist and sexist narratives. For instance, in a section on current issues impacting American citizenship, the first bullet point listed was "increase in diversity." The instructor explained that diversity reduced national unity. Later, the same instructor framed immigrants as a problem and described some immigrants as "illegal." These statements provided a one-sided perspective on diversity and immigration, failed to acknowledge the historical precedence of immigrants and other diverse peoples in the United States, and reinforced any negative associations students might have with diversity by discussing it in generalities without supporting evidence.

In another lesson, the instructor legitimized racist narratives, dehumanizing African Americans.

> On a slide titled, "Abolishing /slavery & The 13th Amendment" describing the Dred Scott decision, the teacher said, "The court initially said `Mr. Scott, you are not a citizen, you are a slave so therefore you do not have the right to be here in court.' The instructor then went further and said, "You are property and therefore you can be taken anywhere (they) want because you are property... Slaves in Dred Scott were defined as property, as possessions, just like you might have a TV set in your living room."

Above, the instructor repeated racist comments regarding the perception that African Americans were inhuman without acknowledging the inaccurate, racist beliefs underlying the Dred Scott decision. After making these comments, the instructor proceeded to the next slide without providing context for the statement or opportunities for reflection. The ignorance of this instructor regarding race relations in the United States extended to current events, as shown below.

> A slide on natural citizenship showed pictures of Presidents Jackson and Obama. The instructor said that historians now think Jackson was born on a boat on the way from Ireland to the US then said the following about President Obama: "President Obama has a Hawaiian certificate of live birth, but there is a major controversy still going on with him because President Obama's father is Ni, uh, Kenyan. Was born in Kenya. And President Obama has some school records from Indonesia that says he is a citizen of Indonesia, so there's a lot of conflict. And this is being

worked out in the Illinois state courts right now." The instructor then goes into a review slide for the section, including a summary point about being a natural citizen where he again said, "That's what we've got a controversy on our current president on."

That the course not only gave airtime to the birther conspiracy theory but framed it as an open discussion that was unresolved perpetuated and legitimized a racist and xenophobic narrative. It's also notable that the instructor only mentioned in passing that there is evidence that Andrew Jackson was not born in the United States but instead chose to focus on the birther conspiracy despite evidence to the contrary. The instructor went on to provide information, such as that Obama attended school in Indonesia, which is irrelevant to his place of birth but furthers the ultimate purpose underlying the birther conspiracy that Obama is culturally "not American" without explicitly calling out his race.

The instructor also played into gender stereotypes. When describing a scenario where there were two candidates for class president, the instructor stated:

> One of them is a girl. She's very attractive. She's real popular, got a lot going on upstairs, and you're friends with her. The other one's a guy. Again, he's captain of the basketball team, great athlete, so highly, highly popular.

It is upsetting that the first characteristic mentioned about the female candidate is her attractiveness and that her intelligence is belittled by the colloquialism "got a lot going on upstairs." The male candidate is also stereotyped as a popular jock. By playing into high school archetypes, the attempt at relating politics to students' high school experiences was overshadowed by essentializing students in a way that likely alienated them.

Acknowledging the Culture of Power

While the previous section detailed patterns in how online courses perpetuated the culture of power, we also wanted to describe instances when the courses at least acknowledged (if not challenged) concepts like racism and other historical contexts. While these examples highlight the beginning steps toward what cultural relevance and an acknowledgment of the culture of power might look like in an asynchronous, online course setting, none come close to the ultimate goal of cultural sustenance and therefore, more often than not, reinforce the inherent limitations of the course systems observed.

Instances acknowledging the culture of power were few and far between, observed in one to 13 percent of lessons in a course. The four content areas and courses upon which our study focused each represented a different context and therefore opportunities for acknowledging the culture of power. For example, the physical sciences instructor briefly discussed the collaborative history of developing the periodic table but fell short by not delving deeper into the historical context in which the field of science was often made exclusive to White men. She discussed how elements were named and may use Latin names, but not why this occurred. In another example of a course acknowledging elements of the culture of power, an ELA lesson incorporated a biography of Maya Angelou where there was a brief (although not critically reflexive) discussion of racism and oppression. Similarly, the course included a detailed discussion of Pacific Island and American Indian cultures, diversifying understanding of literature beyond the White, Western canon. In addition to its somewhat more nuanced and diverse discussion of cultural communities, the ELA course went much further than others to identify and have students reflect on how culture and norms work. In one lesson the instructor asked students to reflect on their own culture and whether there were traditions that allowed the user to explain natural phenomena. Learning about different cultures and how to identify culture from myth is a skill that can help students' function in the culture of power.

In comparison, one of the few examples of the citizenship course acknowledging the culture of power was when the teacher hinted at contradictions in the lives of the founding fathers during the last summary slide of a lesson with, "The founding fathers certainly weren't perfect. We still had a lot of founding fathers who owned slaves. Women's rights. Women didn't get the right to vote, etc." But instead of digging deeper into these contradictions and the systems of inequity they represented, he quickly countered the comment with, "But, men that were running the government, they had a very pure democratic idea," softening, and thus minimizing, the valid concerns raised in the previous statement that acknowledged contradictions between the ideals and practices of early Americans.

In algebra, effort was made to make word problems relevant to students in a general sense. Questions asked students to calculate the total number of miles traveled, price paid for scarves and services, and taxi fare. In one instance, students were told:

> Mustafa's soccer team is planning a school dance as a fundraiser. The DJ charges $200 and decorations cost $100. The team decides to charge each student $5.00 to attend the dance. If n represents the number of students attending the dance, which equation can be used to find the number of students needed to make $1,500 in profit?"

This, and similar, examples provide real-world application, require students to identify pertinent information, and use that information to correctly answer the question. When presenting graphs, sample data included the number of languages spoken at home, the ages of event attendees, and the number of daily phone calls received. Later, students were asked to examine a dot plot showing the exam scores for a ninth-grade class and a histogram showing the age of new social media users. The graphs were followed by questions that required critical thinking, such as "Why does the data presented provide important information? Who might be interested in this data?" However, the instructor answered these questions promptly without allowing students time to think, and similar questions were not asked outside of guided practice. Although these examples highlighted some of the positive practices observed, none came close to realizing cultural relevance and responsiveness.

Limitations

As this study examined only one online course vendor, despite widespread use, additional research is needed to document the breadth of curriculum and instruction provided by online courses. Further, our study sampled the online courses with the highest enrollment in a single, urban emergent school district, which does not preclude the possibility of more culturally responsive or relevant courses offered by the same vendor but in other courses and/or districts. Future research should also extend understanding of how students with different identities respond differentially to the curricular content identified as perpetuating, acknowledging, and disrupting the culture of power in both the short and long term.

We Must Do Better: Opportunities to Disrupt the Culture of Power in Online Courses

Four million public school students in the United States enroll in online courses each year (Gemin et al., 2015). The content of these courses matters and can be easily overlooked by classroom teachers and district decisionmakers given that content is often accessed by students siloed in front of devices and outside of school. This is of concern, as online courses represent a growing, understudied trend in the education sector that provide predominately for-profit corporations with an often-unrecognized influence on students' educational experiences (Boninger et al., 2017; Molnar, 2013). Curricular relevance, responsivity, and ultimately sustenance are necessary to engage students in course content as well as a precursor to the development of critical reflection skills and the cultural flexibility needed to succeed in an increasingly globalized world (Au, 2012; Gay, 2010; Ladson-Billings, 1995, 2014; Paris, 2012; Paris & Alim, 2014). Failure to do so may contribute to not only reduced academic knowledge among students enrolled in online courses but also encourage conformity over proactivity in post-secondary pursuits (Bowles & Gintis, 1976/2011; Karp & Bork, 2014).

As the first examination of cultural relevance and responsiveness in online courses from an explicitly critical lens, this study extends prior research on online learning and other for-profit incursions into the education at a larger scale than available in prior literature (Boninger et al., 2017; Molnar, 2013). Findings can support policymakers, researchers, and educators in designing courses and educational environments that assist students in identifying and disrupting the culture of power in their daily lives (Milner & Lomotey, 2014). We hope our research-practice partnership work ultimately leads to the enactment of culturally sustaining pedagogies in online settings. Our findings also provide nuance to larger policy-level arguments on the disparate quality and relevance of students' K-12 educational experiences in the United States, as the type of emergent urban school district studied is particularly susceptible to the incursion of for-profit companies into the instructional core with standardized, unresponsive "solutions" exacerbating educational opportunity gaps (Apple, 2018; Boninger et al., 2017; Molnar, 2013).

Drawing on the call to action laid out by Apple, Au, and Gandin (2009) for critical approaches to educational research, we set out to bear witness to the types of online instructional spaces typically only experienced by students and use our privileged positions as researchers to systematically examine the culture of power in these spaces. Specifically, we highlighted patterns in how the curriculum designed by one of the largest online course vendors in the United States often lacked cultural relevance and responsiveness, mirroring findings in traditional, face-to-face classrooms (Delpit, 1995). The content perpetuated the culture of power by presenting dominant cultural narratives as fact and centered the experiences and accomplishments of White men. This emphasis alienates students from minoritized cultural backgrounds by invalidating their lived experiences, resulting in psychological strain (Aronson & Laughter, 2016; Gay, 2010; Hipolito-Delgado & Zion, 2017; Steele & Aronson, 1995; Tappan, 2006). Lessons across subjects exhibited a pattern of teaching decontextualized information, which fails to identify – let alone challenge or begin to teach students how to navigate – the culture of power (Delpit, 1995). This type of false neutrality and color blindness minimizes the discomfort of individuals in power by failing to acknowledge the systems that benefit them through the attribution of societal failures to individuals, thereby reinforcing existing structural inequalities (Bonilla-Silva, 2006; Delpit, 1995; Lipman, 2013). Lessons also failed to provide consistent opportunities for critical reflection, such as through the one-sided examination of economic and environmental issues from a neoliberal perspective, which did not prepare students to succeed in an increasingly multicultural, globalized world (Apple, 2018; Au, 2012; Delpit, 1995, Paris, 2012; Paris & Alim, 2014). Further, the citizenship course perpetuated explicitly racist, sexist, and xenophobic narratives. As such, we identified several missed opportunities to name and describe the culture of power at work, including how hegemony and racism work in each course discipline.

As one of the most "upstream" stakeholders, vendors have sizable power, despite low current marketplace incentives, to change the nature of course content (Burch & Good, 2014). In contexts where online learning is necessary, students, practitioners, and communities must help content developers realize that making course content culturally aware, relevant, and responsive is critical to ensuring student engagement; it makes a better product. Vendors looking to improve the cultural responsiveness of coursework within the constraints of online learning platforms can do so by contextualizing the study of each subject and using applied examples, such as the statistics of racialized housing practices, that draw on themes related to the culture of power (Banks, 1993; Gutstein, 2006; Ladson-Billings, 1995). Instructional tasks should provide opportunities for student-directed learning, deep dives, and critical reflection (Apple, 2004; Au, 2012; Banks, 1993; Cammarota & Romero, 2009; Gutstein, 2006; Ladson-Billings, 1995, 2014; Laughter & Adams, 2012; Morales-Doyle, 2017). For instance, instead of just learning the text of the Bill of Rights in the citizenship course, the instructor could support students in an analysis of how the concept of freedom of speech has evolved over time and has been differentially applied to various populations of Americans. Relatedly, instructional activities and assessments must require critical thinking instead of solely remembering and reciting information from the lecture (Apple, 2004, 2018; Gutstein, 2006; Ladson-Billings, 1995; Molnar, 2013). Lastly, multicultural content must move beyond surface and shallow cultural examples to those that acknowledge and integrate diverse values, norms, and worldviews (Ladson-Billings, 2014).

There are also larger questions regarding inherent limitations of standardized, asynchronous online courses for instruction, as these types of educational environments struggle to facilitate collaborative or learner-driven activities that are an essential component of CRP (Bondy et al., 2015; Frye et al., 2010; Hsiao, 2015; Ukpokodu, 2008). For this reason, fully realizing CRP online will likely require integrating at least some opportunities for interactive learning and discussion (Bondy et al., 2015). Further, collaboration with students, educators, and local communities – and subsequent adaptations of content and instructional strategies to local contexts – would further support cultural relevance and responsiveness in online courses.

In fact, our research team currently is in a partnership with district administrators and the vendor of online courses to draw on these study findings in an ongoing process of reviewing and redesigning course content. We are providing specific feedback to remove explicitly biased content, embed more cultural relevance, and explore ways (including through inquiry-based, blended instruction) to improve the cultural responsiveness of the courses. We are optimistic about the potential for this, and similar partnerships, between school districts, ed-tech vendors amenable to open dialogue about CRP, and researchers to improve the quality and cultural relevance of ed-tech content and structures.

Conclusion

Unlike traditional, face-to-face instruction where the district-selected curriculum or an individual teachers' personal beliefs might affect a couple hundred students a year, millions of students in over 16,000 schools nationwide are exposed to the curricular content and underlying ideological assumptions presented by the vendor who developed the courses studied. Given the rapidly expanding role of online learning in our K-12 schools, these courses must be more responsive to the contexts and lived experiences of the students interacting with course material (Apple, 2018; Au, 2012; Ladson-Billings, 1995, 2014; Paris, 2012; Paris & Alim, 2014). Students deserve to, and the future of their communities requires that they, be treated as more than commodities (Boninger et al., 2017; Molnar, 2013). As this study illustrates, exposure to content is not enough without high-quality instruction supporting the development of the critical reflection that fosters student engagement and intellectual skill development. This work should raise concerns that continuing to put any student – but particularly students already facing systemic barriers in their school and community-based lives – in front of courses such as the ones highlighted, which fail to provide opportunities and skills essential for personal, intellectual, and community well-being.

Epilogue

Many systemic and institutional structures contribute to the School-to-Prison Pipeline. In this chapter, we described how one aspect of schooling, online credit recovery courses, intersects with the dynamics of the School-to-Prison Pipeline. First, online credit recovery courses are often rhetorically figured as alternative, educational pathways for struggling students with asynchronous platforms such as the one studied used with students in or recently out of the juvenile justice system. Second, the online formats studied (both the instructional approach and the content itself) can be dehumanizing for students and often involves a teacher-student relationship that is more about monitoring than true engagement and co-constructed learning. These are both patterns indicative of the types of learning environments that facilitate carceral dynamics in schools. Through this research, we highlight how for-profit outsourced online curriculum – that disproportionately serves students from minoritized, low-income backgrounds – perpetuates the culture of power. In particular, we identified the specific contributing factors and characteristics, such as curricular content and educational engagement practices, that reify the culture of power for students positioned punitively within the educational system. Substantial revision of existing online credit recovery programs such as the one highlighted in this study are necessary to disrupt existing systemic inequities present in educational institutions and their contribution to the School-to-Prison Pipeline.

Notes

1 https://www.gminsights.com/industry-analysis/elearning-market-size
2 https://www.jsonline.com/story/news/education/2020/03/13/racial-gap-discipline-still-plagues-milwaukee-public-schools/4880382002/
3 https://doc.wi.gov/DataResearch/DataAndReports/DJC/DJCPopulationReport.pdf

References

Ahn, J., & McEachin, A. (2017). Student enrollment patterns and achievement in Ohio's online charter schools. *Educational Researcher, 46*(1), 44–57. doi:10.3102/0013189X17692999

Anyon, J. (2006). Social class, school knowledge, and the hidden curriculum. In L. McCarthy & G. Dimitriadis (Eds.), *Ideology, curriculum, and the new sociology of education* (pp. 37–45). New York, NY: Routledge.

Apple, M.W. (2004). Creating difference: Neo-liberalism, neo-conservatism and the politics of educational reform. *Educational Policy, 18*(1), 12–44. doi:10.1177/0895904803260022

Apple, M.W. (2018). *Ideology and curriculum* (4th ed.). New York, NY: Routledge.

Apple, M.W., Au, W., & Gandin, L.A. (2009). Mapping critical education. In M.W. Apple, W. Au, & L.A. Gandin (Eds.), *The Routledge international handbook of critical education* (pp. 3–19). New York, NY: Routledge.

Aronson, B., & Laughter, J. (2016). The theory and practice of culturally relevant education: A synthesis of research across content areas. *Review of Educational Research, 86*(1), 163–206. doi:10.3102/0034654315582066

Au, W. (2012). *Critical curriculum studies: Education, consciousness, and the politics of knowing*. New York, NY: Routledge.

Bakia, M., Shear, L., Toyama, Y., & Lasseter, A. (2012). *Understanding the implications of online learning for educational productivity*. Washington, DC: U.S. Department of Education.

Banks, J.A. (1993). Multicultural education: Historical development, dimensions, and practice. *Review of Research in Education, 19*(1), 3–49. doi:10.3102/0091732X019001003

Benjamin, R. (2019). *Race after technology: Abolitionist tools for the New Jim Code*. Medford, MA: Polity Press.

Bondy, E., Hambacher, E., Murphy, A. S., Wolkenhauer, R., & Krell, D. (2015). Developing critical social justice literacy in an online seminar. *Equity & Excellence in Education, 48*(2), 227–248. doi:10.1080/10665684.2015.1025652

Bonilla-Silva, E. (2006). *Racism without racists: Color-blind racism and the persistence of racial inequality in the United States*. Landham, MD: Rowman & Littlefield Publishers.

Boninger, F., Molnar, A., & Murray, K. (2017). *Asleep at the switch: Schoolhouse commercialism, student privacy, and the failure of policymaking*. Boulder, CO: National Education Policy Center.

Bowles, S., & Gintis, H. (1976/2011). *Schooling in capitalist America: Educational reform and contradictions of economic life*. Chicago, IL: Haymarket Books.

Burch, P., & Good, A. (2014). *Equal scrutiny: Privatization and accountability in digital education*. Cambridge, MA: Harvard Education Press.

Cammarota, J., & Romero, A. (2009). The social justice education project: A critically compassionate intellectualism for Chicana/o students. In W. Ayers, T. Quinn, & D. Stovall (Eds.), *Handbook of social justice in education* (pp. 465–476). New York, NY: Erlbaum.

Christianakis, M. (2011). Hybrid texts: Fifth graders, rap music, and writing. *Urban Education, 46*(5), 1131–1168.

Clark, K. F. (2017). Investigating the effects of culturally relevant texts on African American struggling readers' progress. *Teachers College Record, 119*(6), 1–30.

Darling-Aduana, J. (2020). *High school student experiences and learning in online courses: Implications for educational equity and the future of learning* (Doctoral dissertation, Vanderbilt University, Nashville, TN). http://hdl.handle.net/1803/10101

Darling-Aduana, J. (2021). Authenticity, engagement, and performance in online high school courses: Insights from micro-interactional data. *Computers & Education, 167*. doi:j.compedu.2021.104175

Darling-Aduana, J., Good, A., & Heinrich, C. J. (2019). Mapping the inequity implications of help-seeking in online credit-recovery classrooms. *Teachers College Record*, *121*(11), 1–40.

Dee, T. S., & Penner, E. K. (2017). The causal effects of cultural relevance: Evidence from an ethnic studies curriculum. *American Educational Research Journal*, *54*(1), 127–166. doi:10.3102/0002831216677002

Dee, T. S., & Penner, E. K. (2019). *My brother's keeper? The impact of targeted educational supports* (CEPA Working Paper No. 19-07). Stanford Center for Education Policy Analysis: http://cepa.stanford.edu/wp19-07.

Delpit, L. (1995). *Other people's children: Cultural conflict in the curriculum*. New York, NY: The New Press.

Fiedler, C. R., Chiang, B., Van Haren, B., Jorgensen, J., Halberg, S., & Boreson, L. (2008). Culturally responsive practices in schools: A checklist to address disproportionality in special education. *Teaching Exceptional Children*, *40*(5), 52–59. doi:10.1177/004005990804000507

Fine, M. (1991). *Framing dropouts: Notes on the politics of an urban public high school*. Albany, NY: State University of New York Press.

Frye, B., Button, L., Kelly, C., & Button, G. (2010). Preservice teachers' self-perceptions and attitudes toward culturally responsive teaching. *Journal of Praxis in Multicultural Education*, *5*(1), 5.

Gamoran, A. (2009). Tracking and inequality: New directions for research and practice (WCER Working Paper No. 2009-6). Madison: University of Wisconsin–Madison, Wisconsin Center for Education Research. [e.g., August 20, 2009], http://www.wcer.wisc.edu/publications/workingPapers/papers.php

Gay, G. (2010). *Culturally responsive teaching: Theory, research, and practice*. New York, NY: Teachers College Press.

Gemin, B., Pape, L., Vashaw, L., & Watson, J. (2015). *Keeping pace with k-12 digital learning: An annual review of policy and practice*. Durango, CO: Evergreen Education Group.

Goldstein, D., Popescu, A., & Hannah-Jones, N. (2020, April 8). As school moves online, many students stay logged out. *The New York Times*. https://www.nytimes.com/2020/04/06/us/coronavirus-schools-attendance-absent.html

Griner, A. C., & Stewart, M. L. (2013). Addressing the achievement gap and disproportionality through the use of culturally responsive teaching practices. *Urban Education*, *48*(4), 585–621. doi:10.1177/0042085912456847

Gutstein, E. (2006). *Reading and writing the world with mathematics: Toward a pedagogy for social justice*. New York, NY: Taylor & Francis.

Heinrich, C. J., Darling-Aduana, J., Good, A., & Cheng, H. (2019). A look inside online educational settings in high school: Promise and pitfalls for improving educational opportunities and outcomes. *American Educational Research Journal*, *56*(6), 2147–2188.

Heppen, J. B., Sorensen, N., Allensworth, E., Walters, K., Rickles, J., Taylor, S. S., & Michelman, V. (2017). The struggle to pass algebra: Online vs. face-to-face credit recovery for at-risk urban students. *Journal of Research on Educational Effectiveness*, *10*(2), 272–296. doi:10.1080/19345747.2016.1168500

Hipolito-Delgado, C. P., & Zion, S. (2017). Igniting the fire within marginalized youth: The role of critical civic inquiry in fostering ethnic identity and civic self-efficacy. *Urban Education*, *52*(6), 699–717. doi:10.1177/0042085915574524

Hsiao, Y. (2015). The culturally responsive teacher preparedness scale: An exploratory study. *Contemporary Issues in Education Research*, *8*(4), 241–250.

Karp, M. J. M., & Bork, R. J. H. (2014). "They never told me what to expect, so I didn't know what to do:" Defining and clarifying the role of a community college student. *Teachers College Record, 116*(5), 1–40.

Kohli, R., Pizarro, M., & Nevárez, A. (2017). The "new racism" of K–12 schools: Centering critical research on racism. *Review of Research in Education, 41*(1), 182–202.

Ladson-Billings, G. (1995). Toward a theory of culturally relevant pedagogy. *American Educational Research Journal, 32*(3), 465–491. doi:10.3102/00028312032003465

Ladson-Billings, G. (2014). Culturally relevant pedagogy 2.0: aka the remix. *Harvard Educational Review, 84*(1), 74–84. doi:10.17763/haer.84.1.p2rj131485484751

Langlie, M. L. (2008). The effect of culturally relevant pedagogy on the mathematics achievement of Black and Hispanic high school students (Doctoral dissertation). Boston, MA: Northeastern University.

Laughter, J. C., & Adams, A. D. (2012). Culturally relevant science teaching in middle school. *Urban Education, 47*(6), 1106–1134.

Lee, C. D. (2007). *Culture, literacy, and learning*. New York, NY: Teachers College Press.

Lipman, P. (2013). *The new political economy of urban education: Neoliberalism, race, and the right to the city*. New York, NY: Taylor and Francis.

Martin, D. B. (2010). Liberating the production of knowledge about African American children and mathematics. In D. B. Martin (Ed.), *Mathematics teaching, learning, and liberation in the lives of black children* (pp. 3–38). New York, NY: Routledge.

McLaren, P. (2015). *Life in schools: An introduction to critical pedagogy in the foundations of education*. New York, NY: Routledge.

Milner IV, H. R. (2011). Culturally relevant pedagogy in a diverse urban classroom. *The Urban Review, 43*(1), 66–89. doi:10.1007/s11256-009-0143-0

Milner IV, H. R. (2012). But what is urban education? *Urban Education, 47*(3), 556–561. doi:0.1177/0042085912447516

Milner IV, H. R., & Lomotey, K. (2014). Introduction. In H. R. Milner IV & K. Lomotey (Eds.), *Handbook of urban education*. New York, NY: Routledge.

Molnar, A. (2013). *School commercialism: From democratic ideal to market commodity*. New York, NY: Routledge.

Morales-Doyle, D. (2017). Justice-centered science pedagogy: A catalyst for academic achievement and social transformation. *Science Education, 101*(6), 1034–1060.

Oakes, J. (2008). Keeping track: Structuring equality and inequality in an era of accountability. *Teachers College Record, 110*(3), 700–712.

Paris, D. (2012). Culturally sustaining pedagogy: A needed change in stance, terminology, and practice. *Educational Researcher, 41*(3), 93–97. doi:10.3102/0013189X12441244

Paris, D., & Alim, H. S. (2014). What are we seeking to sustain through culturally sustaining pedagogy? A loving critique forward. *Harvard Educational Review, 84*(1), 85–100. doi:10.17763/haer.84.1.982l873k2ht16m77

Powell, A., Roberts, V., & Patrick, S. (2015). *Using online learning for credit recovery: Getting back on track to graduation*. Vienna, VA: International Association for K–12 Online Learning.

Seale, C. (2019, January 30). Forget implicit bias, let's talk about explicit bias in education. *Education Post*. https://educationpost.org/forget-implicit-bias-lets-talk-about-explicit-bias-in-education/

Shevalier, R., & McKenzie, B. A. (2012). Culturally responsive teaching as an ethics- and care-based approach to urban education. *Urban Education, 47*(6), 1086–1105. doi:10.1177/0042085912441483

Siwatu, K. O. (2007). Preservice teachers' culturally responsive teaching self-efficacy and outcome expectancy beliefs. *Teaching and Teacher Education, 23*(7), 1086–1101. doi:10.1016/j.tate.2006.07.011

Steele, C. M., & Aronson, J. (1995). Stereotype threat and the intellectual test performance of African Americans. *Journal of Personality and Social Psychology, 69*(5), 797. doi:10.1037/0022-3514.69.5.797

Tappan, M. B. (2006). Reframing internalized oppression and internalized domination: From the psychological to the sociocultural. *Teachers College Record, 108*(10), 2115–2144.

Tyson, K. (2011). *Integration interrupted: Tracking, Black students, and acting White after Brown.* New York, NY: Oxford University Press.

Ukpokodu, O. N. (2008). Teachers' reflections on pedagogies that enhance learning in an online course on teaching for equity and social justice. *Journal of Interactive Online Learning, 7*(3), 227–255.

Valenzuela, A. (1999). *Subtractive schooling: U.S.-Mexican youth and the politics of caring.* Albany, NY: State University of New York Press.

4

REDIRECTING THE TEACHER'S GAZE

Teacher Education, Youth Surveillance, and the School-to-Prison Pipeline

John Raible and Jason G. Irizarry

> It seems to me that whether the prisoners get an extra chocolate bar on Christmas … is not the real political issue. What we have to denounce is not so much the "human" side of life in prison but rather their real social function—that is, to serve as the instrument that creates a criminal milieu that the ruling classes can control.
> —*Michel Foucault interviewed by Roger-Pol Droit, 1975*

Deciding exactly what social roles the young should be encouraged to play remains highly contested in the socio-political context of education. Particularly in the American context, social institutions such as child welfare, juvenile justice, and schooling—and by extension, the field of teacher education—reflect the unfinished ideological struggles between social and political forces that advocate competing visions of democracy and the related agendas of state agencies that enable different futures for particular children. Although our practice as teacher educators lies in the United States, we can point to certain eerie parallels in other industrialized nations, particularly in societies with similar histories of settlement by European colonial powers and subsequent patterns of widespread immigration. While our concern for the burgeoning problem of incarcerated youth stems from our positions as critical researchers working in the field of multicultural teacher education as it is practiced in the United States, we believe that teacher educators who work in other contexts can benefit from—and contribute to—the perspective advanced here.

As we shall argue, we have found an under-examined link between the surveillance role played by many teachers in public schools and the over-representation of youth of color in the U.S. penal system. We surmise that similar links can be made in other societies with visible minority populations. For example, Aboriginal or First Nations people in Canada account for only 4% of that country's population but comprise almost one-quarter of the population in provincial/territorial custody (Landry & Sinha, 2008). Similarly, according to the Australian Bureau of Statistics (2009), the imprisonment rate for indigenous Australians is 14 times higher than that of non-indigenous prisoners (Australian Bureau of Statistics, 2009). Given similar social dynamics between majority and minority populations across the globe and the historic uses of schooling to manage minority populations (see Spring, 2004), our colleagues outside the U.S. should be able to contribute research that uncovers the connections between schooling in their own societies and the over-representation of minority and immigrant populations in the penal system in their local contexts.

Teaching Teachers to Resist Youth Surveillance

This article addresses one of the profound contradictions in teacher education that results in conflicting goals for educators who work with the young. It asks: How do we prepare future teachers to interrogate their inherited professional roles in the ongoing surveillance, management, and disciplining of youth? How does teacher education move students to care about youth who belong to socio-economic and racial subgroups that have been deemed problematic and "undesirable?" How can teachers resist the urge to collude with the institutional processes that help to create the criminal milieu as described by Foucault in the opening quotation?

To begin to answer these questions, we critically examine the role of teacher education in exacerbating what has come to be known in the U.S. as the school-to-prison pipeline, that combination of personal and institutional failures that leads too many students on a trajectory from the schoolhouse to the jailhouse (Brown, 2007). We begin by addressing ways in which teachers are encouraged, most recently in the name of accountability, to become principally agents of surveillance and behavior management. We also explore the potential for teacher education to serve as a site of resistance to heightened surveillance, particularly of youth from dominated, marginalized communities, and possibilities for providing a counternarrative to the "expectation of incarceration" (Meiners, 2007) for youth that have been effectively written off as problem children. In raising these questions about our field, we aim to redirect the gaze of educators away from a simplistic concern for "deviant" youth (and their management) as the problem, to a more comprehensive understanding that accounts for the intersections between state institutions, including schools, prisons, and colleges of education, and the discourses that create certain views and understandings of the roles of teachers and students. Finally, we call for renewed attention to our collective professional responsibility to promote social justice in and through education.

The Disciplinary Gaze as School Tradition

As alluded to in our opening quote from Foucault (1975), we wonder about the frequently unmentioned yet powerful collusion of teachers with a broad system of youth surveillance and regulation. How might teachers more effectively resist pressures to label, discipline, and, as we shall argue, eventually contribute to the process of criminalizing certain segments of school-age populations, namely students from poor communities of color? In recent years, we have become concerned by shifts in popular views of children and youth in general. In our view, the growing presence of police and metal detectors in U.S. schools, and increasing reliance on medication to manage student behavior, suggest that the experience of school, and indeed of childhood itself, may now be understood in radically different ways compared to during previous generations.

Given the growing pressures for accountability that influence the daily work of teachers and administrators, which scholars have linked to recent economic trends toward privatization and globalization and the ideology of neoliberalism (Giroux, 2000; Lipman, 2003; Sleeter, 2007), our view is that teacher educators must attend more explicitly to the intersections of these issues in our work in K-12 schools and in colleges of education. Alongside teacher educators, pre-service teachers (i.e., those who are currently training to become teachers) must be encouraged to clarify their understanding of the socio-political context of their work and the political nature of the roles they will soon take on while they fashion identities as novice teachers within an increasingly regulated and punitive system of youth-serving agencies that includes schools, law enforcement, the courts, and prisons. We believe that a critical orientation to social justice can facilitate the process of consciousness-raising and role clarification for pre-service teachers and teacher educators alike, thereby improving the chances for future teachers to connect more meaningfully with their students.

It is clear that teachers play a significant role, for better or worse, in the sorting and labeling of young people once they enter school. As Meiners (2007) documents in her recent research, disciplinary action, assessment techniques, pedagogy, and other school practices and policies all too often set in motion a series of actions that "function to normalize an 'expectation' of incarceration" for growing numbers of youth (p. 31). In the United States, the cumulative impact of current practices of surveillance that place children at risk for exclusion from school is nothing short of alarming. According to the National Centre for Educational Statistics (NCES, 2003), school officials meted out three million suspensions and approximately 1000 expulsions during the 2002–2003 academic year alone. When students disengage from (or are pushed out of) school, many are set up for failure in other ways. Increasingly, youth advocates, educators, prison activists, and others are calling attention to the escalating rates of suspension and disengagement from school in terms of a trajectory that effectively moves students from school to prison.

The discourse generated from research on the school-to-prison pipeline provides a way of framing the larger issues that result in the failure of schools to meet the needs of poor students from dominated communities. Wald and Losen (2003) aptly describe the metaphor of the pipeline as the intersection of major American institutions that wield enormous power over the life chances of the young, namely education and the criminal justice system. In our view, the current preoccupation of school officials on behavior management and regulation reflects an age-old tension between *disciplining* and *educating* the young, dating as far back as the Enlightenment. The ways in which schools staffed by ostensibly well-intentioned teachers come to support, to actively participate in, and hopefully to ultimately reject such a system of punishment and regulation is the focus of our analysis.

As Foucault (1977) famously observed, social control has been influenced by the model of the panopticon in prominent social institutions, including in schools, mental hospitals, and prisons. Foucault described the panopticon, based on Jeremy Bentham's 19th century ideas for prison reform, as a central tower around which prison cells would be organized, allowing for ongoing surveillance of prisoners at all times. Key to the panoptic model was the idea that the guards would remain hidden, so that prisoners would never know when they were being watched. In theory, panoptic surveillance becomes highly effective because the prisoners thus guarded—and the non-incarcerated masses that witness from the sidelines—begin to police themselves.

Surveillance and regulation, rather than punishment alone, became normalized throughout western societies as the exercise of power progressed from reliance on brute torture and physical punishment (e.g., public hangings and beheadings) during what Foucault (1975) called the "culture of spectacle" to a more "carcercal culture" through which criminals were incarcerated, disciplined, and potentially, even rehabilitated. The implications of the move toward surveillance and behavior management meant, in Foucault's view, political profit for ruling elites through the criminalization of certain segments of the populace, "political profit in that the more criminals there are, the more readily the population will accept police controls" (p. 26). Importantly for Foucault, the panoptic gaze and its emphasis on regulation influenced multiple emerging social institutions, including prisons and schools.

Educational researchers in recent years have taken up Foucault's interest in power and disciplinary practices, and have written about the role of surveillance and behavior management in public education. For example, Noguera (2003) draws on social reproduction theory to remind us of the traditional functions of schools under the system of American capitalism, which he describes succinctly as threefold: (1) to sort students and determine "who will lead and manage corporations and government, and who will be led and managed by those in charge"; (2) to socialize children into the "values and norms that are regarded as central to civil society and the social order"; and (3) to "operate as institutions of social control as surrogate parents" (p. 344). Noguera underscores how present-day students' experience of school can vary profoundly, depending on their socio-economic and racial status. Such variations can be observed in the approaches to school discipline used with students from diverse backgrounds. According to Noguera, in the differential education designed for students *not* tracked to become mangers, schools contribute to the marginalization of such students, often pushing them out of school altogether, while ignoring the issues that actually cause the problematic behavior. Schools also punish the neediest children because in many schools there is a fixation with behavior management and social control that outweighs and overrides all other priorities and goals (p. 342).

Noguera's analysis begins to connect the dots between discipline practices in modern-day schools, teachers' surveillance of youthful behavior, and the increased chances for involvement with the criminal justice system for students who refuse to conform to school norms and who subvert the official agenda of conformity, accountability, and control.

From Surveillance to Incarceration

As of 2002, the United States—which prides itself on serving as the alleged beacon of liberty for the free world—incarcerated 2.1 million members of its population, by far the highest rate of incarceration of any nation on the planet (Bohrman & Murakawa, 2005, p. 112). Families in poor urban communities— especially among African Americans and Latinos—bear the brunt of the spreading grip of the prison-industrial complex. Over the last two decades, observers of the "new penology" have documented the ideological "shift from rehabilitation and reform to incapacitation and mass warehousing of surplus populations" (Feeley & Simon, 1992; cited in Sudbury. J. [ed.], 2005, p. xvi). In our view, this represents the latest phase of Foucault's carceral culture. Others have noted with concern the unforgiving, punitive assault that specifically targets "dangerous" working class minority children (Lipman, 2003) as "public enemies" in need of containment (Meiners, 2007), positioning minority youth of color particularly as what we refer to as "undesirables."

The origins of the governing elites' antipathy toward racialized undesirable populations have been articulated recently for teacher educators by Noguera (2003), who draws from the insights of sociologist Wacquant (2000). In Wacquant's analysis, lingering hostility toward undesirables can be traced to the quandary faced by ruling elites over the fate of African Americans once the institution of slavery ended. Wacquant has argued "that in the current period, the melding of ghetto and prison through various carceral strategies is the latest method devised for achieving these longstanding objectives" (p. 15), namely of creating and maintaining a pool of exploitable, cheap labor, on the one hand, and on the other, of curtailing growing demands for inclusion of Blacks in the rights and privileges of citizenship.

This history of ambivalence, if not outright hostility, toward a socially undesirable but economically useful population for American capitalism grounds our view that certain populations have come to be represented as threatening, and therefore it is in need of increasingly stringent degrees of social control. In the case of African Americans, once slavery was abolished and the economic justification for the presence of huge masses of Africans vanished, the problem for governing elites became what to do with (and how to manage) the surplus population. Based on his analysis of the status of African Americans, Wacquant argues that African Americans now occupy "the first prison society of history" (p. 121), which represents the fourth phase of the U.S. social order, following from the first phase of slavery (from 1619 to 1865, respectively the year of the first importation of Africans to the end of the Civil War), through the Jim Crow era of legal segregation (1865–1965), to the third phase of the urban hyperghettos (1914–1968).

Similarly Latinos, who, combined with African Americans, account for one-quarter of the US population and more than three-quarters of incarcerated persons in American prisons have experienced similar phases of repression throughout history. For example, inter-country relations in the western hemisphere have been characterized by American domination, including genocide, territorial encroachment, and colonization in Mexico and Puerto Rico (Acuña, 2000; Fernández, 1996). Moreover, there exists a historic legacy of rounding up and removing Latinos from the United States. One million Mexican Americans were deported during the 1930s, blamed in the American popular imagination for the misery of the Great Depression (Cockcroft, 1996; Durand, Massey, & Zenteno, 2001; Kanellos & Esteva-Fabregat, 1994). More recent manifestations of anti-Latino sentiment are evident in the proposal to construct an imposing two-thousand-mile wall (euphemistically referred to as a "fence") along the US–Mexico border. The presence of military personnel and private militia along the American southern border ostensibly prevents admission or reentry for so-called "illegals" and others while restrictions at the northern border with Canada are significantly more lax. Importantly, containment—including the use of detention and incarceration—have always been used to control dominated communities labeled as undesirable, whether they are African American and Latino, or Native Americans who were historically relegated to reservations, and Asian Americans, as evident in the case of the internment camps for Japanese Americans during the Second World War (Spring, 2004; Takaki, 1993; Zinn, 1995).

It is worth remembering, too, how education has historically played a prominent role in various responses to the social problem thus defined. While space constraints do not permit a detailed examination of the contentious history of schooling for African Americans and Latinos, suffice it to say that education has been championed as the liberator and equalizer for communities of color, at the same time that it has been used as the mechanism for their assimilation and social control, depending in large measure on *who* controlled the schools set up for the descendants of slaves, colonized communities, and immigrants (Spring, 2004).

Moreover, we note that students and their families are not merely passive victims of processes of control done to them by others; dominated communities of color have always attempted to resist, subvert, reform, and in some cases take over those processes and institutions which impact the conditions of their lives and their chances for survival (Spring, 2004). These countermoves against social control reverberate in contemporary classrooms and, in our view, should also be taken up in teacher education programs if teachers are to address effectively the real lives of students; hence, our call for increased attention to issues of social justice in teacher education.

Confronting the School-to-Prison Pipeline

As teacher educators, we share with other educational researchers an interest in issues that link minority youth and schooling, such as gaps (i.e., in achievement and opportunity) and dropout rates, sorting and "tracking" students by their perceived ability, and the over-representation in special education classes of youth from poor and dominated communities. Nevertheless, our view of youth has expanded to consider the fate of school dropouts once they leave school, and even more importantly, what happens to them *during* their trajectories away from school participation while still in attendance or at least on the official school enrollment rosters.

In May 2003, the Civil Rights Project at Harvard University convened a conference for researchers and youth advocates on the school-to-prison pipeline (see Wald & Losen, 2003). One finding from that conference indicated that "racial disparity in school discipline and achievement mirrors racially disproportionate minority confinement" in the larger society. Our interest as researchers in the school-to-prison pipeline arises from our drive to understand our own complicity, as teachers and teacher educators, in positioning certain students on previously unexamined trajectories. We are confronted with such questions as: What roles do we play, perhaps inadvertently, in the school-to-prison pipeline? How might we as teachers transform those roles to take up work that more actively counters negative student trajectories? What do teacher educators need to understand in order to cultivate an awareness of and commitment to interrupting pipeline dynamics among pre-service teachers? How can the field of teacher education advance counternarratives that resist the criminalization of youth from dominated communities? How might we more clearly connect the stark parallels between the over-representation of students of color in special education classes, school discipline cases, the child welfare system (e.g., in foster care and other out-of-home placements), juvenile justice cases that result in detention, and the ultimate confinement of imprisonment?

As Wald and Losen (2003) have pointed out, the same punitive mentality that results in the over-representation of youth of color who land in trouble at school extends to the juvenile justice system. African American youth are six times more likely to be confined than white youth for the same offence; Latino youth, more than three times (p. 10). Beginning in the 1990s, nearly all (i.e., 45 of the 50) American states passed laws to make it easier to try minors as adults. According to Wald and Losen, between 1983 and 1997, four out of five youth confined to detention or correctional facilities were minority youth (ibid.). In our view, the growing reliance on zero-tolerance approaches to discipline (i.e., no second chances for youth offenders) translates into diminishing adult understanding of and patience for the mistakes and unwise choices made by the young. The combination of the racism that sustains a view of certain segments of the populace as undesirable, combined with adult ageism toward youth in general coalesces in collective fears that target youth of color in particular.

The 2005 report of the Children's Defense Fund on "Dismantling the Cradle to Prison Pipeline" identified three major risk indicators that set poor young Americans on the trajectory to incarceration: (1) early involvement in the child welfare system, (2) educational failure, and (3) involvement with the juvenile justice system (Murray, 2005). By linking the treatment of minority youth to recent concerns in the U.S. over increased efforts toward racial profiling (the practice of targeting visible minorities for scrutiny by police or security officials at airports), Meiners (2007) flags the complicity of schools in facilitating the transition of certain students into the school-to-prison pipeline:

> Clearly, the grotesque over-representation of youth of color caught up in school discipline policies and in the category of special education illustrates that educators and educational institutions are not exempt from a kind of "racial profiling" endemic to our police systems. Rather, racialized surveillance *prefigures* the practices undertaken by police, customs, and other punitive institutions, and I argue that the establishment of these practices in schools functions to seemingly launch, for individuals caught in these punitive practices and for those who participate and observe, the processes of racial profiling.
>
> *(p. 41)*

Without question, schools play a significant role among an array of adult interventions into the dire circumstances facing youth in the United States. The contradiction is that such well-intentioned interventions too often exacerbate the problems faced by youth rather than provide solutions. For example, in their study of the intersections between high-poverty high American schools and the juvenile justice system, Balfanz, Spiridakis, Neild, and Legters (2003) documented ways in which youth-serving institutions frequently work at cross purposes. Ironically, in an era of cutbacks in social services for those most in need, rather than easing their transition to productive and responsible adulthood, "incarceration. Has become America's social program for troubled youths" (Murray, 2005).

The Role of Teacher Education in the School-to-Prison Pipeline

The links between schools and the prison-industrial complex are becoming increasingly clear. Thus far escaping the inquiry of many educational researchers is the role that teacher education plays in legitimating and reifying the school-to-prison pipeline. Although there are positive aspects of teacher education that do effectively prepare teachers to serve poor students and students of color, there are three detrimental aspects that, from our perspective, contribute directly to the school-to-prison pipeline: the lack of student diversity in U.S. teacher education programs; the over-emphasis on classroom management and control, particularly when it comes to urban youth of color; and the superficial treatment of issues of diversity within American teacher education.

As the American school-aged population has become more racially, ethnically, and linguistically diverse, the population of pre-service teachers enrolled in traditional teacher preparation programs has become increasingly monocultural and monolingual. Currently, 85% of all teacher candidates in the United States are white women, and the composition of teacher education programs can best be characterized by an "overwhelming presence of whiteness" (Sleeter, 2001). Moreover, the majority of pre-service teachers comes from suburban communities and from middle or upper middle-class families (Chizhik, 2003). As a result, pre-service teachers are often disconnected from and unfamiliar with the socio-cultural realities of the urban poor. We do not argue that white, middle-class, female identities are a problem per se. However, research suggests that many women in U.S. colleges enact and actively try to preserve identities as "good girls" (Galman, 2006; Holland & Eisenhart, 1992), which often revolve around conforming to traditional Western gender norms that maintain the status quo, as opposed to challenging injustice and oppression based on age, race, gender, or social class. Despite the highly politicized nature of schooling, American teacher education programs have continued to primarily attract conformist "good girls." At the same time, they have created curricula and experiences that, for the most part, reinforce mainstream identities while failing to help students to develop more critical stances regarding education, particularly for populations that have been traditionally underserved by schools. Moreover, U.S. teacher education has done relatively little to help these pre-service candidates become more critical consumers of educational policies (i.e., high stakes testing or scripted "teacher-proof" curricula) that impact their work in classrooms. This is not to say that men or women of color in teacher education programs are necessarily more critical or make better teachers. Nor do we deny that everyone in the academy, regardless of background, has been socialized to perform racialized and gendered identities in ways that tend to reinforce unequal power relations. However, it is imperative that teacher education as a field addresses the intersections of race, gender, and class, and how these are manifested and reproduced in schools of education. "Good" girls (and boys, too) in pre-service programs need encouragement to interrogate conformity to dominant oppressive norms, and to understand, if not identify with, students often represented as "bad," that is, as dangerous, deviant, and undesirable.

Pre-service teachers often enter higher education with preconceived notions about poor students of color; teacher education, for the most part, does little to change those limited perceptions. In fact, there is evidence to suggest that field experiences and coursework devoid of a systematic analysis of race and class may do more to reinforce stereotypes than to challenge them (Melnick & Zeichner, 1995; Vavrus, 2002). Commenting on the influence of teacher education on pre-service teachers, Banks (2006) notes,

> Educational reform is impeded by the misconceptions and lack of knowledge about ethnic and racial groups that teachers learn in the wider society. Much of the popular knowledge that teachers acquire is either reinforced or is not challenged by the mainstream knowledge they acquire in their undergraduate university education and in teacher education programs. Educators often accept mainstream knowledge and resist other knowledge forms because it reinforces the social, economic, and political arrangements that they perceive as beneficial (C.E. Sleeter, personal communication, 2003). The assumptions and values that underlie mainstream academic knowledge are often unexamined in the school, college, and university curriculum.
>
> *(p. 769)*

When unchallenged, these dominant "good" identities allow teachers to continue to see themselves as the norm and construct student diversity as a problem (Achinstein & Barrett, 2004), thus resulting in the hyper-surveillance of poor, deviant students of color that can lead to school exclusion, and, as data have demonstrated, set them on the pathway to prison.

A major emphasis within the literature regarding teacher education for diversity in the United States has been to prepare teachers to more effectively educate students of color (Dilworth, 1992; Grant & Sleeter, 1999; Ladson-Billings, 1994; Vavrus, 2002). As teacher educators who lead courses that address issues of diversity, we (the authors) have struggled in our own work with the challenges posed by helping pre-service teachers who are often disconnected from, and unaware of, the socio-cultural realities of communities of color, and who, at times, appear resistant to acknowledging the roles they play in perpetuating, let alone combating, oppression. Nevertheless, we have through our teaching and research encountered rare individuals, particularly white women, who perform their identities in ways that allow them to meaningfully connect with, learn from, and teach people of color from dominated communities (see Raible & Irizarry, 2007).

At the same time, we advocate for teacher education programs to more accurately mirror the demographic characteristics of American society at large and the school-aged population in particular. If the national cohort of pre-service teachers and teacher educators were to more accurately reflect U.S. society's demographics, approximately one in four individuals participating in teacher education programs would be people of color, and one in five would come from a home where a language other than English is spoken. While it is important to educate all pre-service teachers to develop the knowledge, skills, and dispositions to work effectively with students of color, we believe that teacher education would be significantly enhanced if, paraphrasing the words of former U.S. Secretary of Education Richard Riley, "our teachers looked more like America" (Riley, 1998). That is, given the increasing diversity among public school students in the United States and the shortage of teachers of color and multilingual teachers, it behooves our profession to pursue diversity within its ranks with a renewed sense of urgency and vigor.

The ability of teacher education to prepare educators to improve the school experiences and outcomes for students of color is predicated partly on its ability to recruit and prepare a more diverse cadre of teachers. At the same time, it is imperative that we recruit individuals from a variety of backgrounds who have connections to individuals and communities of color. We call for the recruitment of pre-service teachers who demonstrate a vested interest in restructuring schools so that they can become spaces where students and teachers engage in a process of liberation, as opposed to the reification of hegemony. Today's students need teachers—from all backgrounds—who understand the dire stakes involved in liberating communities from rigid domination and state control. We emphatically do not argue for minority teachers exclusively for minority students. Instead, we call for teacher education programs to better prepare all teachers to participate in community struggles for self-determination and survival, for family preservation rather than separation of families (for instance, through detention and foster care), in direct opposition to the prison-industrial complex by deliberately interrupting the school-to-prison pipeline.

Second, as a consequence of soaring teacher attrition rates in urban districts, city schools in the United States tend to have a disproportionately high percentage of novice teachers, and are more likely to feel the adverse impacts associated with the national teacher shortage (Howard, 2003; Ingersoll, 2001). Research conducted in the 1980s in the area of new teacher development posited that many novice teachers cited classroom discipline as their most pressing concern (Veenman, 1984). Approximately a quarter of a century later, novice teachers continue to cite classroom management as their greatest weakness (Wang, Odell, & Schwille, 2008). Recent literature suggests that teachers' struggles with classroom management may in fact be a result of problems with curriculum and pedagogy and the challenge to engage learners of diverse backgrounds

(Feiman-Nemser, 2003). This perceived need to gain control of the classroom may be exacerbated by the presumption among many teachers in impoverished schools that urban contexts tend to be more violent, chaotic, and dangerous places in which to work.

Representations of communities of color as inherently problematic are often reinforced in teacher education programs through formal experiences, such as coursework and internships in actual classrooms. In our own work with pre-service teachers, we have become aware of instances where faculty and mentoring teachers have warned pre-service teachers of the potential dangers that may await them in urban schools. For example, on several occasions, students in our programs have reported receiving negative messages from faculty prior to entering their urban field placement sites to "travel in groups," "leave by 3:00" and to "protect your belongings." Pre-service students may enter diverse settings with an array of unexamined stereotypes, for which they then seek—and often find—validation, failing to acknowledge the more hopeful counternarratives that also exist in these settings. Thus, many field placement experiences may do more to reinforce stereotypes about racialized others than to improve teachers' ability to work in cross-cultural contexts (Sleeter, 2001).

We assert that the day-to-day struggles of teachers to effectively work with students of color in urban settings are constrained under a framework that reflects an official discourse of accountability, and are further compromised by teachers' inabilities to reconcile egalitarian notions of schooling (e.g., schools as the great equalizer) with actual institutional structures that reflect a legacy of racism, classism, ageism, and other forms of oppression that impact their work. For example, many pre-service teachers articulate an intellectual appreciation and respect for diversity, yet still refer to members of diverse cultural groups as culturally deficient or inferior. Gaertner and Dovidio (1986) refer to this phenomenon as aversive racism. Quite simply, aversive racists firmly believe they do not discriminate against others on the basis of race while simultaneously unconsciously bearing feelings of uneasiness toward people of color. Moreover, aversive racists often adopt ideologies that "justif[y] group inequalities [and] reinforce group hierarchy," thus "producing and justifying discriminatory behavior" (p. 619). This is particularly troublesome because, since pre-service teachers may uncritically believe that the proverbial playing field is level, they may fail to implicate themselves in their own ineffectiveness in the classroom. Additionally, there may be no incentive for pre-service teachers to change their beliefs or practice without carefully guided and facilitated opportunities for critical reflection.

In sum, because comprehensive, anti-racist multicultural education is marginalized within teacher education programs, often taking the form of an individual course that is disconnected from internship experiences, and because multicultural education is rarely infused throughout the curriculum (Vavrus, 2002), there is as yet untapped potential for teacher education programs to do much more to transform teachers' ideologies and pedagogy in meaningful ways (Ladson-Billings, 1999). Too many teachers leave colleges of education ill-prepared to meet the challenges of successfully promoting the academic, linguistic, and personal growth of students from diverse backgrounds. Underprepared teachers may in fact do more harm than good, particularly by adopting uncritically the roles and practice of surveillance and behavior management that bolster the school-to-prison pipeline dynamic.

Tapping the Potential for a More Critical Teacher Education

As they are currently constructed, teacher education programs do little to prepare teachers to respond to the educational crisis that results in the school-to-prison pipeline. The crisis, of course, is bigger than the pipeline. In fact, from a Foucauldian perspective as noted earlier, colleges of education often prepare teachers to become agents of state-sponsored youth surveillance and managers of deviant behavior, which effectively shapes the educational experiences of students, especially poor students of color, in ways that may serve to push them away from engagement with school. Nevertheless, we hold onto hope that schools can become sites of anti-racist resistance where critical pedagogy moves from rhetoric to practice, resulting in the establishment of multiracial and intergenerational coalitions for social justice based on genuinely caring relationships between teachers and students. Given the far-reaching influence that educators potentially can have on future generations, teacher education potentially has a significant role to play in this transformation of schooling. Key to activating this potential is a commitment to developing a more comprehensive analysis of the role of race, gender, and other differences within the field, and how these dynamics play out in the intersections between institutions such as education, law, child welfare, and the juvenile justice system.

Turning again to the work of Meiners (2007), whose insights illuminate the connections between race and gender in schools, we find support for our view concerning the twin tasks for teacher education. The first addresses the dwindling number of teachers of color in the field, and the need to recruit pre-service students from the very communities from which urban public school students come. The second is developing a comprehensive approach to expanding the ranks of pre-service students currently predominating in the field (namely, white women), so that more teachers come to self-identify as allies in the struggle against racism, and make explicit connections between the work of teaching and ongoing community struggles for social justice.

Regarding the latter task, the multicultural education and racial identity development of white educators have been written about extensively in recent years. Nevertheless, the work of Meiners (2007) is once again pertinent to the present discussion. Meiners draws on the racial contract theory of philosopher

Mills (1997) to suggest ways in which educators might interrogate race in order to develop clarity about their subjectivity as teachers who happen to be white:

> The racial contract constructs. an epistemology of ignorance, or a deliberate scaffolding to protect white folks from a material awareness of the flawed institutions, discourses, and laws created by white supremacy.
>
> *(p. 95)*

Meiners describes how the epistemology of ignorance results in what she calls white cognitive impairment that prevents whites "from knowing the effects of white supremacy they themselves have constructed" (p. 95). Exposing the links between race and gender, Meiners suggests that teacher education can also deconstruct its basic gendered construction, i.e., the "good girl" identities of many teachers. She argues that

> shifting the foundational idea of the concept of the teacher, drawing on other archetypes not the lady, and highlighting teachers and educators whose work, identity, and definitions of teaching radically expose the sexual and racial foundation in education, is one possibility. The field can take responsibility for initiating change to actively challenge the archetype that is currently shaping the profession, and to work to recruit new bodies into the profession.
>
> *(p. 53)*

Our interest in the multicultural identity development of preservice teachers reflects one of the field's primary aims, namely to prepare educators to work effectively in 21st century classrooms. The population of students in the United States has become increasingly more diverse in the past few decades. More than 40% of children enrolled in K-12 schools are students of color, and one in every five students comes from a home where a language other than English is spoken (National Centre for Education Statistics, 2007). It is therefore crucial for pre-service teachers to become aware of issues of diversity *before* they enter their multicultural classrooms. For example, addressing the disparities in disciplinary actions taken against students of color, Banks et al. (2005) maintain that teacher education must help pre-service teachers grapple with the inequities they will inevitably face in schools:

> If we are to create schools where all students have opportunities to learn, teachers must know how to be alert for these kinds of disparities and aware of how to provide classroom environments that are both physically and psychologically safe for all students.
>
> *(p. 242)*

Again, teacher education programs must facilitate the development of critical consciousness, with particular regard to multicultural issues such as race, gender, and class among preservice teachers.

As American society has grown more diverse, the impact of the school-to-prison pipeline has become far-reaching, if not staggering. Between 1980 and 2000, the national inmate population quadrupled, while more than 700 new prisons were built (Bureau of Justice Statistics, 2004). The link between schools and prisons becomes more pronounced upon examination of data regarding the educational attainment of current inmates. Approximately three-quarters of state prison inmates, 60% of federal inmates, and almost seven out of every ten inmates in jail have not completed high school (Alliance for Excellent Education, 2006). While it would be inaccurate to assume that all high school dropouts will commit crimes, it is fair to conclude that, of the people who receive convictions and serve time in prison, the overwhelming majority will not have received an adequate education. Many observers have noted a direct correlation between educational failure and participation in the penal system. As such, with the alarmingly high dropout rates among students of color, it is no surprise that there are now more than three African Americans in jail for everyone in college (U.S. Census Bureau, 2007). The ratio for Latinos is similarly high, at 2.7:1, while the rate for white students is, not surprisingly, inverted, with more than three white Americans in college for everyone serving time in prison (U.S. Census Bureau, 2007).

Conclusion

As critical teacher educators working in the United States context, we aim to encourage more pre-service students to effectively connect with, and forge bonds of solidarity with, poor students of color in order to counter the dynamics that result in widespread school failure, which, as we have argued, too often results in incarceration. An explicitly anti-racist orientation among teachers can be cultivated through the transracialization of teacher identities (Raible & Irizarry, 2007). Transracialization may enhance the multicultural development of individual teacher identities. Yet it is important to bear in mind that transracialization only occurs when close relationships between individuals of different races enable genuine relationships of caring to unfold over time (Raible, 2005).

The related development of what Banks et al. (2005) refer to as socio-cultural consciousness can also facilitate closer connections between teachers and students from diverse backgrounds. Teachers who develop socio-cultural consciousness understand that the life experiences of students (and teachers) can profoundly influence their worldviews, which are understood as anything but universal. Banks and his colleagues argue further that teachers not stop merely at greater awareness, but take responsibility for working actively as agents of change within schools:

> Teachers need to be aware of how the formal and informal systems of the school operate to construct opportunity and how to participate in school-level change processes that call attention to organizational needs and help develop a supportive culture school-wide.
>
> *(p. 255)*

We remain hopeful about the potential for genuine intercultural connectedness to emerge when teachers demonstrate care and respect for students and their lives and concerns beyond the walls of the classroom. We bear in mind the implications of a recent study that found school connectedness, "defined as a student's feeling part of and cared for at school," to be linked with lower levels of substance use, violence, suicide attempts, pregnancy, and emotional distress among young people (cited in Wald & Losen, 2003, p. 12). We view such connectedness as crucial for success in education, and we seek to help pre-service teachers to value connectedness, and to cultivate strategies that foster mutually enriching teacher-student bonds.

We invite teachers, both pre-service and in the field, along with other teacher educators, to rethink their connections to (or disconnections from) urban poor students and their communities. Teachers can be encouraged to meet students on their own turf, and to see them as partners in the educative process, rather than as passive recipients of charity and good intentions. It is simply too easy for educators to fall in step uncritically with the ideologies and social practices that feed into the school-to-prison pipeline. For this reason, critical consciousness about our personal roles in larger institutional structures becomes vital to the ongoing struggle for social justice and democracy. In light of persistent racism and its effects in schools during the present era of accountability, our work focuses on how we collectively (i.e., educators, youth, and their families) might effectively develop cross-cultural, intergenerational, anti-racist alliances, in schools, and within and between communities. This, we have come to believe, is absolutely necessary in order to turn present nightmares into more hopeful futures.

Although it has been estimated that African American boys today have a one in three chance of going to jail before they attain 30 years of age, we refuse to abandon these and other minority youth to such a pessimistic foregone conclusion. Given the dire implications of the "cradle-to-prison pipeline" (Edelman, 2007) of which the school phase is but one (although hardly insignificant) link, we anticipate that more and more educators and families will of necessity find ways to work together to counter this dangerous trend. If schools are to become sites of transformational resistance, teacher education can and must insist on personal introspection and critical analysis as key elements of effective programs. Moreover, teachers must learn to redirect their gaze from the hyper-surveillance of poor students of color that results in viewing them problematically, and begin to see the ways in which institutional structures can either facilitate their oppression or support their liberation.

References

Achinstein, B., & Barrett, A. (2004). (Re)Framing classroom contexts: How new teachers and mentors view diverse learners and the challenges of practice. *Teachers College Record, 106*(4), 716–746.

Acuña, R. (2000). *Occupied America: A history of Chicanos* (4th ed.). New York: Harper & Row.

Alliance for Excellent Education. (2006). *Saving futures, saving dollars: The impact of education on crime reduction and earnings.* Washington, DC: Alliance for Excellent Education.

Australian Bureau of Statistics. (2009). *Prisoners in Australia 2009*. Report. June 30, 2009. Canberra, Australia.

Balfanz, R., Spiridakis, K., Neild, R. C., & Legters, N. (2003). High poverty secondary schools and the juvenile justice system: How neither helps the other and how that could change. *New Directions for Youth Development, 99*, 71–89.

Banks, J., Cochran-Smith, M., Moll, L., Richert, A., Zeichner, K., LePage, P., et al. (2005). Teaching diverse learners. In L. Darling-Hammond & J. Bransford (Eds.), *Preparing teachers for a changing world: What teachers should learn and be able to do* (pp. 232–274). San Francisco: Jossey-Bass.

Banks, J. (2006). Researching race, culture and difference: Epistemological challenges and possibilities. In J. L. Green, G. Camili, & P. B. Elmore (Eds.), *Handbook of complementary methods in education research* (pp. 786–789). Mahwah, NJ: Lawrence Erlbaum Associates.

Bohrman, R., & Murakawa, N. (2005). Remaking big government: Immigration and crime control in the United States. In J. Sudbury (Ed.), *Global lockdown: Race, gender, and the prison-industrial complex* (pp. 109–126). New York: Routledge.

Brown, T. M. (2007). Lost and turned out: Academic, social and emotional experiences of students excluded from school. *Urban Education, 42*(5), 432–455.

Bureau of Justice Statistics. (2004). *Bureau of justice statistics, prisoners in 2003.* Washington, DC: Paige M. Harrison & Allen J. Beck.

Chizhik, E. W. (2003). Reflecting on the challenges of preparing suburban teachers for urban schools. *Education and Urban Society, 35*(4), 443–461.

Cockcroft, J. (1996). *Latinos in the making of the United States: The Hispanic experience in the Americas.* New York: Franklin Watts.

Dilworth, M. E. (Ed.). (1992). *Diversity in teacher education: New expectations.* San Francisco: Jossey-Bass.

Durand, J., Massey, D. S., & Zenteno, R. M. (2001). Mexican immigration to the united states: Continuities and changes. *Latin American Research Review, 36*(1), 107–127.

Edelman, M. W. (2007). The cradle to prison pipeline: An American health crisis. *Preventing Chronic Disease, 4*(3), A43. Published online June 15, 2007.

Feeley, M., & Simon, J. (1992). The new penology: Notes on the emerging strategy of corrections and its implications. *Criminology, 30*(4). Cited in J. Sudbury (Ed.). (2005). *Global lockdown: Race, gender, and the prison–industrial complex.* New York: Routledge, p. xvi.

Feiman-Nemser, S. (2003). What new teachers need to learn. *Educational Leadership, 60*(8), 25–30.

Fernández, R. (1996). *The disenchanted island: Puerto Rico and the United States in the twentieth century*. Westport, CT: Praeger.
Foucault, M. (1975). On the role of prisons. Interview by Roger-Pol Droit. http://www.nytimes.com/books/00/12/17/specials/foucault-prisons.html; accessed February 7, 2008, p. 26.
Foucault, M. (1977). *Discipline and punish: The birth of the prison*. New York: Vintage.
Gaertner, S. L., & Dovidio, J. F. (1986). The aversive form of racism. In J. F. Dovidio & S. L. Gaertner (Eds.), *Prejudice, discrimination, and racism* (pp. 61–89). Orlando, FL: Academic Press.
Galman, S. (2006). "Rich white girls": Developing critical identities in teacher education and novice teaching settings. *International Journal of Learning, 13*(3), 47–55.
Giroux, H. (2000). Postmodern education and disposable youth. In P. P. Trifonas (Ed.), *Revolutionary pedagogies: Cultural politics, instituting education, and the discourse of theory* (pp. 174–195). New York: Routledge.
Grant, C. A., & Sleeter, C. E. (1999). *Making choices for multicultural education: Five approaches to race, class, and gender*. New York: Merrill.
Holland, D., & Eisenhart, M. (1992). *Educated in romance: Women, achievement and college culture*. Chicago, IL: University of Chicago Press.
Howard, T. (2003). Who receives the short end of the shortage? Implications of the U.S. teacher shortage on urban schools. *Journal of Curriculum and Supervision, 18*(2), 142–160.
Ingersoll, R. M. (2001). Teacher turnover and teacher shortages: An organizational analysis. *American Educational Research Journal, 38*(3), 499–534.
Kanellos, N., & Esteva-Fabregat, C. (Eds.). (1994). *Handbook of Hispanic cultures in the United States*. Houston, TX: Arte Publico Press and Madrid, Spain: Instituto de Cooperacion Iberoamericana.
Ladson-Billings, G. (1994). Who will teach our children? Preparing teachers to successfully teach African American students. In E. Hollins, J. King, & W. C. Hayman (Eds.), *Teaching diverse populations: Formulating a knowledge base* (pp. 129–142). Albany: State University of New York Press.
Ladson-Billings, G. (1999). Preparing teachers for diverse student populations: A critical race theory perspective. *Review of Research in Education, 24*(21), 211–247.
Landry, L., & Sinha, M. (2008). Adult correctional services in Canada, 2005/2006. *Statistics Canada – Catalogue, 28*(6), 1–26.
Lipman, P. (2003). Cracking down: Chicago school policy and the regulation of black and Latino youth. In K. Saltman & D. Gabbard (Eds.), *Education as enforcement: The militarization and corporatization of schools* (pp. 81–101). New York: Routledge Falmer.
Meiners, E. (2007). *Right to be hostile: Schools, prisons, and the making of public enemies*. New York: Routledge.
Melnick, S. L., & Zeichner, K. M. (1995). *Teacher education for cultural diversity: Enhancing the capacity of teacher education institutions address diversity issues to*. National Center for Research on Teacher Learning, 116 Erickson Hall, Michigan State University, East Lansing, MI 48824-1034.
Mills, C. (1997). *The racial contract*. Ithaca, NY: Cornell University Press.
Murray, M. (2005). *The cradle to prison pipeline crisis*. Poverty and Race Research Action Council. http://wwwprrac.org/full_textphp?text_id=1043&item_id=9518&newsletter_id=82&header=Education; accessed December 18, 2007.
National Center for Education Statistics. (2003). Suspension and expulsions of public elementary and secondary school students, by state, sex and percent of enrollment: 2000. http://nces.ed.gov/programs/digest/d03/tables/dt147.asp; accessed March 10, 2008.

National Center for Education Statistics. (2007). *The condition of education, 2007*. Washington, DC: U.S. Department of Education.

Noguera, P. (Autumn 2003). Schools, prisons, and social implications of punishment: Rethinking disciplinary practices. *Theory Into Practice, 42*(4), 341–350.

Raible, J. (2005) *Sharing the spotlight: The non-adopted siblings of transracial adoptees*. Doctoral thesis, University of Massachusetts, Amherst.

Raible, J., & Irizarry, J. G. (2007). Transracialized selves and the emergence of postwhite teacher identities. *Race, Ethnicity and Education, 10*(2), 177–198.

Riley, R. W. (1998). Our teachers should be excellent, and they should look like America. *Education and Urban Society, 31*(1), 18–29.

Sleeter, C. (2007). Vice President's invited address: Equity, democracy and neoliberal assaults on teacher education. In: *Paper Presented at American Educational Research Association Conference*, Chicago, IL.

Sleeter, C. E. (2001). Preparing teachers for culturally diverse schools: Research and the overwhelming presence of whiteness. *Journal of Teacher Education, 52*(2), 94–106.

Spring, J. (2004). *Deculturalization and the struggle for equality: A brief history of the education of dominated cultures in the United States*. New York: McGraw-Hill.

Takaki, R. (1993). *A different mirror: A history of multiculturalism in America*. Boston, MA: Little, Brown

U.S. Census Bureau. (2007). Press release. Census bureau releases new data on residents of adult correctional facilities, nursing homes and other group quarters: Annual data also paint diverse portrait of nation's race, ethnic and ancestry groups. September 27, 2007.

Vavrus, M. (2002). *Transforming the multicultural education of teachers*. New York: Teachers College Press.

Veenman, S. (1984). The perceived problems of beginning teachers. *Review of Educational Research, 19*(3), 143–178.

Wacquant, L. (2000). Deadly symbiosis: When ghetto and prison meet and mesh. *Punishment and Society, 3*(1), 95–134.

Wang, J., Odell, S., & Schwille, S. (2008). Effects of teacher induction on beginning teachers' teaching: A critical review of the literature. *Journal of Teacher Education, 59*(2), 132–152.

Wald, J., & Losen, D. (Eds.). (Fall 2003). Defining and redirecting the school-to-prison pipeline. *New Directions for Youth Development: Theory, Practice, Research, 9*–15.

Zinn, H. (1995). *A people's history of the United States 1492–present*. New York: Harper Perennial.

5
UNDERSTANDING THE SCHOOL-TO-PRISON PIPELINE FOR BLACK PROBATION YOUTH

Bo-Kyung Elizabeth Kim, Jessenia De Leon, Camille R. Quinn, Patricia B. Logan-Greene, and Paula S. Nurius

> We black folk, our history and our present being, are a mirror of all the manifold experiences of America. What we want, what we represent, what we endure is what America is. If we black folk perish, America will perish.
> *Richard Wright, writer, 1941*

Overrepresentation of Black Youth in Multiple Systems

In 2019, 696,620 youth under the age of 18 years old were arrested—the lowest since 1980 (Puzzanchera, 2021). While the number of youth in the juvenile justice system has reduced in the last 12 years, the disproportionality of Black youth has persisted (Abrams, Mizel, & Barnert, 2021; Peck & Jennings, 2016; Puzzanchera, 2021). Arrests for both property and violent crimes have decreased but Black youth are still disproportionately arrested for those crimes. The disproportionality is also evident in school discipline. While the number of youth receiving suspension or expulsion has decreased, Black youth continue to be three to seven times more likely than White youth to be suspended and expelled in a given academic year (Henderson et al., 2019; Leaf, 2010; U.S. Department of Education Office for Civil Rights, 2014; Marchbanks & Blake, 2017).

Both in the juvenile justice system and in school discipline, youth eligible for special education are overrepresented. Although the rate of special education in the juvenile justice system has varied markedly by state (9.1%–77.5%), on average, one in three justice-involved youth qualify for special education, over twice the rate observed in the general population (14%) (McFarland et al., 2019). The most common qualifying diagnoses for special education for youth in the juvenile justice system include learning disability (38.6%), emotional disturbance (47.7%), and intellectual disability (9.7%; Quinn et al., 2005). Furthermore,

DOI: 10.4324/9781003262077-5

students with special education status are also overrepresented in school discipline—significantly more likely to receive exclusionary disciplines, such as suspension and expulsion (Anderson & Ritter, 2017; Hurwitz, Cohen, & Perry, 2021; Kalu et al., 2020; U.S. Commission on Civil Rights, 2019). In particular, emotional and behavioral disorders tend to have the highest odds of suspension when compared to all other disabilities (Chu & Ready, 2018; Krezmien et al., 2006; Sullivan et al., 2014; Zhang et al., 2004). Although youth with special education needs are protected by the Individuals with Disabilities Education Act (IDEA), they are disciplined and pushed out of schools, putting them at a greater risk for juvenile justice involvement (Morris, 2016; Skiba, 2002).

Research on the overrepresentation of Black youth in special education, however, is mixed. Many studies have documented the overrepresentation of Black youth in special education (e.g., Ahram et al., 2011; Albrecht et al., 2012; Jordan, 2005; Losen & Orfield, 2002; Quinn et al., 2005; Skiba et al., 2008; Zhang et al., 2014). In a five-year study examining trends of special education, Zhang et al. (2014) report that between 2007 and 2011, the number of Black youth in special education remained unchanged—evidence that Black youth are the largest group represented and continue to be so. In a population-level study across three states, Grindal et al. (2019) found that Black and Hispanic youth were significantly more likely to be identified for special education and placed in separate education settings compared to White youth. Over-identifying Black youth for special education further stigmatizes Black youth as youth with problems. More recent studies (e.g., Elder et al., 2021; Morgan et al., 2017), however, have refuted some of these findings demonstrating that Black youth with special education needs, in fact, are often under-identified, thus, not receiving necessary support and services. Morgan et al. (2017) synthesized and evaluated the quality of existing evidence and concluded that when accounting for school-level factors (e.g., social class, academic achievement, high percentage of minority students), Black youth are far less likely to receive special education than otherwise similar White youth. In another study, Elder et al. (2021) provide a more complex understanding of the phenomena by examining racial segregation alongside special education. They also found that Black students attending schools with a large minority population (exceeding 40%) tended to be underrepresented in special education but those attending schools with less racial/ethnic diversity were overrepresented in special education.

Given these mixed conclusions, examining the experiences of Black youth with special education needs separately would be important especially in the context of the school-to-prison pipeline. It is clear from the literature that youth with special education needs are overrepresented in the juvenile justice system. It is also clear that Black youth are disproportionately involved in the juvenile justice system. The question is, are Black youth with special education needs overrepresented in the juvenile justice system? What is the role of school discipline (e.g., suspension, expulsion) for these youth? In this chapter, we disentangle some of these questions and examine the pathway from special education to the juvenile justice system for Black youth. In a previous paper (see Kim et al., 2021), we explored the pathway from special education to the juvenile justice system for all probation youth in a sample of participants. We found that youth with special education needs recidivated more than the rest of the probation youth. Furthermore, school expulsion/suspension history increased recidivism significantly more for special education youth. Extending the findings of this paper, we seek to understand the unique experiences of Black probation youth within the context of special education and school discipline (i.e., suspension, expulsion) that fast-track them onto the school-to-prison pipeline.

Theoretical Pathways for Special Education-to-Prison Pipeline

The overrepresentation of youth with developmental disabilities in the juvenile justice system has largely been theorized to occur in three ways: school failure, susceptibility, and differential treatment. The school failure theory (Osher et al., 2002) suggests that these youth struggle academically, which increases their likelihood of leaving school (e.g., dropout, suspension, expulsion) and subsequently engaging in delinquency. Of note, while we adopt the school failure theory to guide our conceptual framework, we recognize that the term "school failure" lays unnecessary burden on the student. Since school practices and policies can largely contribute to what the theory refers to as "school failure," we selectively focus on school exclusion experiences (i.e., expulsion, suspension). The susceptibility theory (Keilitz & Dunivant, 1986) posits that the characteristics that accompany their disabling conditions—such as low impulse control, irritability, and poor problem-solving skills—lead to delinquency. The differential treatment theory (Rutherford et al., 2002) suggests that youth with disabilities who qualify for special education simply experience more punitive treatment across school and juvenile justice systems than their peer counterparts. Regardless of the pathway, youth with disabilities continue to penetrate deeper into the juvenile justice system instead of receiving needed services, jeopardizing their future prospect of success.

Conceptual Framework

Based on these three theories and related research findings, we have outlined a conceptual framework to capture pathways by which youth with special education needs get funneled into the justice system. Youth with mental, emotional, and behavioral (MEB) problems in schools are at higher risk for engaging in problematic behaviors, such as early substance use and aggressive or violent behaviors, that might lead to involvement in the juvenile justice system (O'Connell et al., 2009; Figure 5.1, Path A). The pathway to the juvenile justice system for youth with MEB problems might also be mediated through either special education referral/identification (Figure 5.1, Path B+C) or harsh disciplinary practice

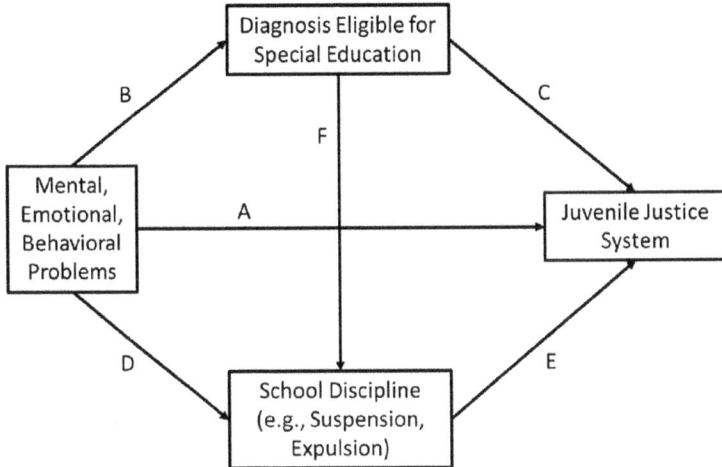

FIGURE 5.1 Conceptual Framework of Special Education to the School-to-Prison Pipeline.

(Figure 5.1, Path D+E). Path B+C and Path A are different in that Path B+C provides a potential opportunity to intervene when youth are identified as having special education needs (Landrum et al., 2003; Morgan et al., 2017). Path D+E represents youth with MEB problems—possibly unidentified for special education needs or other support service needs but labeled as "problem kids" in school—receiving recurring disciplinary infractions and, ultimately, getting involved in the justice system (Morgan et al., 2012, 2015).

Additionally, youth with MEB problems might be identified as needing special education services and, yet, still receive harsh discipline and, in turn, enter into the justice system (Figure 5.1, Path B+F+E). Studies have shown that youth in special education are more likely to experience school failure and exhibit the kinds of behavioral issues that lead to disciplinary problems (Leone et al., 2002; Skiba, 2002), often resulting in suspension or expulsion. In fact, youth with special education needs are seven times more likely than youth without special education needs to be expelled or suspended (Quinn et al., 2005), which increases the likelihood of juvenile justice system involvement in the year following a suspension or expulsion (Fabelo et al., 2011). Once involved in the juvenile justice system, youth with special education needs have a higher likelihood of recidivism than their juvenile justice counterparts without special education needs (Bullis et al., 2002).

While we focus primarily on the failings within the school system, resource-deprived environments (i.e., access to stable housing, family economic hardship) for many justice-involved youth can increase the likelihood of life adversities and conduct problems that bring them to the attention of the juvenile justice system (e.g., Logan-Greene et al., 2020). These adverse experiences are likely amplified in their effects in the case of youth with special needs. Thus, family context from which these youth come also need to be considered.

Unique Experiences of Black Youth

How might these conceptual pathways look for Black youth? Added to the Black youth's experience are racialized interactions and racist experiences at schools, with teachers, police officers, and in courts. In many studies, experiences of Black youth are not examined as the central question but rather in comparison to another group, even though the nature of the experiences might be qualitatively different. For example, when teachers demonstrate helpfulness, attentiveness, and are viewed as accessible by Black girls, they are more likely to attribute these positive attachments to feeling a sense of belongingness (Kalu et al., 2020; Murphy et al., 2013). However, McGlynn-Wright et al. (2021) found that police interactions, positive or negative, increased the risk of future arrest for Black youth but not for White youth. District-wide practice and policy that station peace officers, resource officers, and police officers can be detrimental to Black youth. Likewise, being identified and receiving services as youth eligible for special education among Black students might be a very different experience compared to White or other racial/ethnic minority youth. Does it provide the support students need? Or does it simply label the students?

The conceptual framework outlined above lives in the context of anti-Black racism. Recently, more scholars have suggested the importance of acknowledging anti-Black racism in everyday life of Black individuals (Kendi, 2019). Anti-Black racism resides within societies, institutions, and ideologies of Whiteness, White supremacy, and fear of the Black body (Kendi, 2019), which promotes the oppression of Black people (Dumas, 2016). This form of racism is deliberately directed toward Black people and their resistance to oppression (Benjamin, 2011). The longstanding legacy of anti-Black racism situates Black people as objects of obsession and vigor that harkens back to slavery through the perpetual denial of their humanity (Sexton, 2010, 2015). This certainly rings true for Black students in schools, who are marginalized through stereotype, microaggressions, and discipline (Cole & Cohen, 2013; Kubek et al., 2020; Mendoza et al., 2020). More stark in anti-Black racism is our country's justice system that criminalizes Black individuals, especially Black males. Black individuals are five times more likely to be incarcerated in state prisons than White individuals (Nellis, 2016). While only 13% of Black individuals make up the United States population (U.S. Census, 2019), they make up 38% of the prison population (Carson, 2020). One in four Black youth has had incarcerated parents growing up, over six times more likely than for White youth (Morsy & Rothstein, 2016). This disparity is mirrored in young Black children who are far more likely than any other racial or ethnic groups to be arrested, charged, adjudicated, and incarcerated (Kim et al., 2020). The question is not about how much more crime Black youth commit but why they are being policed and incarcerated more than their White counterparts. Given this context, there's meaning in trying to understand and explain the different experiences of Black youth.

The conceptual framework must, thus, be informed by critical race theory. Critical race theory centralizes race to assess inequities embedded in social, political, legal, and economic institutions, systems, policies, and practices (Bell, 1980; Ladson-Billings & Tate, 1995). Thus, understanding Black youth's educational journey, using critical race theory, can illuminate how race can determine opportunities and pathways for Black youth in schools. When Black youth have MEB problems, how might school personnel react to them? According to the literature, in some settings, school personnel might overidentify these students into special education; in other settings, they might simply overlook the issues as disrupting class or school environment and refer them for office discipline. In both situations, the interaction is racialized. One way or another, Black students are being academically segregated from other students, further marginalizing and stigmatizing them—labeled as problem students needing attention. This might, then, lead to negative school experiences for Black youth and increased likelihood of dropout or suspension/expulsion, which ultimately puts them at risk for juvenile justice involvement. Further, once youth become involved with the juvenile justice system, they are likely to experience further marginalization when they return to the community, as school personnel often stereotype them because they have been identified as "juvenile offenders" or simply as part of the "juvenile justice system." These terms promote stereotypes and stigmatization (Cole & Cohen, 2013; Kubek et al., 2020). Throughout these experiences, Black youth are less likely to receive support within schools, from teachers, and staff or given another chance because of their racial and ethnic identity (Lopez & Jean-Marie, 2021; Munroe, 2017).

What about Black Girls?

Girls, especially Black girls, remain the fastest growing group in the juvenile justice system (Kerig, 2018; Quinn et al., 2021; Tam et al., 2019) who also bear a higher burden of system involvement in the United States (Quinn et al., 2021). However, their growth as a group does not particularly reflect an increase in delinquent acts they commit, which notes a possible difference in how the system responds to Black girls (Javdani et al., 2011; Rubino et al., 2021). Given that, it is necessary to consider an intersectional lens with Black girls in the school-to-prison pipeline. Specifically, intersectionality theory describes the multiple and interlocking oppressions that Black women (and girls) face in society that are related to both race and gender equally (Crenshaw, 1989). This theory centers on the "triple jeopardy" barriers of racism, sexism, and capitalism that Black women (and girls) experience (Aguilar, 2012). The systemic barriers that Black girls experience in schools and in particular, the school-to-prison pipeline support this phenomenon. Further, utilizing an intersectional lens, especially in research, is needed as it indicates variation in the pathways for girls and boys to systems like special education, juvenile justice, etc. (Collins, 2015; Goff et al., 2014).

Summary of Findings about Black Probation Youth

We replicated the analyses conducted in Kim et al. (2021) for Black probation youth only, with the exception of taking out age from the analytic models as one of the covariates. Age was strongly associated with the number of reoffenses for Black probation youth—meaning that those who were younger, by virtue of the way the data were compiled, had more reoffenses; they simply had more time in our dataset to reappear than those, for example, who started in our dataset at age 16 who would have only had one year in our dataset to recidivate. These youth would not have returned to the juvenile justice system but to the adult criminal justice system. While age was positively associated with more reoffenses in the full sample (Kim et al., 2021), it did not conceal the relationship of other predictors, as it did in the subsample of Black youth. We, thus, conducted the analysis without the effect of age.

In a sample of 1,000 Black probation youth, 40% reported having at least one special education eligibility criterion: 0.7% with intellectual disability, 17% with ADHD, 21% with behavioral disorder, and 22% with learning disability. This is similar to what Kim et al. (2021) found across all probation youth, with the exception that a greater proportion of Black probation youth had special education for behavioral disorder and a smaller proportion for ADHD. One in five Black probation youth reported having past and/or current mental health problems. Nearly 93% of youth had at least one experience of suspension/expulsion. Almost half (47%) of Black youth recidivated at least once and 10% had four or more reoffenses (m = 1.06; SD = 1.58). See Table 5.1.

Examining the relationship between special education status and mental health problems, we found that 35% of Black youth with special education status (vs. 46% in the overall sample) had mental health problems whereas 68% of Black youth with mental health problems (60% in the overall sample) had special education status. Relatedly, we examined the relationship between special education status and expulsion/suspension. Over 96% of Black youth with special education status (93% in the overall sample) had an expulsion while 42% of Black youth with expulsion (41% in the overall sample) had special education status. Finally, we examined the relationship between mental health problems and expulsion/suspension history. Nearly 95% of Black youth with expulsion (95% in the overall sample) had mental health problems while 21% of Black youth with mental health problems (21% in the overall sample) had expulsion history.

For Black probation youth, special education status was significantly associated with more reoffenses (Model 1: B =.15; p <.001). While mental health problems were not significantly associated with more reoffenses across all models,

TABLE 5.1 Descriptives

Variables	All Youth (n = 4,317)			Black Youth (n = 1,000)		
	Total	Boys	Girls	Total	Boys	Girls
Recidivism						
Mean Reoffense (0–13)	0.81	0.84	0.71	1.06	1.08	0.98
Any Reoffense (0/1)	38.6%	39.8%	34.5%	47.0%	47.5%	43.8%
Sex						
Boys	76.5%	–	–	76.0%	–	71.7%
Girls	23.5%	–	–	24.0%	–	28.3%
Age (in years)	15.5	15.5	15.4	15.3	15.4	15.2
Mental Health (MH)						
Current/History MH (0/1)	30.3%	29.2%	34.0%	20.4%	18.4%	26.7%
Self-Regulation Skills						
Problem Solving	0.06	0.04	0.13	−0.04	−0.06	0.03
Impulse Control	0.05	0.04	0.09	−0.01	−0.003	−0.02
School Exclusions						
Any Exp/Susp (0/1)	88.9%	90.7%	83.1%	92.6%	93.8%	88.8%
Special Education (0/1)	39.6%	43.4%	27.2%	40.0%	43.6%	28.8%
Behavioral Disorder (0/1)	19.0%	21.1%	11.8%	21.0%	23.0%	14.6%
Learning Disability (0/1)	22.2%	24.3%	15.0%	22.3%	24.2%	16.3%
ADHD (0/1)	19.5%	22.1%	11.1%	17.2%	18.6%	12.9%
Intellectual Disability (0/1)	0.7%	0.8%	0.5%	0.7%	0.7%	0.8%

lower problem-solving skills (Model 3: B = -.123; p <.01; Model 4: B = -.120; p <.01) were significantly associated with more reoffenses. Controlling for mental health problems, problem-solving skills, impulse control, and suspension/expulsion, special education continued to be significantly associated with more reoffenses (Model 4: B =.09; p <.01). Suspension/expulsion was not significantly associated with more reoffenses. See Table 5.2.

Black Probation Youth by Gender

We then examined these patterns by gender. Consistent with Kim et al. (2021), more Black boys (44%) were eligible for special education than Black girls (29%). Rates of past expulsion or suspension were high across the board but higher for Black boys (94%) and girls (89%) compared to the rest of the probation youth (91% and 83% respectively). Prevalence of past or current mental health history was lower for Black boys (18%) and girls (27%) compared to the rest of the probation youth (29% and 34% respectively). See Table 5.1.

Examining the relationship between special education status and mental health problems, we found that 31% of Black boys with special education status

TABLE 5.2 Multiple Regression Models Predicting Recidivism

All Black Youth (n = 1,000)

Number of Reoffenses	Model 1			Model 2			Model 3			Model 4		
	B	SE	β	B	SE	β	B	SE	β	B	SE	β
(Constant)	0.868	0.063		0.842	0.065		0.897	0.065		0.788	0.182		***
Special Education (0/1)	0.477	0.101	0.148 ***	0.421	0.105	0.130 ***	0.296	0.106	0.092 **	0.29	0.106	0.09 **
Mental Health (0/1)				0.234	0.128	0.060	0.169	0.127	0.043	0.168	0.127	0.042
Problem Solving							−0.246	0.102	−0.123 *	−0.240	0.102	−0.120 *
Impulse Control							−0.212	0.119	−0.091	−0.214	0.119	−0.091 **
Exp/Susp (0/1)										0.120	0.188	0.020
Special Ed X Exp/Susp												
F	22.20***			12.81***			16.98***			13.66***		
R-Squared	0.022			0.025			0.064			0.064		

Black Boys (n = 760)

Number of Reoffenses	Model 1			Model 2			Model 3			Model 4		
	B	SE	β	B	SE	β	B	SE	β	B	SE	β
(Constant)	0.900	0.077		***	0.869	0.078		***	0.920	0.077		***	0.709	0.232		***
Special Education (0/1)	0.427	0.116	0.132 ***	0.347	0.121	0.107 **	0.237	0.121	0.073 +	0.230	0.122	0.071 +
Mental Health (0/1)				0.354	0.155	0.086 *	0.258	0.154	0.062	0.255	0.154	0.062
Problem Solving							−0.256	0.120	−0.124 *	−0.247	0.102	−0.120 *
Impulse Control							−0.192	0.137	−0.081	−0.192	0.137	−0.082

(Continued)

	Model 1			Model 2			Model 3			Model 4		
	B	SE	β	B	SE	β	B	SE	β	B	SE	β
Exp/Susp (0/1)										0.229	0.238	0.034
Special Ed X Exp/Susp												
F	13.41***			9.35***			12.04***			9.82***		
R-Squared	0.017			0.024			0.06			0.061		

Black Girls (n = 240)

	Model 1			Model 2			Model 3			Model 4		
Number of Reoffenses	B	SE	β	B	SE	β	B	SE	β	B	SE	β
(Constant)	0.789	0.114		0.798	0.121		0.848	0.119		0.952	0.292		***
Special Education (0/1)	0.645	0.212	0.193 **	0.663	0.227	0.198 **	0.481	0.229	0.144 *	0.49	0.231	0.147 *
Mental Health (0/1)				−0.051	0.232	−0.015	−0.034	0.228	−0.010	−0.035	0.228	−0.010
Problem Solving							−0.206	0.198	−0.112	−0.218	0.200	−0.118
Impulse Control							−0.262	0.243	−0.116	−0.255	0.245	−0.025
Exp/Susp (0/1)										−0.120	0.307	−0.025
Special Ed X Exp/Susp												
F	9.24***			4.63*			5.24***			4.21**		
R-Squared	0.037			0.038			0.082			0.083		

+ p <.10.
* p <.05.
** p <.01.
*** p <.001.

had mental health problems whereas 74% of Black boys with mental health problems had special education status. There was a big discrepancy with girls: over 50% of Black girls with special education status had mental health problems while 55% of Black girls with mental health problems had special education status. Relatedly, we examined the relationship between special education status and expulsion/suspension. Over 96% of Black boys with special education status had an expulsion while 44.7% of Black boys with expulsion had special education status. Similar patterns emerged for girls. Nearly 96% of Black girls with special education status had an expulsion while 31% of Black girls with expulsion had special education status. Finally, we examined the relationship between mental health problems and expulsion/suspension history. Over 96% of Black boys with expulsion had mental health problems while 19% of Black boys with mental health problems had expulsion history. Similarly, over 90% of Black girls with expulsion had mental health problems while 27% of Black girls with mental health problems had expulsion history.

Different associations were found by gender. In Model 1, having special education eligibility was significantly associated with more reoffenses for both Black boys (B = 0.132; p < .001) and girls (B = .193; p < .01). Past and current history of mental health problems was significantly associated with more reoffenses for Black boys (Model 2) but not for Black girls. Having higher levels of problem-solving skills was significantly associated with fewer reoffenses for Black boys across all Models but not Black girls. Holding constant mental health problems, problem-solving skills, and impulse control, special education eligibility was significantly associated with more reoffenses for Black girls but not Black boys (Model 4). For Black girls only, having special education eligibility continued to be significantly associated with more reoffenses across all models. Expulsion/suspension history was not associated with reoffenses for both Black girls and boys. See Table 5.2.

Discussion

This chapter sought to re-conceptualize the role of special education in the context of probation for Black youth. We provided a theoretical rationale of why it is important to examine Black youth separately from other youth and Black boys separately from Black girls. Our empirical findings further strengthen our argument that it is simply not enough to compare Black youth with White youth or use gender as a control variable. This chapter extends the findings of Kim et al., 2021, by examining the possible unique experiences of Black probation youth—boys and girls separately—eligible for special education on the school-to-prison pipeline. Given the aforementioned racialized experiences for Black youth, we sought to unpack the findings—what this might mean for Black youth serving probation.

Like other studies, we found that Black youth were disproportionately represented in probation. Black youth in this particular county made up approximately 7% of the youth population but made up 23% in probation. We, however, did not find an overrepresentation of Black youth among those with special education needs. As recent studies suggest, this may be due to a mix of over- and underidentification of Black youth for special education across different schools. To explore possible avenues through which Black youth get identified for special education as well as discipline, in this chapter, we closely examined the concordance and discordance across special education, mental health problems, and school expulsion/suspension history. Across the board, Path F (see Figure 5.1) is clear. Youth, Black or not, with special education status are disproportionately suspended or expelled, providing clear support for the differential treatment theory (Rutherford et al., 2002). While youth with special education needs are legally protected to ensure suspension and expulsion are used as the utmost last resort, our data suggest that on-the-ground practices have not provided that support.

Given the underrepresentation of Black probation youth in terms of mental health problems, we found that a lower percentage of Black probation youth in special education had mental health problems compared to the overall sample. This was especially true for Black boys. On the flip side, a greater percentage of Black probation youth, and more so for Black boys, with mental health problems had special education status compared to the overall sample. One possible explanation would be that fewer Black probation youth, boys in particular, get into special education for undiagnosed mental health problems. For Black boys with a diagnosis, however, it is clear that they are more likely to be in special education. While being identified for special education increased recidivism for Black boys, when accounting for mental health problems and self-regulation skills, the association disappeared. This is consistent with the susceptibility theory (Keilitz & Dunivant, 1986), which posits that the characteristics that accompany their disabling conditions—such as low impulse control and poor problem-solving skills—lead to delinquency. Meaning that, for Black boys, a more concerted effort in building self-regulation skills and reducing mental health problems might help mitigate the negative impact of being identified for special education. Also, greater efforts need to be made to correctly identify and diagnose mental health problems. Undiagnosed mental health problems can lead to school challenges, and other negative problems in schools. It is imperative that youth receive the support they need, especially in the context where Black youth and Black boys, especially are criminalized. State policies based on race/ethnicity and class with an eye toward public safety, as well as personal and educational accountability center the premise of dispossession. In addition, these policies infuse schools with juvenile/criminal justice surveillance, extracting resources, time, and relationships from teaching and learning while sending these resources into legal surveillance and pursuit, that is, the school-to-prison pipeline.

On top of this, Black girls have been doubly oppressed and marginalized through sexism and misogyny, as girls who need little protection or advocacy. From this lens, it is feasible that Black girls who receive special education services are more likely to enter and re-enter the juvenile justice system rather than receive the support they need. Consequently, a slightly different explanation is needed for Black girls. A greater percentage of Black girls with special education had mental health problems than in the overall sample, meaning that mental health diagnosis seemed to be one of the more common reasons why Black girls received special education. This is evident in the Black girls' experiences of expulsion/suspension. Black girls with mental health problems made up the biggest group among Black girls with expulsion/suspension history. It is interesting that while Black girls were still underrepresented in terms of mental health problems, it seems to be the biggest risk for Black girls. Moreover, being identified for special education was significantly associated with recidivism for Black girls, even after accounting for school discipline, mental health problems, and self-regulation skills. This is consistent with the findings by Kim et al. (2021). While special education services are developed for the purpose of support, it functioned as a risk for Black girls, in terms of entering and re-entering the juvenile justice system. It may be that some girls are mis-identified. It may also be that some girls do not have access to quality special education. It could also mean that other more pertinent issues, like trauma have not been addressed and manifested in different ways.

Criminological theories like social bonding, general strain, and social learning theories, tend to be more gender neutral and assert that boys and girls have the same or similar criminogenic pathways (Ishoy & Blackwell, 2019). Further, general strain theory (Agnew, 2013) indicates that criminal behaviors may result from youth trying to deal with trauma on their own (McKenna et al., 2020), which can also be associated with their academic and mental health problems whether identified or not. It has been estimated that 70% of girls report histories of sexual or physical abuse (Kerig, 2018; Meichenbaum, 2006). Approximately 40% of Black females report experiencing coercive sexual contact by age 18, reflecting a high rate of sexual trauma among girls of color suggesting "trauma-linked youth offenses and recidivism" (Kerig, 2018; Meichenbaum, 2006). Of note, research with feminist pathways theory has initiated needed discourse about trauma and the needs of system-involved girls, especially Black girls. Yet, the knowledge needs to extend beyond describing their experiences to action-oriented research that will solve the longstanding causes of girls' system involvement. This gap must be addressed, as it reflects the paradigm of circuits and consequences of dispossession in which Black and other racial and ethnic minority groups, are treated as embodying danger and worthlessness (Fine & Ruglis, 2009), ultimately leading to their academic failure.

Under the Individuals with Disabilities Education Improvement Act (IDEA), 20 U.S.C. § 1400 et seq. (2004), every child, including children with special education needs as well as children who are incarcerated, has the right to receive a free and appropriate public education in the least restrictive environment. In this chapter, we re-examined the role of special education among Black probation youth, informed by critical race theory and intersectionality. Special education is an important and necessary support. We must, however, understand that the policies, practices, and processes of receiving services through special education also reflect structural and systemic racism. It is time to explicitly acknowledge, name, and address the harms that have been done for youth of color, especially Black youth, on the school-to-prison pipeline.

References

Abrams, L. S., Mizel, M. L., & Barnert, E. S. (2021). The criminalization of young children and overrepresentation of black youth in the juvenile justice system. *Race and Social Problems, 13*(1), 73–84.

Act to amend §48647 of the Education Code. (2019–2020). *Relating to juvenile court school pupils*, Cal. Assemb. B. 1354, Chapter 756 (Cal. Stat. 2019). https://Leginfo.legislature.ca.gov/faces/billTextClient.xhtml?bill_id=201920200AB1354

Agnew, R. (2013). When criminal coping is likely: An extension of general strain theory. *Deviant Behavior, 34*(8), 653–670.

Aguilar, D. D. (2012). From triple jeopardy to intersectionality: The feminist perplex. *Comparative Studies of South Asia, Africa and the Middle East, 32*(2), 415–428.

Ahram, R., Fergus, E., & Noguera, P. (2011). Addressing racial/ethnic disproportionality in special education: Case studies of suburban school districts. *Teachers College Record, 113*(10), 2233–2266.

Albrecht, S. F., Skiba, R. J., Losen, D. J., Chung, C.-G., & Middelberg, L. (2012). Federal policy on disproportionality in special education: Is it moving us forward? *Journal of Disability Policy Studies, 23*(1), 14–25. doi:10.1177/1044207311407917

Anderson, K. P., & Ritter, G. W. (2017). Disparate use of exclusionary discipline: Evidence on inequities in school discipline from a U.S. state. *Education Policy Analysis Archives, 25*(49). doi:10.14507/epaa.25.2787

Bell, D. A. (1980). Brown v. board of education and the interest convergence dilemma. *Harvard Law Review, 93*, 518–533.

Benjamin, A. (2011). Afterword: Doing anti-oppressive social work: The importance of resistance, history and strategy. In D. Baines (Ed.), *Doing anti-oppressive practice: Social justice social work* (pp. 290–297). Halifax, Canada: Fernwood Press.

Bullis, M., Yovanoff, P., Mueller, G., & Havel, E. (2002). Life on the outs—Examination of the facility-to-community transition of incarcerated youth. *Exceptional Children, 69*(1), 7–22. doi:10.1177/001440290206900101

Carson, E. A. (2020). *Prisoners in 2019*. U.S. Department of Justice, Office of Justice Programs, Bureau of Justice Statistics. https://bjs.ojp.gov/content/pub/pdf/p19.pdf

Chu, E. M., & Ready, D. D. (2018). Exclusion and urban public high schools: Short- and long-term consequences of school suspensions. *American Journal of Education, 124*(4), 479–509. doi:10.1086/698454

Cole, H., & Cohen, R. (2013). Breaking down barriers: A case study of juvenile justice personnel perspectives on school reentry. *Journal of Correctional Education, 64*(1), 13–35.

Collins, P. H. (2015). Intersectionality's definitional dilemmas. *Annual Review of Sociology, 41*, 1–20.

Crenshaw, K. (1989). Demarginalizing the intersection of race and sex: Black feminist critique of antidiscrimination doctrine, feminist theory and antiracist politics. *University of Chicago Legal Forum*, 139–168. doi:10.4324/9780429500480-5

Dumas, M. J. (2016). Against the dark: Antiblackness in education policy and discourse. *Theory into Practice*, 55(1), 11–19.

Elder, T. E., Figlio, D. N., Imberman, S. A., & Persico, C. L. (2021). School segregation and racial gaps in special education identification. *Journal of Labor Economics*, 39(S1), S151–S197.

Fabelo, T., Thompson, M. D., Plotkin, M., Carmichael, D., Marchbanks, M. P., & Booth, E. A. (2011). *Breaking schools' rules: A statewide study of how school discipline relates to students' success and juvenile justice involvement*. Council of State Governments Justice Center.

Fine, M., & Ruglis, J. (2009). Circuits and consequences of dispossession: The racialized realignment of the public sphere for US youth. *Transforming Anthropology*, 17(1), 20–33.

Goff, P. A., Jackson, M. C., Di Leone, B. A. L., Culotta, C. M., & DiTomasso, N. A. (2014). The essence of innocence: Consequences of dehumanizing Black children. *Journal of Personality and Social Psychology*, 106(4), 526–545. doi:10.1037/a0035663

Gresham, F. M., Sugai, G., & Horner, R. H. (2001). Interpreting outcomes of social skills training for students with high-incidence disabilities. *Exceptional Children*, 67(3), 331–344. doi:10.1177/001440290106700303

Grindal, T., Schifter, L. A., Schwartz, G., & Hehir, T. (2019). Racial differences in special education identification and placement: Evidence across three states. *Harvard Educational Review*, 89(4), 525–553. doi:10.17763/1943-5045-89.4.525

Henderson, D. X., Walker, L., Barnes, R. R., Lunsford, A., Edwards, C., & Clark, C. (2019). A Framework for race-related trauma in the public education system and implications on health for black youth. *The Journal of School Health*, 89(11), 926–933. doi:10.1111/josh.12832

Hurwitz, S., Cohen, E. D., & Perry, B. L. (2021). Special education is associated with reduced odds of school discipline among students with disabilities. *Educational Researcher*, 50(2), 86–96.

Individuals with Disabilities Education Improvement Act, 20 U.S.C. 1400 et seq. (2004). https://uscode.house.gov/view.xhtml?path=/prelim@title20/chapter33&edition=prelim

Ishoy, G. A., & Blackwell, B. S. (2019). Situational action theory's self-control/morality interaction effects and the moderating influence of being female: A comparison of property and violent offending using a sample of juvenile delinquents. *Feminist Criminology*, 14(4), 391–419.

Javdani, S., Sadeh, N., & Verona, E. (2011). Expanding our lens: Female pathways to antisocial behavior in adolescence and adulthood. *Clinical Psychology Review*, 31, 1324–1348.

Jordan, K.-A. (2005). Discourses of difference and the overrepresentation of Black students in special education. *The Journal of African American History*, 90(1/2), 128–149. doi:10.1086/JAAHv90n1-2p128

Kalu, S. R., Menon, S. E., & Quinn, C. R. (2020). The relationship between externalizing behavior and school and familial attachments among girls from diverse backgrounds. *Children and Youth Services Review*, 116, 105170. doi:10.1016/j.childyouth.2020.105170

Keilitz, I., & Dunivant, N. (1986). The relationship between learning disability and juvenile delinquency: Current state of knowledge. *Remedial and Special Education*, 7(3), 18–26.

Kendi, I. X. (2019). *How to be an antiracist*. New York: Random House.

Kerig, P. K. (2018). Polyvictimization and girls' involvement in the juvenile justice system: Investigating gender-differentiated patterns of risk, recidivism, and resilience. *Journal of Interpersonal Violence*, 33(5), 789–809.

Kim, B. K. E., Johnson, J., Rhinehart, L., Logan-Greene, P., Lomeli, J., & Nurius, P. S. (2021). The school-to-prison pipeline for probation youth with special education needs. *American Journal of Orthopsychiatry, 91*(3), 375–385.

Kim, B. E., McCarter, S., & Logan-Greene, P. (2020). Achieving equal opportunity and justice in juvenile justice (Grand Challenges for Social Work Initiative Working Paper No. 25). https://grandchallengesforsocialwork.org/wp-content/uploads/2020/06/Achieving-Equal-Opportunity-and-Justice-in-Juvenile-Justice-3.pdf

Krezmien, M., Leone, P., & Achilles, G. (2006). Suspension, race, and disability: Analysis of statewide practices and reporting. *Journal of Emotional and Behavioral Disorders, 14*(4), 217–226.

Kubek, J. B., Tindall-Biggins, C., Reed, K., Carr, L. E., & Fenning, P. A. (2020). A systematic literature review of school reentry practices among youth impacted by juvenile justice. *Children and Youth Services Review, 110*, 104773.

Ladson-Billings, G., & Tate, W. F. (1995). Toward a critical race theory of education. *Teachers College Record, 97*, 47–68.

Landrum, T. J., Tankersley, M., & Kauffman, J. M. (2003). What is special about special education for students with emotional or behavioral disorders? *The Journal of Special Education, 37*(3), 148–156. doi:10.1177/00224669030370030401

Leaf, P. J. (2010). Multilevel exploration of factors contributing to the overrepresentation of black students in office disciplinary referrals. *Journal of Educational Psychology, 102*(2), 508–520. doi:10.1037/a0018450

Leone, P. E., Drakeford, W., & Meisel, S. M. (2002). Special education programs for youth with disabilities in juvenile corrections. *Journal of Correctional Education, 53*(2), 46–50.

Logan-Greene, P., Kim, B. E., & Nurius, P. S. (2020). Adversity profiles among court-involved youth: Translating system data into trauma-responsive programming. *Child Abuse & Neglect, 104*(104465), 1–12. doi:10.1016/j.chiabu.2020.104465

Lopez, A. E., & Jean-Marie, G. (2021). Challenging anti-black racism in everyday teaching, learning, and leading: From theory to practice. *Journal of School Leadership, 31*(1–2), 50–65.

Losen, D. J., & Orfield, G. (2002). *Racial inequity in special education.* Civil Rights Project at Harvard University: Harvard Education Press.

Marchbanks, M. P., & Blake, J. J. (2017). *Assessing authoritative school strictness by race: Final report.* College Station, TX: Public Policy Research Institute, Texas A&M University.

McFarland, J., Hussar, B., Zhang, J., Wang, X., Wang, K., Hein, S., Diliberti, M., Forrest Cataldi, E., Bullock Mann, F., & Barmer, A. (2019). *The condition of education 2019 (NCES 2019-144). U.S. department of education.* Washington, DC: National Center for Education Statistics. https://nces.ed.gov/pubsearch/pubsinfo.asp?pubid=2019144

McGlynn-Wright, A. R. D., Crutchfield, M. L., & Skinner, K. P. Haggerty. (2021). The usual, racialized, suspects: The consequence of police contacts with black and white youth on adult arrest. *Social Problems, 00*, 1–17.

McKenna, N. C., Golladay, K. A., & Holtfreter, K. (2020). Integrating general strain theory and trauma-informed principles into the study of older adult victimization. *Journal of Trauma & Dissociation, 21*(2), 187–200.

Meichenbaum, D. (2006). *Comparison of aggression in boys and girls: A case for gender-specific interventions.* Miami, FL: The Melissa Institute.

Mendoza, M., Blake, J. J., Marchbanks, M. P., III, & Ragan, K. (2020). Race, gender, and disability and the risk for juvenile justice contact. *The Journal of Special Education, 53*, 226. doi:10.1177/0022466919845113

Morgan, P. L., Farkas, G., Cook, M., Strassfeld, N. M., Hillemeier, M. M., Pun, W. H., & Schussler, D. L. (2017). Are Black children disproportionately overrepresented in special education? A best-evidence synthesis. *Exceptional Children, 83*(2), 181–198.

Morgan, P. L., Farkas, G., Hillemeier, M. M., & Maczuga, S. (2012). Are minority children disproportionately represented in early intervention and early childhood special education? *Educational Researcher, 41*, 339–351. doi:10.3102/0013189X12459678

Morgan, P. L., Farkas, G., Hillemeier, M., Mattison, R., Li, H., & Cook, M. (2015). Minorities are disproportionately under-represented in special education: Longitudinal evidence across five disability conditions. *Educational Researcher, 44*, 278–292. doi:10.3102/0013189X15591157

Morris, M. (2016). *Pushout: The criminalization of Black girls in schools*. New York: New Press.

Morsy, L., & Rothstein, R. (2016). *Mass incarceration and children's outcomes: Criminal justice policy is education policy*. Economic Policy Institute. https://www.epi.org/publication/mass-incarceration-and-childrens-outcomes/

Munroe, T. (2017). Enriching relational practices with critical anti-Black racism advocacy and perspectives in schools. *Relational Child & Youth Care Practice, 30*(3), 32–45.

Murphy, A., Acosta, M., & Kennedy-Lewis, B. (2013). I'm not running around with my pants sagging so how am I not acting like a lady?: Intersections of race and gender in the experiences of female middle school troublemakers. (Report). *The Urban Review, 45*(5), 586–610. doi:10.1007/s11256-013-0236-7

Nellis, A. (2016). The color of justice: Racial and ethnic disparity in state prisons. The Sentencing Project.

O'Connell, M. E., Boat, T., & Warner, K. E. (2009). *Preventing mental, emotional, and behavioral disorders among young people: Progress and possibilities* (Vol. 7). Washington, DC: National Academies.

Osher, D., Woodruff, D., Sims, A. E., Losen, D. J., & Orfield, G. (Eds.). (2002). *Racial inequity in special education*. Harvard Education Press.

Peck, J. H., & Jennings, W. G. (2016). A critical examination of "being Black" in the juvenile justice system. *Law and Human Behavior, 40*(3), 1–14.

Puzzanchera, C. (2021). *Juvenile Arrests, 2019*. U.S. Department of Justice, Office of Justice Programs. https://ojjdp.ojp.gov/publications/juvenile-arrests-2019.pdf

Quinn, C. R., Boyd, D. T., Kim, B. K. E., Menon, S. E., Logan-Greene, P., Asemota, E., DiClemente, R. J., & Voisin, D. (2021). The influence of familial and peer social support on post-traumatic stress disorder among Black girls in juvenile correctional facilities. *Criminal Justice and Behavior, 48*(7), 867–883.

Quinn, M. M., Rutherford, R. B., Leone, P. E., Osher, D. M., & Poirier, J. M. (2005). Youth with disabilities in juvenile corrections: A national survey. *Exceptional Children, 71*(3), 339–345.

Rubino, L. L., Anderson, V. R., & McKenna, N. C. (2021). Examining the disconnect in youth pathways and court responses: How bias invades across gender, race/ethnicity, and sexual orientation. *Feminist Criminology*, 15570851211003964, 480–503.

Rutherford, R. B., Quinn, M. M., Leone, P. E., Garfinkle, L., & Nelson, C. M. (2002). *Education, disability, and juvenile justice: Recommended practices*. Arlington: Council for Exceptional Children.

Sexton, J. (2010). People-of-color-blindness notes Sexton on the afterlife of slavery. *Social Text, 28*(2/103), 31–56.

Sexton, J. (2015). Unbearable blackness. *Cultural Critique, 90*, 159–178.

Skiba, R. J. (2002). Special education and school discipline: A precarious balance. *Behavioral Disorders, 27*(2), 81–97.

Skiba, R. J., Simmons, A. B., Ritter, S., Gibb, A. C., Rausch, M. K., Cuadrado, J., & Chung, C. (2008). Achieving equity in special education: History, status, and current challenges. *Exceptional Children, 74*(3), 264–288.

Sullivan, A. L., Van Norman, E. R., & Klingbeil, D. A. (2014). Exclusionary discipline of students with disabilities: Student and school characteristics predicting suspension. *Remedial and Special Education, 35*(4), 199–210. doi:10.1177/0741932513519825

Tam, C. C., Dauria, E. F., Cook, M. C., Ti, A., Comfort, M., & Tolou-Shams, M. (2019). Justice involvement and girls' sexual health: Directions for policy and practice. *Child and Youth Services Review, 98*, 278–283.

U.S. Census. (2019). *Quick facts: United States.* https://www.census.gov/quickfacts/fact/table/US

U.S. Commission on Civil Rights. (2019). *Beyond suspensions: Examining school discipline policies and connections to the school-to-prison pipeline for students of color with disabilities.*

U.S. Department of Education Office for Civil Rights. (2014). Civil rights data collection: Data snapshot: School discipline. Issue Brief No. 1. Washington, DC: US Department of Education Office for Civil Rights. https://ocrdata.ed.gov/downloads/crdc-school-discipline-snapshot.pdf

Yoon, S., Quinn, C. R., Shockley, K. M., & Robertson, A. (2019). The effects of child protective services and juvenile justice system involvement on academic outcomes: Gender and racial differences. *Youth & Society, 3*(1), 131–152. doi:10.1177/0044118X19844392

Zhang, D., Katsiyannis, A., & Herbst, M. (2004). Disciplinary exclusions in special education: A 4-year analysis. *Behavioral Disorders, 29*(4): 337–347.

Zhang, D., Katsiyannis, A., Ju, S., & Roberts, E. (2014). Minority representation in special education: 5-year trends. *Journal of Child and Family Studies, 23*(1), 118–127.

6

EXPLORING THE RELEVANCE AND USE OF FUNDS OF GANG KNOWLEDGE AMONG SYSTEM-IMPACTED LATINO BOYS AND YOUNG MEN

The Case of an Urban Continuation School

Adrian H. Huerta and Cecilia Rios-Aguilar

> If a cop ever stops you don't say anything - just be smart, listen… only talk when they talk to you, don't give them any attitude or anything! Because the cop will either take you to jail for the rest of your life and they can kill you and they will get away with it, because the cops can do anything they want to you, so treat a cop like they are God because that's what they want, because with the gun and the badge they think they can do whatever, when they technically can and they can't at the same time.

This quote from Gabe is an example of the *funds of gang knowledge* that many urban Latino young men in this study have acquired. Gabe and the other young men in this study use these varied forms of knowledge as a survival tool on the streets and urban schools. In many communities, youth of color are routinely over-policed by law enforcement, and educators and community members are vigilant of boys of color to ensure that they are adhering to social and cultural norms within their communities (Rios, 2011). For many communities of color, there is a long history of structural racism and marginalization that contributes to the over-representation in gangs, police contact, and the juvenile and adult prison system (Annamma, 2018; Vigil, 1988). Since late spring 2020, the general public has become hyper-aware of police violence in schools and communities, and is not in fact the figment of imagination, but a stark reality that children of color, and adults of color, may easily become the victim of an aggressive police officer and lose their life for trivial occurrences. These cultural realities force some youth to accept that going to juvenile hall and/or to prison is natural – and something they may have to experience as part of growing up due to the embedded racist practices within society (Durán, 2013).

Much of the existing literature on marginalized boys of color provide lenses on how urban contexts affect their trajectories, including the relationship between gangs and deviance, the mistreatment in schools and communities, and the school-to-prison pipeline (STPP) (Huerta, 2018; Noguera, 2003; Rios, 2011). We contribute to these emerging discourses on marginalized Latino young men in urban schools by focusing on – and treating youths' *funds of gang knowledge* as – key intellectual resources that educators and school resource officers can tap into and help humanize and provide context to the lives of vulnerable and marginalized gang-associated Latino young men. Should educators and police officers continue to disregard and dismiss gang knowledge, it will only serve to reinforce the isolating experiences for youth involved in gangs – that they do not matter and their lives are meaningless to adults in schools (Hagedorn, 2017). Unaware to some educators and school resource officers is that youth gang membership can and should be seen as an act of resistance to the constant mistreatment and marginalization in schools and communities (Huerta, 2015; Vigil, 1999). We are aware that some gangs are violent and engage in criminal activities that shake the foundation of communities. But, contrary to what most of the available scholarship and attitudes toward gangs suggest, *funds of gang knowledge* should be seen as tools for educators and school resource officers to build trusting relationships with Latino boys and young men, rather than promote a pathway into juvenile justice systems.

A majority of the literature on the school-to-prison pipeline highlights the mechanisms that contribute to the social reproduction of boys of color in urban schools. Within these arguments and attitudes from educators is the constant use of deficit-oriented frames that perpetuate that boys of color, and those associated with gangs, are terrorists, incapable, and not worthy of any educational investment (Huerta et al., in press; Rios, 2011). However, the reality is that Latino youth, especially boys, are vanishing from the educational pipeline (Saenz & Ponjuan, 2009), where less than one in two Latino boys graduates from U.S. high schools (Schott Foundation for Public Education, 2015). The numbers are even more dramatic for gang-associated youth where only 50 percent earn a high school diploma compared to their non-gang peers (Pyrooz, 2014). Thus, this paper aims to provide a nuanced and multifaceted perspective to understand the complexities of vulnerable lives and on humanizing their experiences. The purpose of this paper, then, is to challenge the existing "politics of representation" (Holquist, 1983) of Latino boys in continuation school settings.[1] To do so, we employ a *funds of knowledge* (Moll et al., 1992; Vélez-Ibáñez & Greenberg, 1992) approach to describe and examine the pedagogical relevance and utility of the gang-specific knowledge and experiences that are embedded in the students' lives. We urge educators and schools to recognize these types of *funds of gang knowledge* as viable, valuable, and legitimate sources of information that many Latino boys and young men must acquire and use to survive in schools and communities. And those educators can use these knowledges as opportunities to forge a deeper understanding of their students' daily lives (Cammarota, 2004; Moje, 2000). Specifically, we aim at answering the following research questions:

> What are Latino boys' attending continuation school funds of gang knowledge? and How can educators use students' funds of gang knowledge to build trusting relationships?

Findings from this chapter are expected to refine existing theories and to begin to build underpinnings to incorporate funds of gang knowledge into the dialogue of asset-based scholarship for minoritized students in urban schools and communities. Educators and others connected to Latino boys must see how the experiences and identities inform their sources of life-knowledge that should not be watered down or disregarded (Carrillo, 2016). Furthermore, the students in this study have experienced a form of a *prisonization* process that builds on deficit models a shared belief that incarceration is the next logical step in the life-course of many other urban Latino boys and young men. Finally, this paper reveals that there is significant educational value in utilizing students' funds of gang knowledge to serve this particular group of students in an urban continuation school. Educators and school resource officers must skillfully tap into these resources if they aspire to help Latino boys, especially those connected to gangs, to accomplish their educational and occupational goals. Failing to utilize these sources of knowledge may continue to perpetuate inequities in the educational system.

Literature Review

Historically, due to the often racist and classist nature of schooling, Latino boys have experienced challenges with academic achievement, educational attainment, and school success, when compared to student peers (Noguera, 2003). These patterns are so common and documented by existing research that focuses on the criminalization of urban youth, the school-to-prison pipeline, and the reasons why Latino boys join gangs. In this review, we attempt to interpret the existing scholarship that examines these topics.

Criminalization of Youth in Urban Schools

The criminalization of students is operationalized through zero-tolerance policies to combat urban violence that shifted institutional responses to student fights, tardiness, and student-educator conflicts (Huerta, 2015; Lopez, 2003), and it means students are arrested, suspended, or expelled for disputes with teachers, counselors, or administrators for often minor infractions (Musto, 2019). These new institutional attitudes and behaviors lead to the constant "push out" of students before diploma completion (Annamma, 2018). The bureaucratic actions of educators or other agents gradually contributed to the STPP (Noguera, 2003), where low-income youth of color are treated like adults for talking back to teachers or fighting with peers, and then subsequently school resource officers create criminal citations which forces youth to be involved in the juvenile justice system (Lopez, 2003). Annamma (2018) helps to showcase how incarcerated girls of color value education, but multiple educational and juvenile justice agents work to strip enjoyment and limit educational opportunities. The presence of gangs in schools further "pushed" educators to embrace the criminalization of urban boys of color and unintentionally redirect students to prisons instead of educational systems (Durán, 2013; Vigil, 1988).

Gangs and Latino Youth

Latino boys have multiple motivations to join gangs during their adolescence such as tensions between parents, perceptions of racism and discrimination in schools, community violence, and poverty, which all contribute to an adolescent's feeling of marginalization (Estrada et al., 2016; Vigil, 1988). If one of the spaces previously listed is void of a nurturing and caring adult, the young man will locate others, including gang members, who can fulfill the gaps necessary to feel validated (Vigil, 1988). One could assume schools would provide the personnel and space to welcome and embrace students who are feeling isolated and marginalized. However, most teachers and other educators are not prepared or supported to make significant changes to alter the "oppressive practices or structures" in schools to meet the needs of gang-involved students (Moje, 2000, pg. 682). Educators must resist the, often, visceral responses to gang-associated youth and instead see an opportunity to humanize and provide support to an individual who lives in vulnerable social condition that may require outside intervention to create a space of equilibrium (Huerta et al., in press) instead of simply transferring students to continuation schools (Hernandez, 2017; Huerta & Hernandez, 2021).

Continuation School Culture

With gang context in the background, we focus on continuation schools which are an extension of this street arena to build funds of gang knowledge for Latino boys. Our focus on continuation schools is grounded in the fact that educators are more likely to critically scrutinize Latinos who are identified or perceived as gang members, and teachers, in this setting, search for opportunities to excessively suspend or expel students from traditional schools (Kim, 2011; Malagón, 2010). Often, educators are more likely to view continuation school students as "troublemakers" (Kelly, 1993), whether the student is gang involved or not.

Continuation schools have a long history in the United States, and the contemporary model of small and adaptive curriculum and learning environment is traced to the 1960s for students who needed flexible structures and curriculums compared to traditional regular school settings (Kelly, 1993). Since then, some alternative schools have transformed into "dumping grounds" for students with academic and disciplinary problems (Brown, 2007; Huerta & Hernandez, 2021). Some models of alternative schools only allow students to be enrolled for short periods of time to fulfill the required suspensions or expulsion mandates of, 20 days to three months, or longer based on the school discipline policy violation (Malagón, 2010) and the students' academic performance in said school (Huerta & Hernandez, 2021). Other alternative schools allow students to permanently transfer and complete all requirements to earn their high school diploma (Hernandez, 2017). However, each school district and state vary in policy allowing students to complete their studies in alternative schools (Kelly, 1993; Lea et al., 2020; Malagón, 2010).

Our study continues this non-deficit perspective to provide needed nuances to the lives of Latino boys. This group, as others in urban spaces, continues to be a target for mistreatment by the hands of educators, law enforcement, and policymakers to disregard the individual and community assets they possess. Due to various demands and unfocused training of how to support and engage gang youth, educators may struggle to see gang members as children, but instead as "thugs" with little hope to change (Huerta et al., in press). Most often, teachers and other school personnel are unable to see the various assets, strength, and resilience that gang-associated Latino young men possess and must endure throughout multiple inequitable social structures that impede their growth and development and hinders trust-building relationships with adults.

Conceptual Framework

(Dark) Funds of Knowledge

It has been over 20 years since the term *funds of knowledge* – the existing resources, knowledge, and skills embedded in students and their families (Moll et al., 1992; Vélez-Ibáñez & Greenberg, 1992) – emerged in the K-12 literature. The research on funds of knowledge has become a standard reference to signal a "'sociocultural' orientation in education that seeks to build strategically on the experiences, resources, and knowledge of families and children those from low-income neighborhoods" (Moll et al., 2013, pg. 172; Rios-Aguilar et al., 2011; Vélez-Ibáñez & Greenberg, 1992). After decades of research, what we know is that the funds of knowledge generated, accumulated, and transmitted by households bring ample possibilities for facilitating the academic success of underrepresented students' education (Neri et al., 2021; Rios-Aguilar & Kiyama, 2017). Indeed, it is the connection between teachers' pedagogical approaches and families' sociocultural, linguistic, and intellectual resources what makes this approach appealing, relevant, and very much needed (Moll et al., 2013).

While most of the available scholarship on funds of knowledge highlights the generous nature of resources inherent in the lives of marginalized students (and their families and communities), some researchers have begun to provide examples of different types of funds of knowledge available to youth. For example, Gallo and Link (2015) describe the existence of politicized funds of knowledge and the influence in schools. They developed the concept while examining the knowledge and experiences with immigration and deportation that children and families undergo in and out of schools. They argue for the need to familiarize better educators to recognize and to respond this type of knowledge. Similarly, Zipin (2009) coined the term *dark funds of knowledge* to describe the challenging knowledge(s) embedded in the lives of marginalized students. Indeed, Zipin (2009) was the first to recognize the absence of students' "dark" and "difficult" life experiences from classroom discussions and activities. Most often, he argued, educators feared integrating students' dark funds of knowledge which centers as a consciousness of crime, drugs, and violence in students' communities and households. These examples signal the need to consider all sources of funds of knowledge, including the vulnerabilities – difficult challenges for living that impact youth and several other household members (Moll et al., 2013) embedded in students' lives and not to focus on their deficiencies.

While we find Zipin's concept and rationale valuable, we also think there is a high risk of utilizing the term *dark* to describe students' funds of knowledge. The risk is to fall again into a deficit mentality and then start attributing "bad" or "dangerous" labels to the varied knowledge(s) these students possess (Dizon, Enoch-Stevens, & Huerta, in press). Instead, we argue that it is more productive to utilize the concept of *Funds of Gang Knowledge*, which is a continuum from less to more complex and controversial knowledge and shows the different shades in knowledge and resources. This expanded notion includes both the funds of knowledge that Moll and colleagues have discussed at length in their research *and* all the more "difficult" knowledge(s) that are also part of students' vulnerable lives.

Challenging Knowledge(s) as Sources of Funds of Gang Knowledge

Moll and González (1997) stressed the importance of having educators "transform students' diversities into pedagogical assets" (pg. 89), but Zipin's (2009) work highlights the deep fear and "institutional denial" (p. 321), which prompts teachers to hold steady the imaginary boundaries of student's home communities filled with poverty and crime to not be blended into schools. The institutional denial can be similar to educators denying the presence of youth gangs within schools. Teachers want to maintain schools as "safe spaces" for their students to escape the harsh realities of their communities (Gallo & Link, 2015), but the strong presence and gradual integration of gangs into schools cannot be denied (Huerta et al., in press). However, we seek to push the theoretical conversation forward by introducing the notion of *funds of gang knowledge*. They include the sharing and preservation of symbols, knowledge, and skills essential for growth and economic survival. As one accumulates funds of gang knowledge, Latino youth may learn about gang networks, drugs, and alcohol, strategies to engage law enforcement, and methods to ease the transition into juvenile hall facilities (see Table 6.1 for a description of funds of gang knowledge available in our sample). The ambition to focus on funds of gang knowledge is rooted in previous researchers' calls to highlight how adolescents "create their own social worlds and funds of knowledge" (Rios-Aguilar et al., 2011, pg. 167). Latino boys who are embedded in gangs create parallel forms of funds of gang knowledge that can be used not only for social and economic survival but for positions of power, resistance from racial oppression, and perpetual marginality in schools and the broader community.

Similar to the original funds of knowledge study, the funds of gang knowledge embedded in students' lives (see Table 6.1) showcase how they operationalize and use their skills related to their social context of urban schools and communities (Neri et al., 2021). This furthers how they learn to "[deal] with changing, and often difficult, social and economic circumstances" (Moll et al., 1992, pg. 73). Gangs similar to households must, "exchange goods, services, and symbolic capital, which are part of each [gang's] functioning" (Moll & González, 2004, pg. 702) to maintain its daily functioning and survival in different spaces.

(Dark) Funds of Knowledge as Pedagogical Assets

In an attempt to better understand youth, Zipin et al. (2012) designed an action research project to help public middle and high school teachers in high-poverty regions in Australia to develop a pedagogy that considered community funds of knowledge. A funds of knowledge approach was used to take a fuller account of diverse and complex spaces of socio-historical life in these spaces. Zipin et al. (2012) found that many students who live in these urban regions did experience dismal violent effects of poverty and racism. In fact, students gave heartbreaking testimony of the "dark" funds of knowledge available to them. These varied sources of challenging knowledge startled (and terrified) teachers (Zipin, 2009). Zipin et al. (2012) argue that, along with other funds of knowledge, knowledge of difficult lived spaces can and should be put to use as assets for curriculum work (Zipin, 2009). They suggest educators have rich curricular conversations about how students can use their agency to re-contextualize potential new futures from their senses of lived realities. In other words, educators should help students valorize their funds of knowledge *and* to develop the capacity to aspire and to imagine more hopeful ways of being and living, however educators sometimes miss opportunities to forge meaningful connectioins with students (Huerta, in press). Another idea of using a funds of knowledge approach is to ask students to carry out curriculum projects that involve residents and family members and to

TABLE 6.1 Sample of Funds of Gang Knowledge

A Sample of Funds of Gang Knowledge	
Names of Rock County Based Gangs by Ethnicity	*Gang Initiation Requirements*
• African-American-based • Latino-based	• Jumped into gang (13 seconds to 1 minute) • Family relationship • Robbery • Continuous evaluation of commitment (are you down?)
Names of Graffiti Crews and Their Relationships	*How to Interact with Law Enforcement and Other Officials*
• Various crew meanings • How graffiti crews merge and expand to new communities	• Activate knowledge about rights • How to act proper in front of probation officers, lawyers, and judges
Regional Affiliation of Gangs and Graffiti Crews	*Parent, Sibling, or Extended Family Member Embedded in Gangs*
• Norteños (XIV) – Northerner Mexican-origin gangs • Sureños (XIII) – Southerner Mexican-origin gangs	• Father • Mother • Aunts or uncles • Brothers and sisters/cousins
Knows How to Advance Their Status in Gang or Graffiti Crews	*How to Survive or Prepare for Juvenile Incarceration Facilities (Juvenile Hall, Holding Cells, or Juvenile Campus)*
• Fight or kill rival gang members • Recruit more members into their group • Write more graffiti around city • Sell larger quantities of drugs • Not allow oneself to be punked	• Stay active and busy in juvenile hall and camps • Don't get punked by other youth • Be aware of rapists • Juvenile camps do not compare to adult prisons
INTENTIONALLY LEFT BLANK	*Knowledge of Drugs and Alcohol*
INTENTIONALLY LEFT BLANK	• Drug wholesale and retail value • Drug measurements • Marijuana • Pharmaceuticals • Methods to combine drugs and/or alcohol

re-imagine collaborating with them to envision a hopeful future together. Sadly, instead, most schools impose severe sanctions against students and their lived experiences. These school-based efforts then twist such dark sides of students' lived worlds into moments where teachers might avoid the emotional work of knowing their students more profoundly. As many educators may become frightened by the contextual and pained lives of their students (Ovsienko & Zipin, 2007). In the following section, we highlight the multiple qualitative research methods used to study Latino boys and their fund of gang knowledge in a continuation school setting.

Methodology

Site and Participants

The site serves between 75 to over 300 students during the academic school year. Monthly enrollment fluctuates based on school suspensions and expulsion, which result in the transfer to Anderson Behavioral School (ABS), a continuation school. A majority of the ABS students attending are low-income and primarily Black and Latino boys and young men. The student data represents one case study drawn from a much larger data set of Latino boys and young men attending three continuation schools in Rock County School District (RCSD). To be eligible to participate in the larger study, the student had to self-identify as Latino, young man and attend a continuation school. Individual student and/or parent/familial gang membership was not a part of the criteria to be eligible for the study (see Table 6.2 for participant information). For a more in-depth understanding about the methods, coding, analysis, and positionality of the authors, please read Huerta and Rios-Aguilar (2021).

Findings

Graffiti Art

Frank is a member of a tagging crew for less than one year. He has attended more than 15 schools in multiple states throughout his life. Frank is unsure about his future goals or career path, or as he says, "freestyling life," but he enjoys art, drawing, and graffiti. Frank's advanced graffiti skills caught the attention of a tagging group, who recruited him to join, and he did so without question. The tagging crew provides opportunities to further Frank's funds of gang knowledge about graffiti skills. Frank shares, "[The graffiti crew] tells me how to do my letters better…Just [how to improve] my letter spacing and stuff [to refine the aesthetic]." Frank's skills are valued, and others in the tagging crew can validate his commitment to improving the art style.

Frank's tagging crew is providing opportunities to learn new techniques to improve his graffiti and accumulate new funds of gang knowledge. He would actively use the new graffiti art information, "I use to get practice [spray] cans and I used to practice [at my house] …on plywood." The graffiti symbols and styles are honored by Frank, but also his tagging crew as they will use their funds of gang knowledge to increase not only their status within the community by writing more. The quality of the graffiti on streets, freeways, and trains are critical methods to promote their group.

TABLE 6.2 Student Names, and School/Community Context

Student Participants

Name	Nationality	Age	Grade	Reason Expelled	Gang Embedded	Family Member(s) Gang Embedded
Carlos	Mexican-American	16	11	Drug possession	No	No
CJ	Mexican and Honduran	19	12	Fighting with student	No	Yes
Emanuel	Mexican-American	16	10	Drug possession and vandalism of school property	Yes	Yes
Frank	Mexican-American	17	10	Drug possession and graffiti tools	Yes	No
Gabe	Mexican-American / Native American	16	10	Threatened school personnel	Associate	Yes
Hector	Central American	15	10	Drug possession	Associate	Yes
Jorge	Mexican-American	15	10	Threatened school personnel	No	Yes
Julio	Mexican-American/ White	16	11	Violence against school personnel	Yes	Yes
Manny	Mexican	15	10	Under the influence of drugs	Associate	No
Oscar	Mexican-American	17	12	Drug possession	Yes	Yes
Rafael	Mexican-American	16	9	Fighting with student	Yes	Yes
Ronald	Mexican-American	14	7	Fighting with student	Yes	No
Santiago	Mexican-American	18	12	Drug possession	No	No

Emanuel demonstrates his creative and unique talents through his graffiti styling, and also leadership within his tagging group. These funds of gang knowledge are necessary for the spaces where he operates, but not valued by his teachers who believe he is, "you're nothing but a fuck up." Below are examples of a teacher responding to Emanuel's graffiti on pieces of paper during a class session:

> [The teacher] was like, "Why are you tagging on the paper?" And I'm like, "It's on paper. Why are you trippin'?" And he's said, "I don't get you fucking kids – you guys are just retarded as fuck, tagging on walls, saying it's art." I was like, "It is art, you just don't see it. I see it". He's like, "you're nothing but a fuck up" and I got mad.

Not all teachers can appreciate the artistic value of graffiti styles created by Latino young men, which is a missed opportunity to forge a relationship with students. Emanuel attempted to reason with his teacher by stating the graffiti art was on paper, which means he is not destroying school property because such as writing on books or etched into the desk on windows. Emanuel claims the teacher said he was "retarded" for believing his graffiti is art. Written literacies are important for youth to demonstrate their abilities, but also a new form of knowledge of creative expression. Emanuel left school for multiple weeks because he was so upset about the negative teacher interaction. Emanuel's resistance is a self-defeating response to how schools embed oppressive structures for youth of color. Although he did not use the words, we believe he was emotionally hurt because he was unable to stand up to the teacher for being disrespectful toward him due to the response. The examples above highlight how peers and teachers respond toward those individuals who possess funds of gang knowledge related to graffiti art. Nevertheless, it helps position why youth, particularly Latino boys, may not trust educators to disclose their gang or graffiti crew status and can feel valued and supported by peers. Emanuel highlights how educators sometimes are unable to see a students' perspective as they try to explain their funds of knowledge to adults unfamiliar with gangs and graffiti crews.

A different perspective is that teachers could stress art is subjective and interpretive but also is not as complicated or controversial as the funds of gang knowledge continuum we present in this paper. Jose, Emanuel, Frank, Manny, Oscar, and Rafael all shared experiences writing graffiti for their essential groups. Teachers could use students' art skills as creative forms of resistance in schools. Original resistance is teacher-student activities that allow students to develop a socio-political awareness of their communities and intersecting identities. For urban youth, this can be an opportunity to not only explore community conditions but also how gangs evolve and remain a staple in urban and low-income communities.

Knowing How to Survive or Prepare for Juvenile Incarceration Facilities

Below, Julio discusses his tagging crew peers describing juvenile hall and youth camp as "kiddy camp," practically comparing juvenile camp to a recreational summer trip.

> **INTERVIEWER:** Does being in a crew help you learn a lot about the juvenile justice system?
> **JULIO:** Oh, yeah. I know the whole inside of [the juvenile hall facility]. I know where E4's at. I know E6. E7.
> **INTERVIEWER:** What does that [represent]?
> **JULIO:** The [holding] units that you go in when you locked up. When I was locked up I already knew a lot of people in there already. And then there was haters in there, too.

Julio is familiar with the layout of the juvenile hall facility, which may have eased his transition into setting. He also pointed out his relationship with people he is friendly with, and also others who are "haters," which may create additional tension. Julio further discusses his experiences in a juvenile youth camp.

> **INTERVIEWER:** Can you give me some examples of the type of stuff [your tagging crew members] would tell you?
> **JULIO:** [My friends would say], "detention is whatever…[Youth Camp] is kiddy camp…Prison is way worse than all of that shit" So when I was going to [Youth Camp], I'd be like "All these fools [my friends] been over here, so if they did it – I could do it, too.

The messages Julio received from his tagging crew friends about the juvenile facility influenced him to see the juvenile hall and youth camp as an effortless experience. Julio held onto the adage, "if they did it – I could do it." This motto may have helped him rationalize the easiness of juvenile youth camp. He further elaborates his experiences:

> What the fuck do I need to start crying and being all sad for? Just because of…being locked up." Once you get locked up, it's not cool. There's a lot of stupid kids [at ABS] that haven't been through nothing. They just get in trouble one time and think they're hard (tough). They'll [say], "Oh, I got locked up" and it was they were in [central] booking for like five hours. That's…nothing…when I went to [Youth Camp], I [said,] "Oh, this ain't nothing. It's only for six months." But then, like, my first three weeks up there, it was sad. 'Cause you miss your family and being home and eating when you want to and doing whatever you want. Going to sleep [at home] when you feel like it.

Julio is the youngest member of his tagging crew, so he is still learning and growing his funds of gang knowledge. Julio differentiates the nuances of incarceration by highlighting others who have simply held in "juvenile booking" offices. He understands the distinction and the role of gang funds of knowledge in preparing for different spaces and environments.

We provide examples for school counselors to build on the students' previous experiences in juvenile facilities. Emanuel, Julio, Oscar, Rafael, and Ronald spent previous time incarcerated in juvenile detention and facilities. School counselors and psychologists should host mentoring sessions for students to channel their emotions from being recently incarcerated. Often there is a stigma in low-income and minority communities for seeking mental-health support, so schools can provide peer and professional services to give students' outlets to process their emotions. If not, students may continue to have outbursts in classrooms when challenged by teachers or others who are attempting to be authoritative with them. We provide further examples in a later section. These sessions must be facilitated by professionals with the licensed and tested training, and educators must recognize there are limitations to how they can help youth as not everyone can meaningfully engage and support Latino young men.

Teachers' Deficit Reactions to Funds of Gang Knowledge

Gabe is not in a gang or tagging crew, but has been actively recruited for years by his gang friends, but does not want to make a full commitment to that lifestyle. Gabe recognizes schools are unable to see any value in the funds of gang knowledge he possesses, and states, "Because [gangs are a] positive thing in certain situations, [but] not everything calls for blood…schools are close[d] minded… and school systems, they are never really going to change." Gabe understands at the school system level, there are impediments to change and adapt to the needs of students involved in gangs. Concurrently he knows gangs are only "positive thing[s] in certain situations," as he identifies the dichotomy and the tension of funds of gang knowledge and schools.

Manny has amassed complex and nuanced funds of gang knowledge, but he is not an official member of the Latino gang in his neighborhood. He grew up with the younger members of the gang and supports them during fights with rivals, helps write gang graffiti, and is mentored by *veteranos* (veteran gang members) in the neighborhood about his life and future goals. He believes teachers can only see gangs as unfavorable, "[Teachers] just want to see [gangs] that way…As in a negative way." Some teachers quickly dismiss the thought gangs or graffiti groups can provide positive and supportive moments for their members and may remove the human element of these organizations. When teachers do this, they risk the chance to learn how these groups sometimes provide the validation or care that is not available in the students' homes and merely focus on the perception of Latino boys and young men who may or may not be connected to a gang and see them as deviant individuals.

Emanuel is a graffiti crew leader and past gang member and believes teachers are only able to see gangs and tagging crews as "terrorists" and destructive in the community. He has been involved in gangs and graffiti crews for more than half of his life and remembers being initiated into a gang at the age of seven or eight years old. Emanuel shares his thoughts about teachers' views of gangs and graffiti crew members:

> [Teachers] think us, gangs and [graffiti crews], we are just out here to terrorize the community. We're not out here to harm innocent people. We are just out here to do our thing, protect our block, and defend it against other rivals. But [teachers] don't see it as that. They just see it as destroying shit.

Emanuel is not timid about challenging or fighting rival tagging crew members. Students may fear and distrust sharing their gang status or funds of gang knowledge with educators because of being reported to school leaders. The focus on gangs adds another level of complexity to their relationship with schools, as students may be removed from school or further pushed to the margins, which may lead to dropping out of school. Rafael shares his fear of being reported and then sent to the Dean of Students' Office for his gang affiliation.

> Because a teacher can't really tell of who is in a gang or not…Teachers [have] called me before telling me, "Oh, are you in a gang?" And, I don't say, "Yes," because [the teachers] will say, "Oh, he's in a gang…Go to dean or something."

Teachers struggle and are unable to determine which Latino young men are in gangs and students often have the awareness to not disclose to their teachers because of the possible result of suspension, expulsion, or additional educational neglect. Teachers should consider humanizing these students as gangs are only a fraction of the adolescents' identity and instead should see how these youths feel valued and are mentored by other adults in gangs. The tension remains about how do educators navigate the potential ethical dilemmas posed by students who are known and active gang or graffiti crew members? We elaborate more on these tensions later in the paper. Although gangs are on a continuum from violent to benign groups, teachers may use this historical knowledge to have students examine their communities. For example, teachers may incorporate class-assignments to read autobiographies from previous gang members turned academics or public intellectuals to show the achievement of others. Lastly, if the youth are seeking out mentors in their communities and are gravitating toward gang members, what role can the schools serve to fill the void of positive mentoring relationships?

Knowing How to Interact with Law Officials

The importance of "knowing" how to interact with police is paramount for Latino young men in this study, and they use their funds of gang knowledge to avoid arrest, unexpected beatings, or mistreatment by law enforcement officers. We position the current context of over-policing boys of color in schools and communities to help others understand why these skills are necessary, relevant, and meaningful for this group of students.

Oscar has long-term aspirations to attend community college and then transfer to a four-year university and then pursue law school to work with juveniles similar to himself. Oscar is the youngest of four siblings and the only one on track to earn a high school diploma. His older brothers were gang embedded for over ten years and spent multiple years incarcerated and unemployed. Oscar has been a member of a tagging crew for over four years, previously held in juvenile facilities, and has sold drugs to supplement his single mothers' low wages from the service industry. He regularly draws from his funds of gang knowledge when he interacts with police, and in the example below, he presents his argument against the police who are trying to search him illegally.

> I have used [my constitutional rights] before. My 5th and 4th [amendments] too. [The police] always [have to] read your Miranda Rights before they arrest you. You have a right to an attorney, and I was like "I want an attorney and I plead the 5th [amendment]." And from there I sit quietly. [The police] tried searching me, and I like "You're not gonna search [me]. I'll use my constitutional rights for you to [not] try to search me. Until my lawyer is present, I won't allow for the searches unless there's probable cause.

Oscar does not hesitate exercising his rights to prevent police from trying to search and arrest him illegally. He shared various examples of police stopping and harassing him without probable cause over the years. Police questioned how and why he possesses such knowledge about his constitutional rights, but he does not share he learned this information from his tagging crew and the internet. The ability to draw his funds of gang knowledge empowers him not to feel as if he is being taken advantage of by the police but also prevents him from being disrespected or "punked" by the police officers who often try to manipulate the law in their favor. Oscar recounts his probation officer talking about other Latino young men on probation and how the juvenile justice system perceives his community:

> When I see my probation officer…he'll [say], "Hey, these kids, they are the fuck-ups, they don't do nothing…[they] ain't gonna make it…you wanna

keep acting like that [ignorant and stubborn]...that's how society wants [you] to be...Like a piece of trash... but that's how he treats all of his kids.

Oscar does not appreciate how the probation officer was depicting other Latino youth and replied, "Like it's all about living and learning. We make mistakes and people sometimes learn from their mistakes." Oscar is aware he's made many mistakes, and that is why he is on probation, but he doesn't appreciate other youth being lumped in a group of "pieces of trash," as he sees himself changing and hopes others can change too. Oscar and others know how to interact with police and other law enforcement personnel. In this example, Oscar shows he can draw from his funds of gang knowledge to cooperate with street police officers and also his probation officer to advocate his position.

Gabe was "born into gangs," so he has built his funds of gang knowledge throughout his lifetime. His father and stepfather are from rival gangs, his best friends are in traditional African-American gangs, his siblings have previously been incarcerated for various reasons, and his mother is affiliated, but not actively involved in gangs. When Gabe discusses his interaction with police, he shared the following story:

> Couple of days ago, I was stopped [by the police] because I was out past curfew. I was with my girlfriend, my little brother and a couple of friends... we had all got stopped and my friend had a jug of vodka, we are under age, so we can't drink - but shit happens...and [the police officer] saw that [bottle of vodka] and he pulled the gun out, he un-holstered it...and put it on the car...

Gabe's father helped him build his funds of gang knowledge about how to act respectfully toward police officers because they feel superior and believe "they are God" and should not counter those ideologies as the results are either being arrested or killed without recourse to the police officer. This information possibly passed through Gabe's mind as he continues with the interactions:

> I told the cops, "No, we are sorry, this is my backpack, we were at a party earlier, we just set [the vodka bottle] down, that's not even ours, you can dump it, you can do whatever, that's cool... We are just walking her home...she lives [in another neighborhood]...I am not going to let her walk home alone...I am not that type of dude...I am definitely not letting my girlfriend walk her alone at night."

Gabe was respectful and apologetic for violating curfew and possessing alcohol as a minor and worked to portray himself as a caring person and gentleman simply walking his girlfriend and female friends' home after a party because of his concern about their safety. He stressed the police officer could dictate the next steps of their interactions by being allowed to "dump" the alcohol and continues to angle his gentleman position.

> [The police officer said], "Okay, we understand," he had holstered his gun and he just dumped the [vodka] bottle, and then said, "All right, we are not going to take you guys to jail, we are not going to keep you here, call your parents, and see what they want to do, if they want to let you guys walk home." and so they called all of our parents and they all said, basically we could walk home, except for mine. My mom wanted them to take me to jail [to teach me a lesson].

This moment highlights the tension Latino boys experience with law enforcement, but also need to have the skills to navigate often stressful encounters with police officers (Brunson & Weitzer, 2011). As Gabe disclosed, the police officer unholstered his weapon and placed it on his vehicle which can send clear messages to Latino boys about who is in a position of authority and controls the situation. Gabe's funds of gang knowledge allowed him not to be arrested that evening. However, if he acted differently, the outcomes might have been grave as stressed by his father in the opening quote, "treat a cop like they are God because that's what they want," which helped Gabe and others understand the power dynamics between himself and local police officers to avoid incarceration or worse – death.

The student interacts with institutional agents on a daily basis, whether these agents are police, teachers, or probation officers, and the students understand there is a power differential between themselves and the adults. Gabe and Oscar both recognized the potential outcomes of disrespecting police or probation officer, the trajectory it will place them on. In the future, these students will understand how to use this underlying information to use for future job placement, as they will have to interact with others in power in their workplace, communities, or other spaces.

"Can't Punk Me!" Knowing How to Advance Status in Gangs or Graffiti Crews

For over a year, Rafael has been deeply embedded in a Latino gang with his two brothers. Although Rafael wants to attend a four-year college in the future, he feels immense pressure to maintain his gang allegiance in order to protect his siblings from rival gang members, "I just had to [join a gang] because I saw my little brother [involved] and I can't leave my brother out." Rafael is reserved and quiet during most class periods, and hardly engages in the loud, boisterous disruptions caused by his guy friends. But simultaneously, he must maintain a strong demeanor not to allow himself to be punked or belittled by others in school, the community, or any other spaces to maintain the "code of the streets." His street and school reputation matter as gangs and tagging crews have a strong presence in ABS. He shares an example of someone trying to challenge him in the classroom.

> Yeah, I got to tell them [what gang I am affiliated with]. I can't be like a wussy, you have to man up, tell them [what gang you are connected to] there was this one person, and I told him, "*What's up?*" But he didn't want to get in trouble, so he sat back down. He just wanted to say, "*What's up?*" I was like "*What's up dawg?*"

Rafael cannot allow himself to be disrespected or punked in the class by a potential rival gang member. The "what's up?" is a method to challenge someone and determine the others' toughness. Rafael indicated he was ready to fight the other student in class if needed but did not further pursue this because it feels he "punked" the other student. The funds of gang knowledge permeate throughout the school and community, and youth understand they must "man up" as Rafael said. He also shared, "I can't be a wussy" and to save face, but also help advance his status within his gang. He had to openly challenge the other students because he has little choice but maintain his reputation.

Gangs and tagging crew promote a level of social delinquency, which includes fighting and violence in or near schools (Curry & Spergel, 1992), which helps members protect their neighborhood, but also increase their street status. Below, Julio shares an example of his tagging crew engaged in a rumble with rivals behind their traditional high school. He provides an example of how a fight developed with a rival tagging crew at another high school:

> One time…some kid came and bumped me [and said,] "Where you from?" and … I was like "Fuck where you from homie," and then he [said], "Let's meet up after school," so I called up my homies and then [they and the rivals arrived at the school in cars at the same time] and they're all, "What's up, fuck where you are from!" So I get out [of the car] and I was like "Get up out the car - What up?" so I punched the [car] window, the window breaks, and then I start punching this fool in his face, and then he pulls out a knife, so I stepped back, I stepped up on the [sidewalk] curb and kick [through] the [car] window, I kicked him in his neck. And then he [stabs] me [in my leg] …and I was [bleeding] everywhere! …I tied my [injury] up with my tank top and we just went down [to the gang neighborhood], 'cause the homie used to live right there. We were just chillin' …

The above case highlights how Julio activated his funds of gang knowledge during and after school to prevent himself from being punked by another person and lead the charge against the other group and sustained an injury. Another person physically hurt him, and the damage can be a symbol of his commitment to his peers and tagging crew, but also allows him to increase his reputation within the tagging crew and possibly at school. It is essential to understand how Julio, and other young men in this study, form and locate their funds of gang knowledge. For instance, Julio joined a tagging crew, which in his mind is a positive step forward compared to being involved in a traditional gang as his entire family is gang embedded. Julio's father spent a considerable amount of time incarcerated for his gang involvement. Julio began accumulating his funds of gang knowledge as young as three or four years old when he started using sidewalk chalk to write the local gangs name on the different surfaces. This was not a malicious action, but only emulating the words, pictures, and symbols he saw in his low-income apartment complex. Whether a Latino young man is refusing to be belittled or punked, fighting rivals, or learning new tagging skills, the culmination of these experiences all contributes to their funds of gang knowledge to improve their reputation and status in a gang or graffiti crew.

Discussion

As shown in this paper, challenging knowledge(s), specifically funds of gang knowledge, are part of students' lives in this one continuation school. This knowledge can be relevant and productive in school settings if educators thoughtfully and courageously incorporate gang knowledge into the curricula and school discourse to engage learners, particularly Latino boys and young men. As Moje (2000) and Zipin (2009) argue, some issues need to be carefully thought out when attempting to incorporate these students' difficult identities and knowledge(s) into urban and underfunded schools. For instance, there may be ethical issues of sensitivity to learners' structures of emotion, identity, self-esteem, and legal risks to self and school for the type of information and trauma experienced in students' homes.

There may be a set of institutional constraints that do not allow teachers and school leaders to utilize these sources of knowledge as parents and outside community members may fear the *glorification* of gangs and the inherent understandings embedded within those groups. The apprehension within school districts to approach new asset-based areas that centers a new lens can be related to the recent attacks on Critical Race Theory in K-12. In 2021, parents believe that youth are taught to "hate White people," or "become social justice warriors," and that "racism isn't real." Similar attacks may happen to new school districts attempting to foster positive relationships with youth involved in gangs.

In another instance, some educators are naturally stressed over the need to cover specific content in class, mandatory testing, and lack of professional development opportunities that hurt teachers to understand the needs of gang-associated youth. Despite these structural conditions, we claim that not incorporating these funds of gang knowledge into the teaching and learning process, particularly in continuation schools, may stimulate the creation of more barriers and sanctions to these students who already feel marginalized and victims of various forms of state violence (Huerta, 2018; Moje, 2000). Whether educators decide to acknowledge students' funds of gang knowledge formally, the current position of teachers and other school personnel may be to continue to perpetuate existing deficit discourses and inequities toward gang-involved youth (Hagedorn, 2017). With the need to push against social norms, school counselors and psychologists may use gang knowledge funds to conceptualize new strategies to address trauma and other possible exposure to violence, in and outside of schools, in supporting Latino boys who are gang-associated. Thus, it is essential to enter this discussion with students with support from either community organizations or other mental health professionals to broach sensitive topics with respect and a humanizing perspective. Suppose no space is provided within schools, Latino boys will continue to operate within the ethos of the "code of the street" and use their funds of gang knowledge to balance their commitments to their gangs inside urban schools. Listening and understanding the students' viewpoint and experiences may shed light on why Latino boys and other boys of color do not trust the police and other social services professionals. The lack of trust is within the current state of the world, where people of color are often victims of state violence that seeks to punish instead of support communities of color.

Again, educators and school leaders must recognize their limitations, ethics, and preparedness to engage youth in rival gangs or graffiti crews. Not every teacher or educator is capable of understanding the potentially hostile street tension that may be unwelcomely introduced into the classroom because of the ill-preparedness of an educator or be prepared to hear harrowing stories of violence, trauma, and death. As Zipin (2009) suggests, it takes conceptual and analytic depth, creativity, courage, extraordinary support, and we add *confianza* (Moll et al., 1992) to make funds of gang knowledge productive in this urban school setting.

Note

1 Continuation schools sometimes are referred to as alternative or behavioral schools, which serve students who have been removed from traditional comprehensive school environments due to academics, behavior, suspension or expulsion (Kelly, 1993; Brown, 2007).

References

Annamma, S. A. (2018). Mapping consequential geographies in the carceral state: Education journey mapping as a qualitative method with girls of color with dis/abilities. *Qualitative Inquiry*, *24*(1), 20–34.

Brown, T. M. (2007). Lost and turned out: Academic, social, and emotional experiences of students excluded from school. *Urban Education*, *42*(5), 432–455.

Brunson, R. K., & Weitzer, R. (2011). Negotiating unwelcome police encounters: The intergenerational transmission of conduct norms. *Journal of Contemporary Ethnography*, *40*(4), 425–456.

Cammarota, J. (2004). The gendered and racialized pathways of Latina and Latino youth: Different struggles, different resistances in the urban context. *Anthropology & Education Quarterly*, *35*(1), 53–74.

Carrillo, J. F. (2016). I grew up straight 'hood: Unpacking the intelligence of working-class Latino male college students in North Carolina. *Equity & Excellence in Education*, *49*(2), 157–169.

Curry, G. D., & Spergel, I. A. (1992). Gang involvement and delinquency among Hispanic and African-American adolescent males. *Journal of Research in Crime and Delinquency*, *29*(3), 273–291.

Dizon, J. P. M., Enoch-Steven, T., & Huerta, A. H. (in press). Carcerality and education: Toward a relational theory of risk in educational institutions. *American Behavioral Scientist*. doi:10.1177/00027642211054828

Durán, R. J. (2013). *Gang life in two cities: An insider's journey*. New York: Columbia University Press.

Estrada, J. N., Gilreath, T. D., Astor, R. A., & Benbenishty, R. (2016). A statewide study of gang membership in California secondary schools. *Youth & Society*, *48*(5), 720–736

Gallo, S., & Link, H. (2015). "*Diles la verdad*": Deportation policies, politicized funds of knowledge, and schooling in middle childhood. *Harvard Educational Review*, *85*(3). 357–382.

Hagedorn, J. M. (2017). Gangs, schools, and social change: An institutional analysis. *The ANNALS of the American Academy of Political and Social Science*, *673*(1), 190–208.

Hernandez, E. (2017). Redefining the experiences of students in continuation high schools: A narrative profile of a Latino youth. *High School Journal*, *100*(4), 264–281.

Holquist, M. (1983). The politics of representation. *The Quarterly Newsletter of the Laboratory of Comparative Human Cognition*, *5*, 2–9.

Huerta, A. H. (2015). "I didn't want my life to be like that": Gangs, college, or the military for Latino male high school students. *Journal of Latino/Latin American Studies*, *7*(2), 156–167.

Huerta, A. H. (2018). Educational persistence in the face of violence: Narratives of resilient Latino male youth. *Boyhood Studies*, *11*(2), 94–113.

Huerta, A. H. (in press). Accessing possible selves with limited college knowledge: Case studies of Latino boys in two urban continuation schools. *American Behavioral Scientist*.

Huerta, A. H., & Hernandez, E. (2021). Capturing the complexity of alternative schools: Narratives of Latino males in an overlooked educational space. *Urban Review*. doi:10.1007/s11256-021-00596-0

Huerta, A. H., McDonough, P. M., Venegas, K. M., & Allen, W. R. (in press). College is…: Focusing on the college knowledge of gang-associated Latino young men. *Urban Education*. doi:10.1177/0042085920934854

Huerta, A. H., & Rios-Aguilar, C. (2021). "Treat a cop like they are God": Exploring the relevance and utility of funds of gang knowledge among Latino male students. *Urban Education*, *56*(8), 1239–1268. doi:10.1177/0042085918794766

Kelly, D. M. (1993). *Last chance high: How girls and boys drop in and out of alternative schools*. New Haven: Yale University Press.

Kim, J. H. (2011). Narrating inquiry into (re)imaging alternative schools: A case study of Kevin Gonzales. *International Journal of Qualitative Studies in Education, 24*(1), 77–96.

Lea, C. H., Crumé, H. J., & Hill, D. (2020). "Traditions are not for me": Curriculum, alternative schools, and formerly incarcerated young Black men's academic success. *Social Sciences, 9*(12), 233.

Lopez, N. (2003). *Hopeful girls, troubled boys: Race and gender disparities in urban education*. New York: Routledge.

Malagón, M. C. (2010). All the losers go there: Challenging the deficit educational discourse of Chicano racialized masculinity in a continuation high school. *Educational Foundations, 24*(1/2), 59–76.

Moje, E. B. (2000). "To be part of the story": The literacy practices of gangsta' adolescents. *Teachers College Record, 102*(3), 651–690.

Moll, L. C., Amanti, C., Neff, D., & Gonzalez, N. (1992). Funds of knowledge for teaching: Using a qualitative approach to connect homes and classrooms. *Theory into Practice, 31*(2), 132–141.

Moll, L. C., & González, N. (1997). Teachers as social scientists: Learning about culture from household research. In P. M. Hall (Ed.), *Race, ethnicity and multiculturalism* (pp. 89–114). New York: Garland.

Moll, L. C., & González, N. (2004). Engaging life: A funds-of-knowledge approach to multicultural education. *Handbook of Research on Multicultural Education, 2*, 699–715.

Moll, L., Soto-Santiago, S., & Schwartz, L. (2013). Funds of knowledge in changing communities. In K. Hall, T. Cremin, B. Comber, & L. C. Moll (Eds.), *The Wiley Blackwell international handbook of research on children's literacy, learning and culture* (pp. 172–183). London: Wiley Blackwell.

Musto, M. (2019). Brilliant or bad: The gendered social construction of exceptionalism in early adolescence. *American Sociological Review, 84*(3), 369–393.

Neri, R. C., Zipin, L., Rios-Aguilar, C., & Huerta, A. H. (2021). Surfacing deep challenges for social-educational justice: Putting funds, wealth, and capital frameworks into dialogue. *Urban Education*. doi:10.1177/00420859211016520

Noguera, P. A. (2003). Schools, prisons, and social implications of punishment: Rethinking disciplinary policies. *Theory into Practice, 42*(4), 341–350.

Ovsienko, H., & Zipin, L. (2007). Making social justice curricular: Exploring ambivalences within teacher professional identity. *Australian Association for Research in Education Annual Conference*.

Pyrooz, D. C. (2014). From colors and guns to caps and gowns? The effect of gang membership on educational attainment. *Journal of Research in Crime and Delinquency, 51*(1), 56–87.

Rios, V. M. (2011). *Punished: Policing the lives of black and latino boys*. New York: NYU Press.

Rios-Aguilar, C., & Kiyama, J. M. (Eds.). (2017). *Funds of knowledge in higher education: Honoring students' cultural experiences and resources as strengths*. New York: Routledge.

Rios-Aguilar, C., & Kiyama, J. M., Gravitt, M., & Moll, L. C. (2011). Funds of knowledge for the poor and forms of capital for the rich? A capital approach to examining funds of knowledge. *Theory and Research in Education, 9*(2), 163–184.

Saenz, V. B., & Ponjuan, L. (2009). The vanishing Latino male in higher education. *Journal of Hispanic Higher Education, 8*(1), 54–89.

Schott Foundation for Public Education (2015). *Black lives matter: The schott 50 state report on public education and Black males*. http://blackboysreport.org/

Vélez-Ibáñez, C. G., & Greenberg, J. B. (1992). Formation and transformation of funds of knowledge among US-Mexican households. *Anthropology & Education Quarterly, 23*(4), 313–335.

Vigil, J. D. (1988). *Barrio gangs: Street life and identity in Southern California*. Austin: University of Texas Press.

Vigil, J. D. (1999). Street and schools: How educators can help Chicano marginalized gang youth. *Harvard Educational Review, 69*(3), 270–288.

Zipin, L. (2009). Dark funds of knowledge, deep funds of pedagogy: Exploring boundaries between lifeworlds and school. *Discourse: Studies in Cultural Politics of Education, 30*(3), 317–331.

Zipin, L., Sellar, S., & Hattman, R. (2012). Countering and exceeding 'capital': A 'funds of knowledge' approach to re-imagining community. *Discourse: Studies in the Cultural Politics of Education, 33*(2), 179–192.

7
RISING UP AND BREAKING DOWN

Youth Resilience and Institutional Failures in the School-to-Prison Pipeline

Keybo Wyze Carillo and Patricia Burch

Introduction

When researchers talk about the school-to-prison pipeline, there is a feeling of inevitabilityand a highly determinate process and outcomes. Once you are in the pipeline, you are stuck. The fact that some students may find themselves incarcerated at age 14, but find a way out of the pipeline doesn't get discussed. Neither is the possibility that, while wrongly incarcerated, some teenagers continue to grow and develop. This is the story of a young man caught inside the school-to-prison pipeline who grew artistically and intellectually in spite of what was happening to him. His is a story of creative power and resilience – made even more impressive by the fact that at every turn, schools and society were letting him down.

But there is never only one story. One story is about Keybo Wyze Carillo, a talented young man who found his way out of the school-to-prison pipeline toward a career as a successful hip-hop rapper and to becoming the rock to his family and inspiration to his younger siblings. The other story – one that was unfolding at the same time – is the story about failed policy and institutions, about lack of accountability, about lack of care, about racism without race, about a series of decisions and choices that did unspeakable harm and left Carillo on the precipice with his life (his actual life) in the balance.

The themes of the chapter recall findings from a larger body of work on how the organization of education polices "subtract" resources from low-income youth (c.f. Valenzuela, 1999). Students receive "subtractive schooling" when teachers fail to forge authentic, caring relationships and feel alienated from school (Brockenbrough, 2015; Noguera, 2003). They are subtracted through policies that fail to view students' cultural and ethnic identities as assets (Nishina et al., 2019; Huera and Rios-Aguilla, this volume). They are subtracted when schools

DOI: 10.4324/9781003262077-7

compromise on our nation's basic social contract of equal educational opportunity and when administrators routinely disregard policies to share educational records with juvenile facilities or with public schools (Burch, this volume). These day-to-day policy decisions are what youth and other intended beneficiaries of education policy experience (Lipsky, 1980). The day-to-day policy decisions carry the signals and messages about white privilege, even when they are not explicitly about race (Harper, 2012). They are micro-decisions that intersect with a broader discourse that extends beyond schools and the criminal justice system. They intersect with structural inequalities such as housing segregation, economic stagnation, and the expansion of private sector solutions to public sector problems.

The Study

Keybo Wyze Carillo and Patricia Burch met in the summer of 2019 as part of consulting work Burch was doing in New York City. Carillo was in his mid-20s and had recently obtained his GED from Pathways to Graduation, a not-for-profit organization in New York City. He was contemplating a move to the West Coast to further his music career as a composer and performer. Carillo was also involved in a program where formerly justice-involved youth would conduct workshops for middle school students in detention centers. This work was organized by the New York City Department of Education, District 67 and a not-for-profit known as Counseling in Schools. In what follows, we present excerpts from our actual conversations, including passages from interviews with Carillo's mother, along with field notes based on these conversations.

Relatively early in the project, the research team (Burch and Carillo) realized that if a rich, youth-centered account of education in the school-to-prison pipeline was to be created, we needed to suspend some of the norms of traditional academic research. Our primary mode of data collection would be the interview, but keep as much of the original text unedited. We rejected the binary of researchers and participant. Burch interviewed Carillo and Carillo interviewed his mother. We both participated in the research. Carillo interviewed Burch about how she felt after listening to his music and what it meant to her. Burch interviewed Carillo about the meaning of the music and what he intended.

We didn't want to reproduce external conceptualizations of the school-to-prison pipeline; we wanted this to be a story that could exist as a narrative and be used by one of the authors (Carillo) as grist for a performance or a song. This creative output was identified as equally, if not more important, as an academic output.

These approaches also directed our attention toward the importance of creativity as a dimension of resistance. Carillo's music was central to the story and to how he made it out of the pipeline. Our conversations began with a discussion of school, but ultimately focused on art and music, and on how one finds themself through one's art. They both focused on artistic expression as a refuge from loneliness and despair. Our joint decisions and oversite of the research also led us away from more conventional accounts of justice-involved youth as "anti-school." The narrative and the music created by Carillo present a student whose achievement is nurtured, both through social processes and specifically in and through family, but also through individual spiritual journeys and hard creative introspection.

The Beginning

BURCH: The first time I met Carillo, I was struck by his commanding presence. Carillo was dressed all in silver; an immaculate tracksuit. With his hair in perfect braids, Carillo was so tall he had to lean back from the table where lunch was being served. His legs were too long to fit there. But there was something else I felt in his presence. It was an emotional intelligence that included a wariness of me, a white middle-aged woman; a professor from a private university. I gave a spiel about what I was trying to do and why and how much I had to learn from him. I noticed during my comments that Carillo tipped his chair further away from the table and me, his body language suggesting caution. His eyebrow cocked, Carillo asked "What are your real objectives here?" as if to say, "Give me the truth, not the research spiel." The truth was this, I told him. I was at the very beginning of understanding what it meant to try to be a student inside of a detention center; I had read the research but it was facts and figures, and I couldn't picture it or feel it. I made a plan to spend the year talking to young men and women who had been inside of these detention centers and found a way out. Would he teach me about this?

There were other students at the lunch. At the end of the one-hour meeting, Carillo asked me if I would share something about myself. Was there something painful that had happened to me in childhood? It was a reasonable request and I shared a story. Carillo later explained that he asked me to share something painful for a reason. He wanted to make sure that I understood how important his own story was to him. It was a personal story, but also as an artist, the stories he told were grist for his creative output. Did I get that? If he was going to share something about his life, I should share something too; something personal that made me vulnerable.

Carillo offered the opportunity to follow up with him after our first conversation, which I did several months later. We decided to conduct our conversations over Zoom (which was free and Carillo had used before). It was before COVID and the fatigue of using Zoom had set in. Carillo and I agreed on a process. After our conversations, I would share the transcripts and he would review them for accuracy. Via Google Docs, we would talk through and agree on emerging themes and I would cross check facts with him. Much of our communication happened over text messages, as was Carillo's preference. We agreed that when it came to Carillo's parts of the story, the rhythm should be preserved. The commas he placed would stay commas. The periods would not be inserted for grammatical precision. He would share his music and poetry with me via text and via SoundCloud. He started to do this as we got into the story and he felt like it was the best way for me to understand what he went through. This was also the reason he wanted to keep the commas where they were in the text. His parts of the story should stay poetic in their rhythm. The rhythm as in his music was part of the meaning.

During our first interview, which took place in early February 2020, I asked Carillo to tell me about his surroundings – the sounds, signs, and smells around him – as he conducted the Zoom call. It was evening on the East Coast and he was sitting outside of his apartment in the Bronx.

> **CARILLO:** *It is nighttime.* My cousin is getting a haircut. But, before we went to the barbershop, we went to get some food. And not even a block down right at the end of the block that we were on there was a bunch of cops. There – everything is blocked off. They got the news van out there. Of course, me being curious. I asked what was going on. They said that there was just a shooting over here earlier in the day. I was like OK, that's nothing new here. There were people going about with their day. I am walking down a really busy strip. There are barber shops, and chicken spots, nail salons and cash checking bodegas, a bus stop, a subway station. It's a split intersection so you have the option of walking in the middle of the intersection. There are police officers on the corners. There's a project building where people live. There are many more people than usual given that earlier in the day, there was a shooting. Cops on every corner, people getting on and off the train heading home or going somewhere, like to meet up with friends or get food from the store or just talk to someone they seen walking by that they knew. Everyone seems to be rushing around, no matter what, even if there was a shooting earlier. Those of us who live in the area are affected by the shooting that happened earlier in the afternoon. Is it one of our family members or just the fact that someone got hit by a stray bullet? Someone's kid could have got hurt. Someone might be arrested, if not for whatever they think the person did, then for something else. The cops are everywhere. One cop, on the corner I just passed, just took a look at me. I am going to go back inside.
>
> **BURCH:** Carillo went inside and we continued the conversation, but not after many minutes, with me staring at his Zoom shot. The sounds of the city now silenced. Everything on mute. The community in which Carillo now lives as an adult and which he left as a child, is a vibrant community that feeds him physically, spiritually and financially. He works there and his friends are there. It is also a place where the police and media "park" themselves for

days with their cars and vans on the curb, on the sidewalk, "in your face" in surveillance mode. They are mainly there after a shooting, he later explains. Sometimes he will see the neighborhood and the cops on the news. The media is broadcasting the violence to the rest of the world and making money off of it, he says. Inside the community, people still have to go about their day, and get things done, get a haircut, get food – with the knowledge that one of their neighbors might have been murdered or that one of their sons or daughters will be arrested and pushed around in that arrest, or worse. When Carillo gets back on our call, he tells me the story of his very first school. His early memories of school were positive, he says without reservation. "I did well at some things."

CARILLO: *When I was in the schools in New York*, there always seemed to be one teacher there who cared about you. What I loved about that was that it wasn't so much that the teachers that you had didn't believe in you, or want to support you. I think they were more challenging you to challenge yourself. They knew you were showing them some attitude, but it didn't. It didn't stop them from teaching you, it didn't stop them from challenging you with it and stop them from, you know, trying to help you and support you and that.

BURCH: Carillo's positive experience with school didn't last. His situation changed. His mother decided to leave the Bronx and move near her sister, in a city in the Poconos in Pennsylvania. Carillo decided to interview his mom when we got to this part of the story in our conversations. There were facts he wanted to cross check with her memory. Carillo's mom told him that she thought life out of New York City would be better for her kids. Rent in New York was very expensive. Carillo found the new school in the Poconos hard on his mental health. He recalls, "If you go back to the beginning, I didn't always hate school, but what I came to learn is that they say things to make you hate it." Listen.

CARILLO: *In the beginning*, when I first started school in New York, I guess I did well. They gave me all of these certificates saying that I was a good student. The fact is, one day, while my mom was at work, I ripped up the certificates. I had gotten in a fight with someone over something, something got said, and then there were blows. They put me in suspension and now they called my mom and said they were going to expel me. My mom picked me up and had to go back to work after that and I just remember hitting stuff in the house and ripping up all the certificates that I had gotten. I was worthless, why should I have those awards? They meant nothing, I didn't deserve them. It was so disappointing.

So, it was just like, all right. I guess I'm not going to be a student. I'll figure out what I'm gonna do from here and see if I can find anything better. It just got worse from there. That's when I think all hell broke loose because now, I'm not in school.

I don't have any real responsibilities at that age. So now I'm just doing whatever the hell I wanted. It was my eighth grade and I was in the school across the street. We had just moved to this new state from the Bronx. It was a different kind of state, a commonwealth or something. They had the three strikes you are out law. This meant that they could put you in prison the third time you did something wrong. It felt like they were looking for that chance.

First day of school in this new state, my English teacher asked me if I was smart due to the fact that I was coming from New York. The teacher, who happened to be white, did the typical, you know, "Welcome the new student to the class" or whatnot. And she asks me to come up to the front. So, when I'm up there, she asked me where I was from. And I'm like, "I'm from New York. I'm from the Bronx." She was like, "Oh, another one – from the Bronx," rolling her eyes. And then in front of the whole class, "Are you smart?" I just kind of looked at her and said, "Yeah. I'm smart." This gave me a very bad taste for that school. The teacher was white. She looked at me – saw my skin color – and let me know in a hush voice, meant for me, but also loud enough so that the whole class could hear … that, that I wasn't welcome at the school – that she believed that I would be trouble and that given my skin color, she didn't believe I was smart. I would have to prove it. She said all this even though she didn't say it. It was in the question and the way she looked at me. I remember how she looked at me. She looked at me as if to say, I am better than you; I don't want you here; I don't want your family here; I can make life very difficult for you in this school. I stared back at her and my stare said it all too. It said: I believe you can, but I believe more in myself. After that day, she did her best to keep me down.

She was always sending me to detention, and it came to the point, where I was asked to go straight to the in-school detention room when I arrived at school. It seemed like I spent more time in the room for in-school suspension than in an actual classroom – hers or any other teacher. When you are in in-school suspension, you're in a room, you can't talk. You can't move. You can't do anything besides the work that they give you to finish or whatever backed up work, you have. And the teachers are just sitting there, just making sure you're not sleeping. They are making sure you're not on your phone and making sure you're actually doing what you're supposed to do. They don't pretend to do anything else. Even if you just put your head in your hands and try to sleep, they stop you from that. They give you busy work, stupid work, to make you feel like you deserve it. That experience in that school, with that teacher, who looked at me and saw trouble, was when everything started to break down. In a recent conversation with Keybo at her kitchen table Carillo's mom agreed:

MOM: It was difficult for you. The school had different kinds of expectations of you, which was more of the discipline part, you know, um, you know, consistent sitting still things still and listen, you know, kind of controlling more of how you thought – not letting you be a free thinker or … They put more pressure on you about what you wasn't good at instead of trying to help strengthen the things you were good at.

CARILLO: Yeah.

MOM: You know, it kind of made me not want to have you in school. You didn't enjoy it. A lot of confrontations or disagreements with the teachers, the counselors, the principal, you know, nobody was there to kind of advocate for you. They didn't take your education seriously.

CARILLO: You are right; they didn't, but neither did my friends. They didn't act like real friends. They encouraged my ignorance. If I went to school, if I was like waiting for the bus. And I was like, "You know what, I'm gonna go to school today and get suspended purposely."

MOM: Seriously?

CARILLO: Yeah, they just said, "When are we going to do this, we are doing this together." Like instead of being like, "Yo, bro. There is no reason for you to do that, you're ready." They were like, yeah, we are ready. We're gonna figure out how we go and do this so we can stay home for the next week or something. It didn't take me and my friends long to figure out how to get suspended. I figured out how to get kicked out. So, they would send me out of school.

BURCH: When Carillo and his mom talk about the pipeline, they talk about the early good years, where there were caring teachers and awards. They talk about the shock and trauma of teachers who criminalized and humiliated Carillo on his first day of school. They remember the blatant racism in how the one teacher introduced Carillo to class. Carillo remembers all this. He remembers being excluded from school and detained in a suspension class, day after day. In theory, he was in school, in practice, he already had been excluded from it. All of this was happening to them in the context of a new neighborhood where the family experienced hardship due to poverty and racism, and where Carillo's efforts to care for his family put him at risk of arrest. It was also the beginning of Carillo's serious growth as a musician, where he started writing his own lyrics. The lyrics were about the breakdown of his life and the music was a way to help him process. The lyrics also were the place for Carillo to figure out who he was, what he stood for, and to protect his identity and self-worth in the face of school exclusion.

MOM: I wanted a better life for all of us so we moved up there. At the time, my sister (your aunt) was living up there. I figured by moving out there, I was moving up, that would be somewhat better and it turned out to be the complete opposite. So, it wasn't better. At the time, you (pointing at Carillo) were about 14, your sister was about 13. The other one was 11 or 12 and you all had a 3-year-old sister at the time as well. I didn't want the younger ones to go through the same things as the older ones did, because we had bounced around so much already, from Brooklyn to Harlem to the Bronx back to Harlem.

CARILLO: We were moving around because things were difficult and you were just trying to find a place for us to survive.

BURCH: Carillo shared the recording of his conversation with his mother. After I had listened to it, we talked about it. I heard in his mother's voice, the extreme betrayal she felt at being let down by the school system she had been led to believe would be better for him. Wasn't that part of the American dream and what she saw in the news and on television – that schools in the suburbs were, by definition, better than schools in the city? The rent was lower in the Poconos, and maybe the family wouldn't have to bounce around as much. For Carillo, the move had elements of a culture shock. The new city was very different than New York City. It seemed to Carillo like a city organized to keep kids like him under control and out of sight. In some ways it was easier to get to school. The bus picked him up right in front of his home; he and his sisters didn't have to take public transportation. But there were other, harder things. There were no sidewalks, and no places to hang out. There were more white people who treated you like you were a criminal in and out of school, and there was less chance of getting work because of that. You had to walk in the street to get to the store. The only store was a Walmart and it was four miles away.

Around that time, Carillo started to get more and more into his music. Music had been a big part of Carillo's life for a long time. He was always singing, dancing, "and teaching the family dances," recalls his mom. But with the move to Poconos, the interest in music became more serious and necessary. Carillo started writing and rapping more, recalling,

> Jay Z was an inspiration of course, and that song of his, 'Breakdown' really spoke to me. Jay Z sings, 'Look, I just shed tears homie and now I ain't too proud to admit it. Just seen my father for the first time in a minute; And when I say a minute I mean years man; Damn, a whale could have swam in them tears fam; 'Cause as I left them I reflected on my younger days; When it was just me and my brother and my mother played father, 'cause no other man bothered.'

About the time he was getting into his music, Carillo was also coming to grips with the absence of his father, and the emotional hurt caused by his father's decision not to be a part of his life, "from the very first, from birth." Carillo talks about his family both as a source of incredible strength and also a source of extreme pain and disillusionment. His mother comes up in the conversation a lot. Carillo talks about his mother as "an incredibly generous person," someone who brought people into their house throughout his life, not just family, but friends, "to shelter them, make them meals" even people who had "done wrong to her and took from her." The generosity of her spirit confounds him at times:

> "I don't get why she keeps doing that but she does," he said. Carillo clearly has been influenced by her giving spirit, by the power she derives by caring for people and seeing everyone, even strangers, as family. You hear this influence when Carillo describes his vision of what he wants to be for his sisters. He wants to be present and connected from the start. He describes this extended family "from the same father, but people who I never met" as part of what drives him as a person. In his vision of the future, "we are all sitting around the table and telling each other stories, and eating good food, and while our meeting is long in coming, it serves us … my sisters and I."

There was a time in his life when Carillo felt completely alone and desperate. The year was 2008. Carillo got into a fight at school and was sent to a juvenile detention center about 40 miles from his hometown. When the fight broke out at school, the administrators called the police and Carillo was put in handcuffs. This time, rather than being expelled, he was required to stand before a judge who sentenced him to five months in a residential camp. The sentencing occurred without a lawyer. The camp was run by a for-profit agency. Although neither Carillo nor I were aware of this fact at the time of the conversation, we both later learned the very same facility was the focus of an FBI investigation about possible kickbacks between the judges in charge of youth sentencing and the for-profit camp. One of the judges at the center of the scandal was elected in 1996 on a "get tough on crime" platform – a platform reflective of a similar policy under Presidents Bush and Clinton, a platform which Clinton later admitted had the effect of increasing the incarceration of African Americans. Two judges were charged with creating a scheme where they would get money (incentives) for sending youth to the for-profit juvenile detention facility. The scandal was called, "Kids for Cash." The for-profit facility opened after a state-run facility closed and the scandal was able to persist under the radar for many years, in part because the facility's owners were powerful businessmen that ran a national chain of for-profit juvenile facilities across the country. As for profit facilities, they were exempt from state audits, so they operated more under the radar than government-run facilities.

Carillo found himself inside of that system, caught in a public *and* private school-to-prison pipeline where school administration, under a code of conduct, responded punitively and aggressively to any misdemeanor, which also landed Carillo in court and in front of a judge who benefited financially from each juvenile lock up. For Carillo, the sentencing was the beginning of a very dark winter – where he was separated from his mother and family – and came under even more pressure from the system to conform to the identity of a school failure. When I asked Carillo about his time in "lock-up," how he referred to it, he talked about the isolation. I sensed clearly that it represented a very low point in his life; a point where life itself lost meaning.

CARILLO: *It was a lock-up facility for whoever got in trouble.* It was something like a small boot camp. I stayed there three months. When you are young, they don't send you like to automatic jail. I guess in certain places they try to give you a chance. Everything you did, they told you when and how you did it. There's a uniform that you have to wear. You are locked up. This place was in the woods; they brought us there in some sort of van or something. I guess at that time I was only 14 or 15 so they weren't putting me behind bars or nothing crazy because the charges were just me getting into a fight in a school. When I got in a fight I already was on probation and so the judge recommended three months in the detention center. It was hell because I never been away from my mom or my family. And that was the longest time I spent away from her. I mean I done overnights away from her, but not in a cell, and so this was bringing me away from my family not willingly. It was long enough for me to know that it was something I would never want to do again. There was something just about the experience that really got to me. It was not having my freedom to be able to do what I wanted to do. Time is not mine. And you're telling me what I can and can't do and when to do it. When to wake up, eat, go to the bathroom, shower, where to shower.

And what they called school wasn't school. Like they had a class or something. I mean, but it really wasn't a real class. It was just a bunch of kids are sitting at the table and they brought some teacher in but the teacher didn't try to teach anything. I sat there with the other kids and we just sat there. We couldn't do much else. Pretty much we were waiting there until we went to the place where we would go to eat and then where we slept. We weren't allowed to have anything electronic. No headphones, no nothing that they thought you could us to kill yourself with or anything like that. They kept me away from music, but when I could, I would work with these lyrics. I would write these songs in my head. It was a way for me to work out some of these feelings of being stuck in there.

BURCH: Carillo found himself thrust into a position and setting where he was expected to "do time" in the classroom. The prison school offered the symbolism of classroom – time set aside for schooling and even a designated space – the classroom, which he was "walked to – required to keep his hands in front of him clasped together" every day. Carillo commented to me later that he would have preferred it if there had actually been no pretense that he actually was in school. It was humiliating for him as an intelligent creative young man to sit in a classroom that looked like a classroom and be offered, absolutely nothing educational. By Federal and state law, Carillo should have had the opportunity to continue his coursework towards graduation. Federal law guaranteeing students in juvenile residential centers with equal opportunities to learn under the law, failed to guarantee Carillo, minimal opportunities to learn. For Carillo, these institutional failures, however painful, were expected. He explains,

CARILLO: *It was like they never even considered me part of the school, even before I went to lock-up.* After I got out of the lock-up, I tried to go back to school. I tried to re-enroll. They told me they didn't have my transcript from when I was when I was in the other school. They tried to put me in as a freshman, and I just said, forget it. It got crazy from that point forward. They said they couldn't find my transcript. My Mom tried to get them to find it. It caused a lot of arguments. But somewhere in there, I really didn't care. They didn't try to call the other school to find out if they can get my transcripts. Instead, they just said, "you have to start school all over again." I was supposed to be a junior; they said I had to start over as a freshman.

I knew it wasn't going to be like a movie, with everyone smiling and welcoming me back, but I wanted something different to happen when I walked back into what was supposed to be real school. I wanted someone to say, "Welcome, oh you are back, how has everything been? Are you okay? Are you ready to start this you know school year and get back on track? "

BURCH: That didn't happen. Carillo however was still making music. He had started to see himself as a hip hop artist, as a musician, with something important to say. The lyrics of the songs at that time, which he had started to perform, reflected his reality. However, he also notes that it was a period of transformation. The music was reflecting his reality and transforming that reality. The first song he recorded on SoundCloud and distributed was Diddy Bob. Diddy Bop is a real, direct, and "in-your-face" song. Listening to the song, a young musician, named Luis Mendez, living on the West Coast, wrote,

> The rapper maintains a strong and punchy flow consistently, and delivers his lyrics with a powerful voice. His fast rapping is filled with heavy rhyme patterns. It is very bass heavy and has dark, gritty keys and synthesizers work with Carillo's bold energy. The song reflects the rapper's refrain – the importance of adaptations to life which become necessary when you live a harder life with more challenges in your way.

Mendez goes on to say,

> The biggest adaptation is the need to toughen up and grow quickly, picking up an 'eat or be eaten' mentality early on in life. This mentality can

be seen in the lyrics whenever the rapper (Carillo) talks about his success and his desire to make the most of every day. In the song, the rapper also shows us that it can be difficult to attach to people when you start earning good money because some people may want to be with you for their own benefit. This is another adaptation that the rapper brings up, making it clear that if he gets too attached, he runs the risk of getting played.

In the song, as in life sometimes, things got worse before they got better. Carillo picks up the story for us again.

CARILLO: *Things got worse for me after that school thing where they didn't have my transcript.* My attitude got worse. The things I was doing like outside of my home got worse; it was more partying, it was more fighting, it was more, you know, selling drugs. This was when it really went to hell because at least when I was in elementary school, I wasn't worried too much about, I mean, getting into selling drugs because you know I had sports. I figured you know I play football and basketball. I don't really have time to be outside because I'm always tired from practice. But after that, like, it was just like, all right, what am I going to do to kill time?

I'm fighting more. I would go to parties from the parties. I'm in trouble and we start something at the party. The cops are being called or I'm with a friend. We get into an incident like on our way out. We get pulled over. And then other situations start to happen. We're going to stores. We're stealing, we're doing this; we are doing that. Everything just kept adding up to the point where, if I'm not mistaken, a friend of mine said he seen my face on the board in a police station. Pennsylvania is a commonwealth state so they make their own laws; they would give you maybe nine months in jail for just a bag of weed. I realized that I was putting my mom at risk and these were hard times for her.

My mom thought life in the Poconos would be better for us. Real hard times. Not having heat, not having water, not having light. I remember a month without having any electricity in the house. The little ones used to play like games to kill time during the nighttime. They used to play hide and go seek or manhunt with the neighborhood kids. Because of the electricity being off, we would just bypass going to sleep and by that time, with that, it was two, three in the morning, so that way you know it's only like maybe five, six, seven hours we were going without electricity. We tried to make do that way.

We also tried to make light of the situation because my mother is not one to give up the game and say, "What are we going to do?" My mother is someone who is going to buckle down. She's going to figure it out. During the day, my mom would like to go out, look for work. There were times we used to have to go to like Walmart from where we live. The store would be maybe like two or three miles out from where we live. I used to walk to Walmart and shoplift meat.

This way, my family we could have food to eat. We would take a book bag and one of us will be on the lookout and make sure nobody's looking, make sure there's no cameras in that section and then put it in the bag and they we would buy something small maybe for like $4 just to play it off and we'll would walk right out the store. And then my mom tried to whip up whatever she could with what we brought home so my sisters and I can eat something and try to save whatever she could for the next day. It was definitely a struggle. *I watched my mother break down. I've watched my sisters, you know, kind of drift apart.*

I watched my own self break in many different parts of my life. So, everything that happened was from a breakdown. No matter what, nobody expects to go through that kind of stuff. And if you're not doing good in life, then what are you doing, but breaking down in certain ways. If I don't have a home, what do I have? I tried to give the answer to that in another song I wrote. The lyrics go like this:

> I guess it's time for me to finally dig deep and shed off all the pain that's deep inside that makes me feel weak;
> Fatigue showing on my face I crack smile but I'm beat;
> Late at night I toss Nd Turn my mind keep running no sleep
> Another night gone
> I'm thinking like how could clear my mind of senseless thoughts that are bringing me down;
> I heard a voice inside my head that told me don't make a sound Close ya eyes and cross your legs and pick ya head up you should always be proud.

The song is about me and my fight but it is also about me and my family. At the end of the day we are family who share the same blood. Like, no matter what happens, we have to stick together. I think that's the rule for any kind of fight for anything worth anything in this world, you know, no matter what the situation, no matter what the outcome, we are still a family, and we must stay together. Sometime later, the family left Pennsylvania and we moved back to Brooklyn. I found a GED program and got my degree in 11 months. A friend of mine told me about it. I was feeling pressure to finish high school and take care of my family. My mother said to me, "Don't put it on your shoulders." But I always felt that me being the oldest child, it still did fall on my shoulders. So that my little brother and sisters could see that, no matter how hard things got my older brother still finished school. Now, they're able to look up to me and say my brother did things we didn't even think were possible for him. They didn't look up to me before. They're looking up to me now, because of the GED and the music and performing.

BURCH: Around that time, Carillo started performing more. School was going well; the music was going well. One process fed the other, synergistic energy that propelled Carillo away from the low point of being incarcerated, of feeling out of control in his life. His first performance was in Brooklyn at a local restaurant. Fifty people showed up to hear him play. He recalls being nervous, because of the size of the crowd, and because of the music. The music had shifted as well. Carillo's point of reference was still his life, but he was tapping into a different emotion, joy rather than anger.

CARILLO: I used to use my anger more when I wrote the songs, as the anger shifted, so did my lyrics. I don't care to put on a certain image if that's not who I am. I want my fan base to be authentic, and I don't want them to just know me for one kind of for me being a "rah rah person" in the street, if I'm not doing those current things at that moment. As I started to perform more, I started to realize what the performing meant to me. Whenever I am performing, I feel a sense of belonging. I feel more of myself then when I am not performing.

BURCH: Carillo's fans hear and feel in his work (early songs and later songs) a power, a man that has learned to value his freedom in life and his pace of living and working. Carillo makes many comments about his refusal to be limited and constrained (in his work, romantically, and in life overall). Despite the challenges he must adapt to, Carillo declares that he's reached a new level in life, and that his experiences have made him stronger and pushed him to work hard to pursue his dream without anything holding him back. He knows to avoid any "leeches" and "leashes" in life in order to move at the pace he wishes. Some people may get overwhelmed and feel hopeless when life is hard and seems to try to hold you back, but Carillo uses this to feed his drive and move forward.

The second story is very different. Carillo's story is also a story of repeated institutional failures – accountability failures on the part of both public and private school officials. Despite federal law, neither public nor private agencies did anything to help Carillo re-enroll in school. His original public school did not share educational records with the for-profit camp after Carillo was sentenced and when he was incarcerated. The for-profit camp did not ask for the records and did not conduct an initial educational evaluation. Judges (sworn to oath) and motivated by greed committed Carillo and others to a detention center. Both public and private agencies deserted Carillo, leaving him in a liminal and painful pause in his educational development and his progress toward a degree.

The public judge who sentenced Carillo to three months in the privately operated and managed camp had close financial ties to the school-to-prison industry (Siskak and Balsamo, 2020). He likely felt that he could get away with the crime (financial kickbacks for each student sentenced to the facility) because he understood it would be very difficult to uncover the pattern in his sentencing given how little private agencies are required to report, and the high levels of aggregation of the data reported.

The private camp where Carillo spent three months was likely under directives from its board to fill the beds. Even at that time, public pressures were building to close juvenile camps, specifically for-profit juvenile camps nationwide. Even as the state was reporting a decline in incarcerated juveniles, the for-profit center was filling more beds. Public school students were sent to the private camps without choice; and in the case of Carillo, without knowledge they were exiting a public system and entering a commercial enterprise where much more could fly under the radar. The public schools failed to create meaningful alternatives to residential juvenile centers for students like Carillo, yet the shareholders and executives of the camps financially benefited. Before entering the private prison, Carillo spent his PUBLIC school days in a kind of in-school prison or suspension room. The school was receiving revenue from his seat time. Yet he didn't have access to the same curriculum his peers did. He was kept in the room for hours at a time. Both public and private institutions failed Carillo, and both sets of failures did indescribable harm. But Carillo believed, in his own words, in the presentations he gives now.

Conclusion

There is never one story. We have told two. The first story is a story about a young man's journey out of the school-to-prison pipeline and that trauma. It is also about how these very experiences became part of the fabric of a life, a fabric which Carillo then drew on as an artist. The experiences became part of the creative juices that became the means for further resistance. The artist Keybo Wyze Carillo understands what he must do to stop, in his words, "the leeches and the leashes." He used that power to reclaim his life.

The second story is about a school system that failed an extremely talented and creative young man, and about the failures of accountability and policy within that system. This is a system that sends individuals like Carillo the message they should be treated with suspicion and not respect. They are understood as angry and oppositional, but also expected to exercise personal responsibility. Where abuses of power happened, as in the Kids for Cash Scandal, redress does not happen.

These failures continue. One of the judges who sentenced Carillo was released from prison early due to supposed health risks during COVID. He had six years left on his sentence in a low-security Miami prison. He was in a low-security prison even though he accepted a share of the $2.8 million from the builder of the for-profit center where Carillo and hundreds of other youth were sent for minor violations (National Public Radio, 2014). This is the same individual who, when interviewed about his crimes in 2017, expressed no remorse, saying:

> Look, this was a finder's fee. We needed this center built. I was always yelling at kids because that's what they needed because parents didn't know

how to be parents and so forth. So what's the big deal now? I mean, everybody was celebrating me all these years and now they're not happy with me anymore just because I took this money?

In a world that seems to put so little value in the capability and creativity of young men like Carillo, while showing compassion for judges convicted of hurting these youth, the system has failed. When actions demonstrate a greater and more deserved compassion for incarcerated youth, the abolition of the school-to-prison pipeline will be in motion.

Acknowledgment

The authors would like to thank Monica Cabrillo, David Kener, and Marie Polinsky for making the connection that led to this collaboration and for their efforts on behalf of court-involved youth.

Biblography

Associated Press. Pa. Judges Accused of Jailing Kids for Cash. https://www.nbcnews.com/id/wbna29142654

Brockenbrough, E. (2015). "The discipline stop": Black male teachers and the politics of Urban school discipline. *Education and Urban Society*, *47*(5), 499–522. doi:10.1177/0013124514530154

Harper, S. R. (2012). Race without racism: How higher education researchers minimize racist institutional norms. *The Review of Higher Education*, *36*(1), 9–29.

Lipsky, M. (1980). *Street level bureaucracy: Dilemmas of the individual in public service*. New York: Russell Sage Foundation.

Nishina, A., Lewis, J. A., Bellmore, A., & Witkow, M. R. (2019). Ethnic diversity and inclusive school environments. *Educational Psychologist*, *54*(4), 306–321. doi 10.1080/00461520.2019.1633923

Noguera, P. A. (2003). The trouble with black boys: The role and influence of environmental and cultural factors on the academic performance of African American males. *Urban Education*, *38*(4), 431–459. doi:10.1177/0042085903038004005

Siskak, M., & Balsamo, M. (2020). *Kids for cash judge released over virus concerns*. New York: Associated Press.

Valenzuela, A. (1999). *Subtractive schooling: US Mexican youth and the politics of caring*. New York: SUNY Press.

INDEX

Page numbers in **bold** refer to tables and *italics* refer to figures.

abstraction 68
access to education 14–20, 24–25
accountability: policies 24; and surveillance 24, 82, 83
African Americans: history in US 86; incarceration rates 87–88, 95, 96; online courses 70–71
age, and reoffense rate 106
Anderson Behavioral School (ABS) 126–137
aversive racism 92

behavioral problems *see* mental, emotional, and behavioral (MEB) problems
Black Lives Matter 36, 38
Black youth: girls in the juvenile justice system 105–106, 107–110, 112; overrepresentation in multiple systems 100–102; probation youth by gender **107**, 107–110; special education services 101, 106, 110, 111; special education-to-prison pipeline 102–113; unique experiences 104–105
Burch, Patricia, interview with 142–156

capitalism, racial 32–36
Carillo, Keybo Wyze, interview with 141, 142–156

Census of Juveniles in Residential Placement (CJRP) 12
citizenship courses 66–73
civil rights: discipline 87; policy design 23; principles 8–9; racial equity 35–36
Civil Rights Act 8, 22
Civil Rights Data Collection (CRDC) 13
classroom management, as challenge 91–92; *see also* discipline
color blindness 6, 56–57
community advocacy, School Resource Officers case study 36–46, 48–50
continuation school case study 126–137
continuation school culture 121–122
creativity, role of 21, 128, 142–143, 151, 155–156
criminal justice system: existing perspectives 3; privatization 17–18; *see also* juvenile justice
criminalization of youth 24–25, 120–121
criminological theories 112
critical curriculum studies 58–59, 74
critical race theory 3, 136
cultural narratives: online courses 66–67; socio-cultural consciousness 95–97; teacher education 81–82
Culturally Relevant Pedagogy (CRP) 56, 59–60, 61–62, 65, 75

culturally responsive online courses 64–65, 73–75
curricula: accountability 24; critical curriculum studies 58–59; funds of knowledge approach 124; Midwest online course case study 60–73; online courses 20–21, 56–57

dark funds of knowledge 123, 124–126; *see also* funds of gang knowledge
digital learning *see* online courses
disabilities *see* students with disabilities
disciplinary gaze 83–85; *see also* surveillance
discipline: classroom management as challenge 91–92; harsh discipline 3–4, 7, 22, 23; race radical discourse 38–39; racism in schools 87–88; School Resource Officers (SROs) 43–46; societal relational level 3–4; and surveillance 82–87
discrimination, online courses 70–71
diversity in the United States 90–93

education policies: access to education 14–20; policy design 5–6; recent attention 8–10
educational evaluations 18–19, *19*
educational expertise 33
Elementary and Secondary Education Act 24
emotional problems *see* mental, emotional, and behavioral (MEB) problems
English learner (EL) students 8, 15
Equal Educational Opportunities Act (EEOA) 8
Every Student Succeeds Act (ESSA) 8, 9
expulsions *see* continuation school case study

funds of gang knowledge 123–124, **125**, 130–136
funds of knowledge 122, 124; *see also* dark funds of knowledge

gang participation 21; continuation school case study 126–137; continuation school culture 121–122; dark funds of knowledge 123, 124–126; funds of gang knowledge 118–120, 123–124, **125**, 130–136; Latino boys 121; literature review 120–122

gender: Black girls in the juvenile justice system 105–106, 107–110, 112; criminogenic pathways 112; patriarchal narratives 66–67; stereotyping 71; teacher education 93; white, female teachers 89–90
graffiti art 126–128, 131

harsh discipline: Civil Rights Act 22; juvenile justice 7; policy design 23; race evasive policies 22; societal logics 3–4
hidden curriculum 58–59
history of the US, lessons about 66–73

incarceration rates **11**, 11–14, 85, 95, 96
Individuals with Disabilities Education Improvement Act (IDEA) 23, 112–113
institutional denial 123–124, 136
intersectionality 105

juvenile justice: Black youth 100–102; early reform efforts 7; funds of gang knowledge 129–130; incarceration rates **11**, 11–14; privatization 17–18; racism 88; recent policy attention 8–10
Juvenile Justice Delinquency Prevention Act (JJDPA) 7
Juvenile Justice Reform Act (JJRA) 7, 9
Juvenile Residential Facilities Census (JRFC) 13

Latinos: continuation school case study 126–137; continuation school culture 121–122; funds of gang knowledge 118–120; gang participation 121; history in US 86; incarceration rates 95; literature review 120–122

marginalization: discipline 85; gang participation 118, 119, 121; online courses 55, 57, 60; stereotyping juvenile offenders 105
mental, emotional, and behavioral (MEB) problems 102–103, 105, 106–110, 111
multicultural identity 94–95

neoliberal therapeutic discourse 40–42, 49
neoliberalism: and accountability 83; online courses 56–57, 68–70; prison industrial complex 24; School Resource Officers (SROs) 40–42, 48–49

No Child Left Behind Act 22, 24
normative cultural narratives 66

online courses: applying a critical lens 58–60, 74; classroom context 63–64; culturally responsive-aligned features 64–65, 73–75; culture of power online 54–56, 65–73; curricula 20–21; curriculum mixed methods study 60–73; disrupting the culture of power 73–76; expanding private sector in K-12 curriculum 56–57; trends in 54, 73
Online Curricular Responsiveness and Relevance Protocol 61–62
outside of school policies 2, 5

Parkland, Florida school shooting 33–34
patriarchal narratives 66–67
police officers, interacting with 132–134
police presence in schools *see* School Resource Officers (SROs)
policy design: education policies 5–6; outside of school policy 2; School Resource Officers case study 36–46, 48–50; school-to-prison pipeline 6–10, 22–26; subtractive schooling 141–142
political economy perspective 3, 23–24
Positive Behavioral Intervention Services (PBIS) 23
positivist framework 66, 68
poverty: funds of knowledge approach 124; racial capitalism 32, 35; School Resource Officers 37–38, 41, 42
power: online courses 54–56, 59–60, 65–73; youth surveillance 84–85
prison industrial complex 23–24, 89
privatization: criminal justice system 17–18; educational evaluations 18–19, *19*; online courses 56–57

race evasive policies 6, 22–23
race neutrality 6, 56–57
race radical discourse 38–39
racial capitalism 32–36
racial contract theory 93–94
racial justice 23; *see also* Black youth; Latinos; students of color
Racial Justice Allies 38, 39

racism: discipline in schools 87–88; existing perspectives 2–6; School Resource Officers (SROs) 34, 42, 46–48; societal relational level 3–4; in the United States 1
residential placement facilities *12–13*, 13–20
restorative practices 43

Safe Schools Act 22
school failure 102
school overcrowding 33
School Resource Officers (SROs): adoption of 20, 31–32; official anti-racism 46–48; policymaking and community advocacy case study 36–46, 48–50; racial capitalism 32–36
school shootings: Parkland, Florida 33–34; School Resource Officers case study 36–46
school-to-prison nexus 4–5, 31–32, 43, 48–49
school-to-prison pipeline 1–2; existing perspectives 2–6; inevitability 141; Latino boys 119; online courses 55, 76; persistence of the problem 10–21; policy design 6–10, 22–26; School Resource Officers 31; special education-to-prison pipeline 102–113; students of color 1–2; subtractive schooling 141–142; teacher education 87–93; youth-centered account project 142–156; youth surveillance 83–84
sexism 105–106; *see also* gender
slavery, teaching about 67–68, 70–71
social messages: American context 81; culture of power online 55; hidden curriculum 58–59
societal relations: discipline and racism 3–4; education policies 5–6
socio-cultural consciousness 95–97
special education services: access to 14–17; Black youth 101, 106, 110, 111; eligibility 21
special education-to-prison pipeline 102–113
students of color: existing perspectives 2–6; incarceration rates **11**, 11–14; School Resource Officers (SROs) role 36–46; school-to-prison pipeline 1–2; suspensions 5; urban contexts and gangs 119; *see also* Black youth; Latinos; racism

students with disabilities: overrepresentation in juvenile justice system 102; policy design 23; suspensions 5; *see also* special education services
subtractive schooling 141–142
surveillance: disciplinary gaze as school tradition 83–85; and incarceration 85–87; resisting youth surveillance 82
susceptibility theory 111
suspensions 5; *see also* continuation school case study

teacher education 81–82; critical analysis 93–95; disciplinary gaze as school tradition 83–85; funds of gang knowledge 136–137; resisting youth surveillance 82; school-to-prison pipeline 87–93; socio-cultural consciousness 95–97; from surveillance to incarceration 85–87

teachers: classroom management as challenge 91–92; critical race theory 3; diversity 90–93; institutional denial 123–124, 136; online courses 54–55, 63–64; predominance of white women as 89–90; reactions to funds of gang knowledge 130–131; role in youth surveillance 82–87; students of color 2–3; youth resilience case study 145–146
trauma: criminological theories 112; funds of gang knowledge 137; racial capitalism 32; School Resource Officers 39, 40–41, 47; youth-centered account 155

vendor-developed online courses *see* online courses

white, female teachers 89–90
white supremacy 35–36, 94

zero tolerance 3–4, 22, 33, 44, 88, 120

For Product Safety Concerns and Information please contact our EU representative GPSR@taylorandfrancis.com
Taylor & Francis Verlag GmbH, Kaufingerstraße 24, 80331 München, Germany

www.ingramcontent.com/pod-product-compliance
Ingram Content Group UK Ltd.
Pitfield, Milton Keynes, MK11 3LW, UK
UKHW021054310326
469517UK00018B/183